Don Watson's book, *Death Sentence*, was the Australian Booksellers' Association Book of the Year 2003. His previous book, *Recollections of a Bleeding Heart*, won the *Age* Book of the Year, the *Age* Non-Fiction Prize, the *Courier-Mail* Book of the Year, the National Biography Award and the Foundation for Australian Literary Studies Colin Roderick Award. His essay, *Rabbit Syndrome*, won the Alfred Deakin Prize. In addition to books and essays, he writes films, and gives occasional seminars and lecture on writing and language.

D1106659

WATSON'S DICTIONARY

of

WEASEL WORDS,

CONTEMPORARY CLICHÉS, CANT & MANAGEMENT JARGON

DON WATSON

V

VINTAGE

A Vintage book
Published by Random House Australia Pty Ltd
20 Alfred Street, Milsons Point, NSW 2061
http://www.randomhouse.com.au

Sydney   New York   Toronto
London   Auckland   Johannesburg

First published by Knopf in 2004
This paperback edition first published by Vintage in 2005

National Library of Australia
Cataloguing-in-Publication Entry

Watson, Don, 1949–.
Watson's dictionary of weasel words, contemporary clichés,
cant and management jargon.

ISBN 1 74051 366 5.

1. Business – Slang – Dictionaries. 2. English language –
Jargon – Dictionaries. I. Title.

658.0014

Cover illustration copyright E. H. Shepard under the
Berne Convention, colouring copyright 1970, 1971 by
E. H. Shepard and Egmont Books Ltd., reproduced
by permission of Curtis Brown Ltd., London
Cover design by Yolande Gray
Internal design by Yolande Gray
Typeset by Midland Typesetters, Australia
Printed and bound by Griffin Press, Netley, South Australia

10 9 8 7 6 5 4 3

Introduction

In *As You Like It*, Jaques says he can suck 'melancholy out of a song as a weasel sucks eggs'. The President of the United States is no less like a weasel when he says a search of Iraq has found '*weapons of mass destruction-related program activities*'; and the Prime Minister of Australia is a match for his American friend when he asks us to recognise a distinction between '*core*' and '*non-core* promises'. Our two leaders have sucked the meaning out of the words; and the result is just as melancholy. They are shells of words: words from which life has gone, facsimiles, frauds, corpses.

Weasel words are the words of the powerful, the treacherous and the unfaithful, spies, assassins and

1

thieves. Bureaucrats and ideologues love them. Tyrants cannot do without them. The Newspeak of Orwell's *1984* is an invention, but also a satire on real states such as the Soviet Union where death from starvation and abuse in slave camps was recorded by officials as 'failure of the heart muscle'. Were any five words ever more melancholy than this?

Totalitarian states use weasel words to hide truth and slew or complicate meaning. They use them, as they use clichés and other dead forms, to exercise and maintain power. Language, as Stalin knew, is an essential instrument of terror. For all the people who were killed or imprisoned as 'enemies of the revolution' in the empire he ruled, or as 'enemies of the Reich' in Hitler's Germany, a great many more were cowed, gulled or anaesthetised into dull-witted obedience by the bastardised and depleted language of those regimes. To speak the words the powerful speak is to obey them, or at least to give up all outward signs of freedom. Stalin was not the first tyrant to be so feared that those around him preferred to imitate even his malapropisms than give him any reason to think they were not in awe of his authority.

The same mimicry can be expected wherever the official language is a kind of code that we must at least appear to understand, or be excluded. It happens in democracies, and in businesses and government departments. Today it is found everywhere the language of the information age is (compulsorily) spoken; everywhere the management revolution has been; everywhere marketing goes. This is language without possibility. It cannot convey humour, fancy, feelings, nuance or the varieties of experience. It is cut off and cuts us off from provenance – it has no past. This dead, depleted, verbless jargon is becoming the language of daily life. The death of language is not being brought about by absent commas and misplaced apostrophes, or even by neglected grammar. Foolish as that neglect is, the real disease is in the system: in the new models of business organisation, in the triumph of economics. It is there in the cant of *competitive advantage* and *human resources management*, *transparency*, *accountability*: in the clichés, *consumer*, *client*, *key*, *core*, *going forwards*, *at the end of the day*, *outcomes-based*. It is there in the pompous lunacy of management jargon which reaches from the world's biggest corporations and government agencies, including military and intelligence agencies, to primary schools where children now use PowerPoint in English presentations and are taught to call the conclusions of their history essays *product*. Language has been made the machine of business and politics in the information age. But it cannot survive the experience and maintain its power to amuse, enchant, invent, comfort. It can't carry ideas and sentiments, bear the culture and be the culture's chief glory. It can't be machinery first and language second. It can't live with the new tyranny.

It was in a democracy that the term 'weasel word' first appeared: in the United States, around the end of the nineteenth century. In 1916 Theodore Roosevelt declared that the 'tendency to use what have been called weasel words was "one of the defects of our nation"'. 'You can have universal training or you can have voluntary training, but when you use the word "voluntary" to qualify the word "universal", you are using a weasel word,' he said: 'it has sucked all the meaning out of "universal".' Teddy's Presidential cousin, Franklin, later complained about the same tendency in speeches sent him from the

State Department, a place where one should expect to find it. The affairs of states make for weasely professions, and none more so than diplomacy. But diplomacy, along with fullblown espionage, may be the only ones where weasel words have a claim to being justified.

Politicians readily convince themselves that weaseling is no less essential in their affairs. When certain remarks of Richard Nixon's turned out to have been untrue, his minders described them as 'inoperative'. John Howard and his ministers chose words that persuaded the public to believe that the refugees on a sinking boat had thrown their children into the sea, and that the government was right, therefore, to stop them landing in Australia. These people seeking asylum in Australia were 'not the sort of people' Australians wanted in this country. It is possible that only weasel words could put Howard and his ministers beyond the reach of their better feelings, and give them up to bastardry. More direct and pungent language might have made the lie unbearable. This is not to assume that there were better angels in their nature to be found, but to remind us that this language anaesthetises both the users and the used. It poisons politics: the politicians, the media, the public service and the voters.

At a recent Senate hearing into that incident, a senior public servant was asked if the Prime Minister or his staff had indicated to her the 'importance and significance' of her evidence: had they, in other words, leaned on her? She replied, 'I do not recall that being particularly the case.' As Teddy Roosevelt might have said, it can be the case or not the case, but when you use 'particularly' to qualify 'the case' you suck all the meaning out of it. And this, as anyone can see, was the intention from the start.

Politicians and their hirelings do not have the habit to themselves. They just have less shame than the rest of us. Bill Clinton's, 'It depends on what the meaning of "is" is', lays claim to being in a class of its own. This is *world's best practice* weaseling. But he was only following a universal instinct to use weasel words, clichés and jargon as shields against attack, as camouflage to escape detection, as smokescreens or vapour to blind or repel anyone sniffing out the truth about us. We use them with intent, and we parrot them without thinking. Adverbs and adjectives do a lot of the work: *perhaps, maybe, possibly, basically, realistically speaking*. But then, through our employment, education or our addiction to fashion, we have likely developed a habit and forgotten the other way of communicating; so that we might say that *realistically speaking, the bottom line is basically that we will evaluate the issue in its context, and basically commit ourselves to endeavouring to achieve a more appropriate scenario with better outcomes for all stakeholders*. Habit or instinct, the effect is the same: we escape with the truth (even if it is not known to us), just as the weasel, also acting from habit or instinct, escapes with the substance of the egg. Escape is made easier of course by the soporific effect that dead words have on our fellow human beings.

'Dead' is the right word. Language, as Toni Morrison says, is part system, part a 'living thing over which one has control'; but in the main it is an 'agency – an act with consequences'. The more we listen to the public language of our times, the more we are driven to believe that it has been gutted for the specific purpose of denying us that agency, denying consequences, denying control over a living thing. We are left with the system, the shell: 'a suit of armour . . . from which the knight departed long ago'. We might resist this deceit more fiercely if we could only stay awake. Getting angry when people write to say we must *ensure that we develop a shared understanding of the core initiatives and to discuss key issues that emerge*, is like sounding off at a cloud of ether. Just as we begin to feel the irritation the lights start going out: *in addition, each construct requires the central office staff to engage deeply with the concepts that underpin each of the initiatives . . . [and] . . . a range of processes have been used to explore issues and gather feedback from different stakeholders to inform our thinking.*

It is likely that by the time readers of this newsletter, from a deputy secretary in a branch of an education department, came to the part about 'gathering *feedback*' they were incapable of gathering anything. Had it been their first contact with such words, an intelligent reaction might have been conceivable: but in education departments this is Standard English. The words are to information age workers what sugar cane is to a cane-cutter, peas to a pea-picker, rivets to a worker in a rivet factory; but cane, peas and rivets are more easily defined and the work that goes into producing them has a clearer shape to it than *information processing* – or *knowledge management* or *implementing strategies for key deliverables* in *HR*.

Ten words in one paragraph from this typical 'communication' are management clichés. *Core, key, initiative, engage, ensure, understanding, underpin, processes, stakeholders, issues*: these and about fifty others will appear in every internal document, every press release, flyer, annual report, internal memo, advertisement, presentation, strategy meeting, workshop, letter and speech. Another hundred or so will turn up almost as often in a relentless, stupefying stream. Workers these days will see and hear *issue, deliver, deliverables, drive, drivers, implement, focus, customer-focus, strategic, operational* – and in every case, if they still have memories and retain the will to remember, they could call up a dozen other better words.

But they must wonder – where wonder is still possible – if it is worth recalling living words when their colleagues use the dead ones and people higher up in the organisation insist on them: when the corpses are part of the culture, the corporate DNA. And when on the radio talk shows before and after work, politicians and business people talk about *expanding the package, exiting the industry, an output management focus*, a *serious issue as we go forward* and '*inviting anyone who's had an impact from this historic rezoning and increasing of the environmental protection of the reef to apply for structural adjustment*'. Far from questioning this drivel, the interviewers parrot it back. They never ask what is meant by *output management focus*. They never say, 'Spare us the jargon, the spin you've rehearsed. Spare us any rezoning that's "historic".'

After eight or ten hours of this every day, who will have the strength left to resist the fatuous ten-second grabs on radio and TV news? Will anyone be watching the interview later in the night? Not when they know they are likely to hear from their masters the same words they have heard all day:

> Well, the rules will say that you have to be negatively impacted and you will have to prove to the adjustment authority that you have been negatively impacted, and I

think all Australians would agree that saving the Barrier Reef, saving it for future generations, protecting that unique environment is absolutely vital and they would want to ensure that anyone who was negatively impacted was able to get structural adjustment and assistance because of that decision.

If in your darkening brain a light still flickers, you might wonder if the government minister means to say that people adversely affected by new regulations will be paid compensation. But when the interviewer mentions this, the minister barks: 'No, it's not *compensation*. It's *structural adjustment and assistance following the historic rezoning.*' *Compensation*, we can safely presume, would *negatively impact* the politics of the *package*. It would be tantamount to using the word 'money', for God's sake! And when they get a whiff of money the mob always leaps to the conclusion that at least some it is theirs. Say *compensation* and the whole country will want some. So stick to *structural adjustment and assistance* and don't forget *historic rezoning* – *historic rezoning* is very good, it makes it sort of . . . historic.

By now who cares? Not the interviewer. He lets it pass. No one is alert enough to notice that as much as the Barrier Reef, the language needs saving for future generations. And did we think or hear ourselves say, as we shuffled off to bed, that an interactive television might be less *negatively impactful* on our *lifestyle*? As we *go forward*?

This Dictionary was prompted by the public response to *Death Sentence: The Decay of Public Language*. It has grown (or been *leveraged*?) from that book, and it is a kind of companion to it. It fills out the argument with examples that convey more vividly, I think, how far the decay has spread. If it induces irritation, curiosity, laughter or rage – above all, if it provokes rebellion – the Dictionary will have fulfilled its purpose. As Morrison said, this language 'must be rejected, altered and exposed'.

People may use the Dictionary for the practical purposes of discovering what these new-fangled words and phrases mean, but they should be warned that it does not provide this enlightenment in every case. Without wishing to escape my obligations, I would say that most often it fails because the words in fact have no meaning, or at least not one that can be described. Moreover, it is possible that no meaning has ever been intended for them. Readers are more likely to see this if they read the entries aloud, either to themselves or to a group. This is also the most amusing – if not the only bearable – way to read this Dictionary. It is, as well, the best way to appreciate what life is like for people who must speak, read and hear this language every day of their working lives.

By this I mean people in private and government employment, people who teach and nurse and provide other forms of care, unemployed people, schoolchildren. Increasing numbers of people. Most people. People who work in organisations that have taken on this language as earlier organisations took on assembly lines and Taylorism. *Death Sentence* can be called successful insofar as it sold well; but also because hundreds of people wrote thankful, angry and amusing letters. Of these a large proportion contained examples they had encountered at work; or in their children's school reports; in correspondence with their bank, insurance company, their parents' nursing home, a government department or some recently privatised public utility. These people confirmed for me that *Death Sentence* was a small assault on a large but not impregnable enemy. This Dictionary may be seen as another charge against the walls – or, rather, into the swamp. Many of the entries are drawn from the letters I received after the publication of *Death Sentence*. Others I have picked up at seminars and talks for companies, government agencies and departments. The frustration of the people who work in them, the sense they have that this language is stupid and oppressive and that it denies them a fundamental right, was one inspiration for this second book. The other was the way our leaders imitate the emptiness of management jargon to weasel their way past our better instincts.

I hope this Dictionary proves useful in an ever-widening campaign of mockery and other forms of resistance. *Translate* it into a *tool* of derision. *Migrate* it to a satirical *skill set*. The Dictionary nurtures the subversive hope that the next edition will be smaller, and the one following smaller still, until this original edition becomes a relic of a brief age when the language slipped from our grasp. But we took it back. We made de-weaseling a *key competency* and began to see that not only had our leaders and our institutions mugged us, we had mugged ourselves. We decided to fight back. *So we could move on.*

Aa

able to be (not)

What would have been done had it not been for the intransigence of objects.

'Unfortunately the potholes in the footpath were *not able to be* filled.'

City Council spokesperson

'The objectives outlined in our strategic plan were *not able to be met* . . . Unfortunately some of the timetables were *not able to be* kept.'

New South Wales Railways

about (it's)

1. Concerning, regarding, in relation to, etc.
2. The story is: the real story; the crux, the gist, the deep structure, meaning, profoundest reaches, etc. A *known known*. ('It's *about* jobs.' 'It's *about* greed.' 'It's *about* her nose,' etc.)

'Football in the end is *about* tradition.'

Fox Footy Channel, April 2004

'*At the end of the day* it's *about* the score on the board.'

Fox Footy Channel

'It's *about* deciding what is likely. The probability of things happening in the future. It's *about* what's going to happen potentially.'

Industry Training Board

about-face (massive)

> 'It is a tale told by an idiot, it's *about* sound and fury,
> It's *about* nothing.'

See *takeout*

about-face (massive)

1. Sudden change of standpoint or attitude (military). Pivot to face the opposite direction.
2. To alter or change; get in a consultant; adopt the principles of *quality management*.

> 'Leadership of a massive *about-face* at CSA . . . Catherine will explain how CSA has been turned around from being the most complained about Federal agency.'
>
> Governance seminar

absolute certainty

1. Beyond a doubt; scout's honour; on impeccable authority, based on irrefutable evidence; watertight, indisputable, ironclad; London to a brick; bet your arse (or ass) on it.
2. Not necessarily the case.

> 'We do know, with *absolute certainty*, that he is using his procurement system to acquire the equipment he needs to build a nuclear weapon.'
>
> Vice President Cheney, 8 September 2002

See *known knowns, absolute fact*

absolute fact

1. Not fiction; even more factual than a fact; incontrovertible, and there are pictures to prove it.
2. *Absolute* humbug, hogwash, eyewash, dupery, flimflam, deceit, japery, lie, etc.

> 'It is an *absolute fact* children were thrown in the water . . . if you don't accept that, you don't accept anything.'
>
> Peter Reith, September 2001

See *absolute certainty*, *known knowns*

absolutely

1. Totally, completely, utterly, entirely, compellingly – yes.
2. Possibly not; the truth may lie elsewhere; it is not really possible to tell with these things; if it suits you to believe it, that's okay with me. Whatever.

> 'Do you, Audrey . . . forsaking all others . . . for richer for poorer . . . (etc.) take Gunther for your lawful wedded husband?' '*Absolutely.*'

> 'Answer the question: *Absolutely* or No?'

absolutely not

1. No. Emphatically no.
2. Depends which way you look at it. Pass?

> 'Reporter: So there was never any question of any Party funds or other funds from any other source . . .

abuse (prisoner)

Tony Abbott: *Absolutely not, absolutely not.*
Reporter: . . . being offered to Terry Sharples?
Tony Abbott: *Absolutely not.*'

ABC, August 2003

'Answer the question: *Absolutely* or *Absolutely Not*?'

abuse (prisoner)

1. Torture lite. Murder, rape, terror, humiliation.
2. 'Unacceptable behaviour and unacceptable treatment': John Howard (June 2004).

'. . . allegations that the United States *abused* prisoners in its custody.'

9/11 Commission, July 2004

'The prisoner shall be taken hence to a place of execution and *abused* by the neck until he is dead.'

accelerated collaborative event

An ACE.

Central to this was an *Accelerated Collaborative Event* (ACE) which enabled a broad cross-section of our *people* to have *input* into our *people approach*, and has resulted in six project teams working to *embed* the *key initiatives* across our firm.'

Ernst and Young, '*Quality* in Everything We Do'

acceptant

1. Accepting?
2. The stage before *supportive*. To be basically *in agreeance*.

> 'The team, whether or not it is *acceptant* of the change, now puts itself on the curve and soon heads for the very natural drop into the Valley of Despair.'
>
> Change Agents

> 'That Harry should love Barbara was something Belinda could never be *acceptant* of!'

access

1. (n) Right of entry, admission or use. Entrance.
(v) To open, get into.
2. A right or entitlement to services. (As in: '*Access* and Equity.')
3. Meet or meeting. (As in: 'I managed to *access* the Minister for half an hour.')

> 'Language is a *key issue* of *access* for people from any non-English speaking culture. It affects the individual's ability to *access* and use services and knowledge of services.'
>
> Human Rights Commission

> 'Fourscore and seven years ago our fathers brought forth upon this continent a new nation, conceived in liberty, and dedicated to the proposition that all men are created equal and should have equal *access* . . .'

> 'Access your VIP Lifestyle.'
>
> VIP tel Brochure

accidental learning

1. Unintended learning?
2. A kind of learning of which arranging words is not a part.

> 'Sometimes you find yourself "role modeling" someone else in handling a situation unconsciously, that *enhances* the way you "used to think". Of course this can be positive or negative, and depends on your skills of then managing the result you get.'
>
> Melbourne University Leadership & Professional Development Program

accountable / accountability

1. Answerable, as in general we all need to be. In times past there was less *accountability*: 'In those days there was no King in Israel: every man did that which was right in his own eyes.' (Judges 21.25) But such a *scenario* is quite unthinkable now.
In our day businesses are *accountable* to their boards and their shareholders; indeed 'to all their *stakeholders*'. To be *accountable*, they must also be *transparent* and have good *governance*.
   Even in football and other team sports, players are *accountable* to each other, their fans, the coach, the club, the guernsey, tradition, the code, and community standards. They play *accountable* football, netball, lacrosse, etc.
2. Condition *achieved* by *transparency*.
3. Duties, tasks, work requirements, job, etc.
4. Integrity, honesty, decency, truthfulness; candid, open, forthright, sincere, fair, just; fair dealing, honest

injun, straight arrow, straight furrow, straight down the line, straight etc.

'Your *accountability* will extend to include the *implementation* and analysis of *customer* research for *value* proposition, *communications* and *product* development, identifying business *opportunities* that are in line with *customer* acquisition and retention *strategy*, you will plan and project manage *customer communications* including advertising, DSM and point of sale material.'

Suncorp job advertisement

'Mick likes guys who are *accountable* when they tag, but *at the end of the day*, you've still got to try to win the ball yourself.'

AFL footballer

'. . . players again slumped back into inefficient and *unaccountable* football, both teams guilty of coughing the ball up . . .'

australian.rules.com.au

'He's being *accountable* for Adam Goodes tonight.'

Football commentator, Channel 7

'Five hens laid every day, but the sixth was not *accountable*.'

accountability moment

A US election in which $US800 million was spent on advertising.

THE PRESIDENT: Well, we had an *accountability moment*, and that's called the 2004 election. And the American people listened to different assessments made about what was taking place in Iraq, and they looked at the two candidates, and chose me, for which I'm grateful.

Washington Post, 16 January 2005

accounting irregularity

1. An indiscretion involving money.
2. What, in a decontextualised *scenario*, might be interpreted as approximating or simulating fraud. White collar crime. Theft motivated by excessive zeal, *commitment*, *passion*, *core values*, etc., but unarmed and usually not involving actual break-in. *Accountable* theft.

'*Accounting irregularity* may be death knell for World Com: World Com, the second largest US phone company, admitted on 25 June that it had improperly booked its operating expenses in such a way as to hide $3.8 billion in costs over the last five fiscal quarters. The expenses were reported as capital expenditures to be depreciated over time, allowing the carrier to post $1.38 billion in net income for 2001 instead of more than a billion dollar loss.'

Spectrum online, 27 June 2002

'Thou shalt not *account irregularly* . . .' (8th Commitment)

See *competitive environment*. (Note: The shredding of files by accounting companies is not called an *accounting irregularity*.)

achieve

1. To succeed at what you're doing, to accomplish, complete the task, do it.

Outcomes, *goals*, *success*, dreams, *missions*, *purposes*, *visions*, *accountability*, etc., are all *achieved*. Companies do not make themselves more transparent, they *achieve transparency*. They do not succeed, they *achieve* success. Some companies have '*achieved* thorough immersion in the NLP [Neuro Linguistic Programming] experience'. Many have *achieved* their *values* through *commitment* to them – even *passionate commitment*. Children *achieve learning outcomes*. *Closure* is also something to be *achieved*.

'*Achieve implementation* success.'

Consultancy document

'And more, much more than this,
I *achieved* it my way.'

'Climb every mountain; ford every stream,
Follow every by-way: till you *achieve* your dream.'

acronyms

'DEAL, the electronic application lodgement system for medical devices, is being developed as part of the overall *Strategic Information Management Environment* (SIME) computing development at the TGA, and as such is dependent on the delivery timetable for other systems such as the Australian Register of Therapeutic Goods (ARTG).'

Department of Health and Ageing (DHA)

across the board

1. Everyone and everything; without exception.
2. *Whole of government*, *whole of organisation*; *holistic*: 'We've made changes *across the board*.'

action / actioning / actioned

'You took the part that once was my heart,
So why not take me *across the board*.'

action / actioning / actioned

Do, doing, done.

'Demonstrate and articulate *innovative* methodologies that
will *enhance* your ability to have your ideas heard (influence),
and *actioned* (*project managed*) [sic].'

Melbourne University Leadership & Professional
Development Program

'And more, much more than this,
I *actioned* it my way.'

See *implement, implementing, implemented*

actionable

1. Subject or liable to an action at law.
2. Something from which actions may result; as in
'actionable outcomes', 'actionable predictions', etc.

'A 360 "jamming" session (kind of like *brainstorming* but with
a mechanism that delivers *actionable outcomes* rather than
useless "crazytivity") provided the breakthrough.'

Effective Clutter Busters

'Call me irresponsible
Call me unreliable
Throw in *actionable* too'

action item

1. Task, job, thing to do.
2. Disaggregated objective.

> *'Action Item* FAB.05.0509.001
>
> 1 Source further notes on Board feedback on the *Strategic* Overview presentation of 4 April 2005 from the Chief Executive Officer's office and forward to the Chairman and Board members. (Liaison Officer).'
>
> Finance Advisory Board Meeting, Gold Coast City Council

> 'Don't send a boy on a man's *action item.*'

action plan

Plan of action, plan to do something, plan, etc. Similar to strategic plan. Strategy of *implementation*. (As in: *Action plan* for *implementing* the *key strategy*.)

> 'An e-business standards *watchdog* last month unveiled a comprehensive *action plan* aimed at kickstarting the adoption of Public Key Infrastructure (PKI) technology.'
>
> Computerworld, March 2004

> 'The *Action Plan* identifies seven *key strategy* areas for preventing the *uptake* of illicit drug use . . .'
>
> Department of Health and Aged Care

> 'The best laid *action plans* o' mice an' men
> Gang aft a-gley.'

actualisation, self-actualisation

Satisfaction of needs, wants, aspirations. Becoming the sum total of your personal wishes. Selfishness, narcissism. Me.

actualised needs

> 'The dominant trend is now towards *self-actualisation*, where people want companies and *brands* that add to their personal development and quality of life.'
>
> Direct marketing agency

> '. . . till you *actualise* your dream.'

actualised needs

1. A marketing formula based on Maslow's Hierarchy of Needs.
2. Satisfied, fulfilled or realised *needs*, e.g. a BMW, blender, jet-ski, a promotion, partner, aftershave, an expensive education for children.

Aspirationals seek to *actualise* their *aspirations*.

> 'This study presents an idea for early *actualisation* of potential *needs* and techniques for *value* diagnosis and evaluation through the evaluation formula V=N/C based on my experience.'
>
> Paper to the 1992 International Conference of the Society of American Value Engineers

> 'And more, much more than this,
> I *actualised* it my way.'

actualisers / self-actualisers

1. People who *achieve* their objectives, *implement* their *plans*, etc.
2. People who satisfy their *needs*. 'Inner directed' people. Not 'sustenance' or 'outer directed' people. Ambitious, capable, egocentric people. Fetishists, exhibitionists, solipsists, narcissists, megalomaniacs, etc. People who are becoming more numerous.

'And more, much more than this,
I *self-actualised* it.'

See *large group awareness training, est.*

address

1. (n) Where one lives.
2. (v) To speak to, confront, look at, look into,
examine, consider, *engage*, solve, etc.
The only thing to do with a *problem;* or an *issue* or a *need*
(the means of *actualising* it); or an *agenda, core agenda,* etc.

What one does with an *ongoing issue.* What one is
determined to do when one intends to do nothing.

'The company *addressed* the consequences of an unsuccessful
attempt at becoming a *global* integrated real estate business.'

Annual report

'I'll *address* that bridge when I come to it.'

advance

(v) To dig

'Test pits will be *advanced* with the use of a shovel.'

Environmental Hygienist report, 2003

'He that *advanceth* a pit shall fall into it.'

See *terrorists*

advices

More than one *advice.*

aerial ordnance

'No further *advices* will be issued unless thunderstorms redevelop.'

'Son, let me give you some *advices*. Be good in terms of your *behaviours*.'

aerial ordnance

Bombs dropped from the air; missiles, etc. Counter-insurgent and anti-terrorist device.

'The *aerial ordnance* broke down into: 611,500 pounds napalm, 3,218,500 pounds explosives, 1230 250-pound bombs, 3318 500-pound bombs, 380 750-pound bombs, 247 1000-pound bombs, 387 2000-pound bombs.'

See *daisy cutter*, *smart bomb*, *dumb bomb*, *bunker buster*

agenda

1. Program, schedule, plan, list of items, esp. for a meeting, ambition or *strategy* (Hence, *agenda* for *change* or *change agenda*, *agenda* for *reform* etc.)
2. Secret, hidden, unconscious, self-interested, wicked, *plan*, (as in: 'But the real *agenda* is a takeover').
3. An ideology, doctrine or obsession frequently opposed to one's own, or to common sense or the broader interest (e.g. feminist, gay, environmentalist, *bleeding heart*, national, right-wing, left-wing, neo-liberal *elitist*, socialist (now rare), murderous – anything).
4. Government *agenda*, as in: 'Consult with *stakeholders* to *advance* government *initiatives* to

support the "smart state" *agenda*.' (Consultant to
Queensland Studies Authority).

> 'Radical feminism, male lesbians, transsexuals, musical condoms
> with suspenders, and lots a drummers drumming are all mani-
> festations of a political *agenda* with roots in the 1960s.'
>
> Rush Limbaugh, *See, I Told You So*

> 'Look like the innocent flower,
> but have an *agenda* under it.'

> 'The best laid *agendas* o' mice an' men,
> Gang aft a-gley.'

agenda (hard and soft)

Wet and dry *agendas*; *main game* and fairy floss *agendas*;
real *agendas* and window dressing; wheat from the chaff,
sheep from the goats, etc.

> 'In common with the other services, the public picks out a
> very specific set of *priorities*, and rejects as unimportant those
> who seek to *achieve* what might be called worthwhile social
> goals. It is the "*hard*" *agenda* the public seeks, not the "*soft*".
> social *agenda* which producers find it convenient to target.
> The *soft agenda* might be easier to do and easier to measure,
> but it is the *hard agenda* which people want.'
>
> Adam Smith Institute

> '*Third wardrobe* leaders who balance the *hard and soft agendas* in
> *driving change* will be those who *deliver* the greatest success for
> their companies over *the longer term*.'
>
> Jeff Floyd, *Australian Chief Executive*,
> October 2002

aggressive accounting

Accounting that hides problems and inflates revenue. Scam, robbery, white collar crime.

'Mr Bush profited personally from *aggressive accounting* identical to the recent scams that have shocked the nation.'

Paul Krugman, *Guardian*, July 2002

See *accounting irregularity*

aggressive timeline

1. Who knows?
2. *Going forwards aggressively*, with intent, speedily. Fast track. Do it before you go home tonight. Get a wriggle on. Mush! Get your arse into gear, etc.

'It's *very key* so we want an *aggressive timeline* on the *implementation* architecture.'

Victorian Education Department

'Thus the heavens and the earth were finished to an *aggressive timeline* . . . and he rested on the seventh day.'

See *very draft*, *very key*

aggressively pursue

To seek cost reductions, performance *enhancement*, *value-adds*, *change agility*, etc., as the young Clint Eastwood might have pursued them. Managerial macho. *Downsizing* as a 'make my day' experience. To *robustly* pursue. In the manner of George W. Bush.

'Recognising the *strategic* importance of increased scope and scale in a deregulated industry, ENERGEX *aggressively pursued* a multi-utility *strategy*.'

Energex Queensland

'With all the positive changes transpiring within the band, members Joe and Jamie *aggressively pursued* their song writing talents.'

La Tropa F band

See *aggressive timeline, aggressive accounting, shock and awe*, etc.

'Climb every mountain
Ford every stream
Follow every byway
As you *aggressively pursue* your dream'

'*Aggressively pursue* and ye shall find.'

agility

1. Nimbleness, spryness, litheness, athleticism.
2. *Flexibility*.

'Ms Larson has an MBA plus a second Masters in Organisational Development. She co-presents this simple, yet highly applicable *change* model with the intention that Black Belts add *change agility* to their *skill set*. Thus building nimble *change embracing cultures* that are based on discipline, facts and data.'

Developing Black Belt Change Agents

'Change. Definition: *change* reflects the ability to be *agile*, initiate or adapt to work effectively in a variety of situations and with different people.'

Victorian Department of Treasury and Finance

'As *agile* as a treasury official.'

agreeance

Agreement. Condition of being *acceptant*.

> 'Have we secured their *agreeance*?' '*Absolutely*! I'm in complete *agreeance* with you, Barry.' 'Both parties are in *agreeance*, then.'

agreed outcomes

Whatever is desired in common. The team responsible for *achieving* the *outcomes* for them is in *agreeance in terms of* how *core* they are.

> 'Wilt thou, Nigel, take this woman . . .'
>
> Solemnisation of *Agreed Outcomes*

See *group think*

aircraft

Non-helicopter aerial vehicle.

> 'When asked why the Black Hawks had not been entered on the mission sheet detailing the *aircraft* in the air that day, the USAF serviceperson responsible said: "We don't consider helicopters to be *aircraft*." '
>
> *New Scientist*, April 2003, on why two USAF fighter planes shot down two US army helicopters in Iraq in 1994

> 'It's a bird! It's a plane! It's a *friendly-fire incident*.'

alert but not alarmed

Counter terrorist mind-set. Alert but relaxed and comfortable. Half-coiled like a worn spring. As the roe is before it sees the lion.

> 'By now, you have probably seen or heard the public information campaign encouraging Australians to be *alert but not alarmed*.'
>
> John Howard, *Let's Look Out for Australia*

align

1. To arrange in a line as sometimes our stars are.
2. To adjust the parts of a mechanism to make it work effectively.
3. To get it sorted.

Now considered essential in companies with the potential for *synergies* and *deliverables* (as in: 'Objectives: to *align* our understanding of our *organisational values* and their *impact* on the way we plan and deliver services'). *Aligning* is a close relation of *maximising synergies*, which is a distant relation of astrology.

> 'It is important that the *strategy* is based heavily on *input* from current owners so that *outcomes* are closely *aligned* to their needs and will therefore *enhance* the experience of owning a thoroughbred in Victoria.'
>
> Letter to thoroughbred owners from CEOs of Racing Victoria and Thoroughbred Racehorse Owners Association

> '*Aligned* Missions, Values and Visions . . .'
>
> Consultancy document

See *harvest*

---

ally

1. Friend, partner, fellow member of an alliance.
2. Vassal, client state, colony, *coaling station*, etc.
3. Neither of the above.

> 'They [the terrorists] lost an *ally* in Baghdad.'
>
> President George W. Bush

See *sovereignty*

alpha

1. The first or most important part of something.
2. Something which *value adds*. Something which *enhances lifestyle* or wellbeing, like a new refrigerator, dog or baby.

> 'I believe we can significantly add *alpha* to our *outcomes* if we get *proactive* on the *change drivers*.'
>
> Corporate document

> 'And more, much more than this,
> I added *alpha* my way.'

anniversary

The date on which a person who receives unemployment benefits (see *job seeker*, *volunteer*) is required to work for them again (see *mutual obligation*).

> 'The *job seeker*'s MO *anniversary* date will be set from three weeks before they finish ISca2.' 'Referrals to CWCs in subsequent periods of MO.'
>
> Department of Employment and Workplace Relations

anti-American

1. To exhibit (i) profound loathing of the United States
(ii) dislike of the United States (iii) loathing or dislike of
some aspects of US policy and influence (iv) dislike or
disapproval of the United States relative to some other
country including one's own (v) sympathy for a declared
enemy of the United States (vi) loathing, dislike, distrust
or disapproval of a particular US administration,
president, ambassador, etc. (vii) less than uncritical
admiration for United States foreign policy or the
ANZUS Alliance.
2. The ABC.
3. Un-Australian.

The degree to which one is *anti-American* depends on:
(i) the degree to which one is *anti-American* (ii) the depth
to which they want to bury you.

'Mr Speaker, I think that says it all about the Labor Party.
Its *anti-Americanism* stands there for all to see.'

Alexander Downer, February 2004

'Having a go at the ABC for questioning the US military
for not being completely honest or forthright? The only
surprise is that Richard Alston managed to keep a straight
face while detailing the ABC offences . . . *Anti-American* is
now defined as the failure to be gullible enough to believe
all the tripe you are force-fed or lacking the zeal that allows
you to suspend all sense of reality or questioning and just
cheerlead like our brave American media brethren.'

Crikey.com, May 2003

Anzac

1. Australian and New Zealand Army Corps.
2. Legend of heroism, mateship, fair go, digger spirit, apotheosis of the bushman. Australian *icon*. Typical Australian.
3. Supreme sacrifice, confirmation of the national character. Supreme sacrifice in defence of the *Australian lifestyle*.
4. Superiority of the Australian soldier; inferiority of the British soldier; rank inferiority of the French, Indian soldier; peculiar absence of the New Zealand soldier; non-existence of the Canadian soldier; etc. Invisibility of the female gender.

> 'But *Anzac* stood, and still stands, for reckless valour in a good cause, for enterprise, resourcefulness, fidelity, comradeship, and endurance that will never own defeat.'
>
> C.E.W. Bean, *ANZAC to Amiens*

> 'Well *Anzac* Day does have a very real feeling, very special feeling. It's something that people believe belongs to Australia alone, and it has an "Australianness" about it that none other has.'
>
> John Howard, ABC, April 1999

See *cut and run*, *Australian lifestyle*

appreciative inquiry

1. *est*-influenced form of management analysis that stresses the positive, and professes a belief in 'world betterment' through enlightened management.
2. A new *paradigm* in baloney?
3. Process based on strength.

'*Appreciative Inquiry* is a strength-based *process* which *engages* a range of *stakeholders* in collaboratively identifying what is working well then compiling those compelling features into a system for positive *change*.'

TAFE Staff Training & Development Department

'At the heart of our *practice* is *Appreciative Inquiry* (AI), an approach that draws on the strengths and *values* of an organisation in order to *implement* its *change agenda* and *achieve* its highest goals . . . We always seek to *enhance* the *core* strengths that *"give life"* to an organisation while *growing* its economic vitality, ecological integrity and organisational health.'

Appreciative Inquiry Consulting

'An exciting new *paradigm* for human development and social innovation.' 'There is something of wonder when we shift our gaze to the vital *core* that gives life to the human system.'

Appreciative Inquiry and the Quest

appropriate

1. Suitable, proper, fitting.
2. Convenient. Useful. Advantageous. Whatever.

'Titan is *committed* to full cooperation with government investigations into these matters. Should evidence arise of unethical or illegal behaviour, we will take *appropriate* action.'

Statement by Titan Corporation CEO, May 2004

Question: 'Mr Secretary, in the event of any conflict with Iraq, would you like to see Australia on board?'

Secretary Powell: 'I think that's *hypothetical*, and the President does not have any war plans on his desk [sic!]. And as he has said to all of his friends, that as we go down this road to try

33

to do something about this despotic regime that develops *weapons of mass destruction* and threatens the region and the world, he will consult widely with our friends and *allies* around the world. But I would not pose such a question at this time because it wouldn't be *appropriate*.'

Press conference after meeting John Howard, June 2002

'And having passed through that first stage, I think it is *appropriate* now that we turn our gaze to the second stage.'

John Howard, address to the Liberal Party, 1997

'And more, much more than this, I did what was *appropriate*.'

arena

1. Stadium, field, etc.
2. Realm, sphere, domain, department, ambit, subject, category of study or business.
3. *Target market*.

'The US REI equity advisory business comprised companies that dominated the slow growth, defined benefit pensioner *arena*.'

Superannuation document

artistic gateway

Not capable of sustainable revitalisation.

'Sustainable revitalisation is not something purchased like a new suite of street furniture or an *artistic gateway*.'

Vital Places consultancy

aspirational

A political and marketing category.
1. (i) (n) One who *aspires*, has ambitions, wants, etc.
(ii) A class of people or political constituency – said to
be new or 'of the future' – who want something better
for themselves, want to 'get on' (as if we all don't; as if
their parents and grandparents didn't). (iii) Working
people who don't see themselves as working class.
Ditto customers and companies that cater to them
(as in: '. . . *aspirational* companies like Virgin').
(iv) People with 'higher-purpose *commitments*'; (adj)
aspirational voters, shoppers / shopping (as in: 'buying
slightly above their true station in life'), *customers*.
2. (n) Social climber; grasper; upstart; philistine;
(adj) greedy; materialistic; meretricious; selfish.

'Estates like these are home to the *aspirationals* . . .'

ABC radio

'Our writings on the "*aspirational* gap" have *focused* more on how
lifestyle brands should help *customers actualise* their *aspirations*.'

New York Times

'Dasoni [bottled water], said a spokeswoman, was designed
to meet the "*aspirational*" *needs* of *customers*.'

Daily Telegraph, UK

'. . . as he was *aspirational*, I slew him.'

'Australia is *aspirational* . . .'

Consultancy to Australian Tourism Commission

See *lifestyle*

aspiration (aesthetic)

Desire to *actualise* vanity.

> 'While, to be fair, a large number of cosmetic patients undergo operations due to natural physical deformity, accidents or the like, what about those *aesthetic* punters out there with more superficial *aspirations*?'
>
> *GQ Magazine*, Spring 2003

> 'Follow every rainbow,
> till you *achieve* your *aspirations*.'

assertive, assertiveness

1. Self-confident, self-assured; pushy.
2. A necessary quality that can be acquired with *tools*.

> 'The goal of being an *assertive* communicator is to project self-confidence thus gaining the respect of others. For people to understand or respond to your ideas or views, you need to be able to articulate what these are. Our *Assertiveness* Course is a practical *workshop* designed to give you the *tools* you need to *communicate* with *clients*, colleagues or business partners in a view [sic] to maintaining a good working relationship.'
>
> Odyssey training

> '. . . as he was *assertive*, I slew him.'

assessment regime

How things are assessed.

> 'QSA should *progress* the *assessment regime*.'
> Consultancy document for Queensland Studies Authority

asset footprint

The footprint of an asset. The kind of footprint that preserves integrity and creates platforms.

'The review will establish an *asset footprint* that preserves the *brand* and style integrity of our wines while creating an efficient and simple production and distribution platform.'

Southcorp media release, 2004

asset structures

Buildings and equipment.

'While our electricity *asset structures* are solid and sound, we have already commenced onsite inspections of all facilities within the region of the earthquake.'

Hydro Tasmania, November 2004

'Joshua fit de battle of Jericho/And de *asset structures* came a tumblin' down . . .'

asymmetrical warfare

Warfare in which the belligerents are so mismatched the weaker must find the flaws in the stronger and exploit them ruthlessly. As in guerrilla warfare; Vietnam; Iraq; David and Goliath, etc.

at peace / at one

1. Resting, calm, assured, resigned; in a state of grace; gone to God.
2. Agreed, of the same mind, on the same wavelength.

3. In *agreeance* with the suggestion, plan, *strategy*, *implementation* architecture, etc. *Acceptant* of it. I'll buy it. I'm satisfied. We can *move on*. *Closure*.

'I'm *at peace* with that. Is everyone *at peace* with that?'

attitude

1. Outlook, opinion, standpoint, manner, posture, etc. (As in: 'He has a curious *attitude* to underwear.')
2. Character, personality; being ('What *attitude*!').
3. Also *attitude problem* – the *wrong attitude*; *attitude* that needs to be *addressed* by *large group awareness training*, *Neuro Linguistic Programming*, *re-engineered*, *downsized*, etc.

'Let's have an *attitude* of being appreciative of where we are because we know where we have come from, and let's never fall into the trap of being satisfied with where we are at and stop *growing*.'

Hillsong Church

'Thou shalt not bear false *attitude*.'

'He that is not with me has an *attitude* problem.'

attrited

Killed and wounded in large numbers, decimated at least, much reduced – 'pureed'.

'The enemy's troops in that region have been heavily *attrited*.'

Iraq War, 2003

'*Attrite* them all! The Lord will know his own!'

'Thou shalt not *attrite*.' (6th Commitment)

See *degraded*, *lit up*

Australian lifestyle

1. The style of life in Australia. Bushfire prone.
Easygoing; fair go; she'll be right; slip, slap, slop; lucky
country, etc. Not up yourself. Just like us. Not 'not the
sort of people we want here'. Relaxed and comfortable.
Democratic, tolerant, rich multicultural diversity, etc.
Crocodile hunting. Mateship, stick together in adversity.
Alert but not alarmed. Sport. *Anzac* spirit. Greatest
shareholding democracy in the world. Aussie! Aussie!
Aussie! Oi! Oi! Oi!
2. A handful of clichés useful in politics, media,
marketing, etc. *Enhanced Australian lifestyle* – what
aspirationals seek i.e. *achievement* of *envisioned*
personal *goals*; *implementation* of *goals*: private school,
share portfolio, etc.

'To think they gave their lives to defend our *Australian
lifestyle*.'

Football commentator on Anzac Day

'*Lifestyle* Funeral Services'

Geelong, Victoria

'I love a sunburnt *lifestyle*,
A land of sweeping plains.'

See *commitment*

Australian people (the)

1. The people who live in Australia or call themselves Australian. Australians. Australians all. Aussies.
2. A rhetorical construction popular with politicians. 'If I know *the Australian people* they will want to stay the course.' '*The Australian people* are not the kind to *cut and run.*' '*History* shows at times like this *the Australian people* stick together.' 'I don't think Australians want to see those kinds of people coming to their country . . .' etc. The *sovereign* people of whom one is an obedient servant – whose duties are more easily filled when one has *access* to opinion polls.
3. Reliable sign of populism, emotional blackmail, political slumming, abandonment of truth, principle, etc. ('Australians are a pragmatic people' = 'It is incumbent upon me to reject a more honourable course.')

See *ordinary Australians*

author

(n) Writer; (v) To write. (As in: 'Tolstoy *authored War and Peace.*' Lincoln *authored* the Gettysburg Address.) *Authors* of English curricula sometimes speak of '*authored* texts'.

'It is *authored*.'

'The *authoring*'s on the wall.'

'It is *authored* all over your face.'

Bb

back-ended

(adj) More at the back than the front. (v) To put more at the back.

'*Back-ended* capital returns.'

See *reticent*

balance

1. Poise, equilibrium, steadiness. Weighed.
2. Whatever serves the status quo; the government, the board; mediocrity, dullness, timidity. Propaganda.

'Whereas some . . . make almost no attempt at *balance*, others . . . do make a genuine effort to be fair.'

Tom Gross, 20 June 2004

'". . . *balance*", the BBC's crudely applied device for avoiding trouble . . .'

Tim Llewellyn, January 2004

See *on balance*

ball-park

Approximate figure or amount, estimate. How much roughly? Am I thinking along the same lines?
(n) What's your *ball-park* on that? (v) Get him to *ball-park* it. (adj) A *ball-park* figure will do.

'What's the *ball-park* of that doggy in the window?'

baseload

1. The minimum amount of power that an energy company must make available to *customers*.
2. Any other minimum; e.g. minimum *customer* requirement. The US Marines speak of *baseload management*.

Baseload is a close relation of *Guaranteed Service Level* (*GSL*), a *commitment* of privatised public utilities. (As in: 'as part of its *commitment* to *customer service*, Powercor Australia has *Guaranteed Service Levels* (*GSLs*) for a number of activities that our *customers* have told us are important . . . One of our *GSLs* is that we will restore power to all *customers* in 12 hours of a supply interruption being reported . . .') etc.

'How to debottleneck *baseload* LNG Plant.'

www.gasprocessers.com

battler

1. Low-income earner. One who battles in life; struggles to make ends meet; an honest, down-to-earth *ordinary Australian* on low to average wages. Salt of the earth. Incarnation of Henry Lawson, *Anzac*, John Curtin, Slim Dusty, Delta Goodrem, etc. A worker. A socialist (archaic). Residing in a caravan park.
2. Loser. Honest no-hoper. Not effectually self-interested; poor bastard, etc.
3. Not a yuppie, not New Age, not a member of the *chattering classes* or *elite*. Drinks instant coffee. Not politically correct. Person who really needs a 4x4, but can't afford one. *Aspirational*, not. Person who used to

vote for the Labor Party, but now votes for anybody.
Voters of influence.

> 'Howard, by contrast, strikes a chord with traditional work-
> ing people because he understands that *battlers* want a hand-
> up, not a handout.'
>
> Tony Abbott

> 'These are some of the most *battling* Australians.'
>
> Kim Beazley

> 'Howard Shafts *Battlers*'
>
> workers.labor.net.au

bed down

1. Go to bed, settle down for the night, hit the hay, hit
the sack, etc. Encamp as animals do: 'At night they *bed
down* in the open away from trees and bushes.'
2. To put in place permanently, or at least until the next
consultancy. To set in concrete. Organisations like their
values and *behaviours* to be *bedded down*. Also their
strategies, *goals*, technology, etc.

> 'The trend is expected to accelerate as banks *bed down* CRM
> as a *customer management* and *marketing tool* : . . .'
>
> *Australian Financial Review*

> 'Now I *bed me down* my goals.'

bedrock understanding

1. A kind of understanding that, like bedrock, is deep
and unshakable and therefore should not need
reaffirming.

behavioural accountabilities

2. Understanding that needs reaffirming.

> 'This is not directed at gay people. It's directed at reaffirming a *bedrock understanding* of our society.'
>
> John Howard, April 2004

behavioural accountabilities

1. *Accountable behaviours*?
2. Things that 'form the cornerstone of the *HR Strategy* and will *underpin* all people-related programs and activities'. (Victorian Department of Treasury and Finance).
3. Things that turn a Department into a *culture*.

> 'I am pleased to be launching the *Behavioural Accountabilities* to you and I look forward to watching the Department evolve into the culture we *aspire* to [sic], as we all continue to *ensure* that we reflect these *behaviours* in our day-to-day life.'
>
> Victorian Department of Treasury and Finance

behaviours

More than one behaviour.
Behaviours are often *key*. For instance, 'knowing the personal *drivers*' and 'evaluating content of work and *quality*' are *key behaviours*.

> 'As members of the Department of Treasury and Finance, it is important that we all demonstrate *behaviours* reflective of both the *organisational aspirations* of the Department, and the specific work *accountabilities*, *deliverables* and *outputs* for which we are individually responsible.'
>
> Victorian Department of Treasury and Finance

'Our *outputs* have tended to be about what we do — our *behaviours* are *focused* on how we do it.'

> Victorian Department of Treasury and Finance

'These *behaviours*, generally referred to within the organisation as "The Eight Behaviours", are as follows:
1. . . . Ruthlessly seeking to understand, through the use of *dialogue* . . .'

> Leadership@City of Port Phillip

'If your *behaviours* don't improve, Shane, your *punishments* will be severe.'

behaviours (challenging)

More than one challenging behaviour. Madness, lunacy, mental disorder.

'Respite services have been expanded with a *focus* on carers in rural and remote areas, and services for carers of people with dementia and *challenging behaviours*.'

> Australian Government, Department of
> Health and Ageing

'Many children present with persistent conduct problems but not all meet the criteria for Disruptive Behaviour Disorder (DSM-IV, Diagnostic and Statistical Manual of Mental Disorders from the American Psychiatric Association). At the primary care level it is more relevant to examine the group of *challenging behaviours* known as Disruptive Behaviour Disorders . . .'

> Fact Sheets for Health Professionals,
> Victorian GP Network

believe

1. To deem it so; to judge or accept as true; to know in one's heart.
2. To think idly. To think maybe and say for sure. Whatever. Make-believe. Almost *known*.

> 'We *believe* he has, in fact, reconstituted nuclear weapons.'
>
> Vice President Cheney, 10 October 2003

belt

See *quality tool belt*

benchmarking

(n) A surveyor's mark for observing tides; hence, a standard by which the performance of an individual or organisation can be measured.

(v) 'Learning, sharing information and adopting *best practices* to bring about step changes in performance.' (Public Sector Benchmarking Service UK).

(adj) *Benchmarked,* the state of an organisation, individual or activity after *benchmarking*; that is, more efficient, successful or competitive.

Whatever is the best is called the *benchmark*: Microsoft, Manchester United, Sachin Tendulkar, Catherine Zeta-Jones, etc.

> 'Full cost allocations will assist in the promotion of *benchmarking* and *contestable* service *delivery* in line with the government's *commitment* to national competition policy.'
>
> Victorian Department of Treasury and Finance

'You're the top. You're the Colosseum,
You're the top. A *benchmarked* Museum.'

benchmarking partnerships

More than one *benchmarker*; *aligned benchmarkers*:
benchmarkers acceptant of each other's *benchmarks*.

> '*Benchmarking Partnerships* are owners of AQC *Benchmarking* &
> Appointed by Asian Productivity Organisation as *Bench-*
> *marking* Experts & Authorised Delivery Partners of Business
> Excellence Australia, a Division of Standards Australia
> International Limited.'
>
> Queensland Government

best of breed

1. The best example (of Angora rabbit, White
Orpington hen, Jersey cow, etc.) in the show.
2. 'The *strategy* of selecting the best *product* of each type
(and *integrating* them yourself), rather than selecting one
large *integrated* solution from a single vendor.'

Also applied to people, but so far only in their organisational contexts.

> 'Wherever appropriate, these "*best of breed*" products are
> *integrated* to provide a seamless legal office *utilising* industry
> standard, client/server infrastructures.'
>
> Consultancy

> 'The people that run these institutions are there supposedly
> because they are the *best of breed* in their profession, because

they have that experience and understand the importance of the work before them . . .'

Senator Lundy (ALP, ACT), February 2004

best practice

The best or equal to the best; the *benchmark*; that to which all procedures should conform; what organisations seeking *continuous improvement* try to *achieve*. Commonly International *Best Practice*, *world's best practice*.

'In order to qualify as a *best practice*, the activity in question must be evaluated both by independent experts and by the people who are directly concerned.'

UNESCO

See *Key Performance Indicators (KPIs)*, *world's best practice*

Bible

What one swears on.

'Well, there never was a *Bible* in the room.'

Texas Governor, Bill Clements, asked about repeated lying

big-step improvement

Not a small step; possible *sea change*, *about-face* or even *paradigm shift*. A big step forwards for the organisation is sometimes a big step backwards for employees.

'CIP-*continuous improvement process*: a never-ending effort to expose and eliminate root causes of *problems*; small-step improvement as opposed to *big-step improvement*.'

Consulting group

See *business process re-engineering*

black armband

1. (n) Worn as a sign that we remember the dead.
2. (adj) Historians and others (see *elite*, *chattering classe*s, intelligentsia, *café latte*) who, according to G. Blainey, J. Howard and various Australian neocon equivalents, recognise only the dark side of Australian history, particularly the dispossession and treatment of Aborigines. Historians actually holding to such a bizarre perspective have not been convincingly identified, but the charge was never intended to be a *surgical strike*. Attendance at *Anzac* Day ceremonies or keeping photos of the dead on one's mantelpiece are not designated *black armband* activities.

'So long as the *black armband* view is influential . . . Australia's future as a legitimate nation is in doubt.'

Geoffrey Blainey, 1997

'This *black armband* view of our past reflects a belief that most Australian history since 1788 has been little more than a disgraceful story of imperialism, exploitation, racism, sexism and other forms of discrimination.'

John Howard, 1996

bleeding hearts

1. *Liberals* in the modern American sense; timorous, pussyfooting, equivocating, spineless. Suckers, fools. People without *moral clarity*; not *plenty tough*. Social democrats, meliorists, ordinary liberals. People whose hearts bleed at every sign of injustice.
A *bleeding heart* is not incurable. Many who begin with the condition go on to become successful right-wing curmudgeons.
2. People whose hearts bleed at *some* signs of injustice. *Black armbanders*. Jerks. Macbeth – '. . . too full o' the milk of human kindness' (cf. Lady Macbeth – '. . . make thick my blood.') No stomach. No ticker, etc.

> '*Bleeding hearts* left exposed as fools.'
> *Sydney Morning Herald*, 15 October 2002

> 'Please help me mend my *bleeding heart*, and let me live again.'

blue-chip

1. Casino chips of the highest monetary denomination.
2. Wealthiest *customers* or *clients*; *clients* requiring special services, including regular cocktail parties and private rooms, known as 'relationship marketing', etc. Privileged *clients*.

blueprint

Overarching framework for *strategies*.

> '*Blueprint* Sponsor Group: This group brings together *key people* across the Office of Education, the Office of

Learning and Teaching and the Office of *Strategy* and Resources who are responsible for *Blue Print* Strategies 3–7 . . . By addressing the interdependencies of the *initiatives*, within the overarching framework of the *Blueprint*, the group is able to support a cohesive *communication strategy* to principals and schools.'

Newsletter, Office of School Education, Victoria

blunt force trauma

Blows. Whacks. Thumps. Punches. Kicks. Hits. Beatings. Bludgeonings, etc., unto death or amputation. Also known as *unlawful knee strikes*.

'Pentagon officials . . . said last fall that both had suffered *blunt force trauma* to the legs.' 'Private Brand, who acknowledged striking a detainee named Dilawar 37 times, was accused of having maimed and killed him over a five day period by "destroying his leg muscle tissue with repeated *unlawful knee strikes*".'

New York Times, March 2005

'How would you like a *blunt force trauma* on the nose?!'

'And David put his hand in his bag, and took thence a stone, and slung it, and the Philistine suffered *blunt force trauma* in his forehead . . . and he fell upon the face of the earth.'

body attachment

Arrest of a person for failure to pay his or her medical bills. (US)

border protection

1. Protecting borders from weeds, pests, drugs, terrorists, crime, disease, etc.
2. Protecting borders from people smugglers.
3. Protecting borders from *queue jumpers*, *illegals*, etc.; from people who are not refugees.
4. Xenophobia. Wedge politics. Scare campaign. To incite fear and loathing.

> 'The *challenges* that Australia now faces in relation to *border protection* include people smuggling, often organised on an international scale; internationally controlled rings of illegal drug traffickers; well-organised and resourced terrorist groups; transnational crime syndicates; the relatively new phenomenon of sophisticated cyber crime; new outbreaks of old health challenges such as tuberculosis; outbreaks of foot and mouth and other potentially devastating diseases; threats to native wild life, and illegal fishing operations in Australian waters.'
>
> John Howard, October 2001

bottleneck

Something requiring *debottlenecking*. Sometimes a person is a *bottleneck*.

bottom line

1. An accounting term. The last figure on the balance sheet.
2. What matters. The only thing that matters. Don't ask me about anything else.

'The *bottom line*, but Tony, yes, but *at the end of the day* — if you'll let me finish, you asked me the question after all Tony, and I'm trying to answer it — *at the end of the day, the bottom line* is what is an *appropriate* response in these circumstances.'

Australian politician

'All animals are equal, but the *bottom line* is some are more equal than others.'

bottom up

1. (i) Capsized; defunct, kaput. (ii) Face down.
2. *Bottom(s) up!* Drinking salutation or toast; Cheers! Here's to a long *lifestyle* and a happy one!, etc.
3. Change that does not *cascade* or *trickle down*. Trickle up.

'Creating Break Through Project *Teams* to work on the critical *issues* identified by the *Vision* Setting or by other means is a proven method for creating *bottom up change* . . .'

www.growconnect.com.au

brand, branding

1. (n) Distinguishing name or trademark. To distinguish with a *brand*.
2. Advertising. *Marketing*. Something built on big ideas.

Examples of *brands* built on big ideas include Fcuk, libragirl, Toyota Kluger and Quickcheck Kiosk. ('Our *challenge* was to create a design that allowed passengers to easily navigate the system and perform various options whilst *ensuring* that the *brand* values of friendly, professional and *service-orientated clients* were clearly enunciated throughout the design [sic].')

Branding frequently means changing a perfectly good name into an obscure, silly or pretentious one: National Bank of Australia to National Australia Bank; Kardinia Park to Skilled Stadium; Australian Opera to Opera Australia, etc.

> 'What we make are *brands*. *Brands* are built on big ideas, not necessarily big budgets and we are *committed* to *leveraging* the power of the "big idea" in the way that works best.'
>
> Whybin Lawrence TBWA Advertising

> 'Make your *brand* a cause and your cause a *brand*.'

> 'The Government is also seeking to gain greater recognition and more effective *branding* through its Active Australia program. Federal Government *branding* of visibly successful programs will *achieve* this.'
>
> Active Australia www.activeaustralia.org

> 'Thou shalt have no other *brands* before me!'
>
> (1st *Commitment*)

See *rebranding*

brandbirth

An idea?

> 'The resulting *brandbirth product* concepts are then sanity checked, shaped and *scoped* for potential *market* testing.'
>
> Growth Solutions Group –
> 'addicted to rigorous fact-based thinking'

bullet points

PowerPoint presentations and corporate documents of all kinds invariably contain a list of *key points* marked by dots called *bullets* (•). *Bullets* are believed to make an argument easier to follow. Because they represent the argument boiled down, they are also supposed to represent the truth distilled. *Bullet points* are child-like statements of the obvious and in combination suggest relationships that do not exist. They are, as Edward R. Tufte has said, 'faux analytical', and may diminish the cognitive abilities of those who regularly use them. People who use *bullet points* regularly may soon find it hard to write sentences.

Bedding down the Dead
1. Overview
   - Man that is born of woman
   - Short time to live
   - Full of misery
2. *Agenda* (Almighty's)
   - Pleased to take the soul of dear exited brother
3. *Agenda* (Ours)
   - Put his body in ground (*core commitment*)
4. *Implementation*
   - Ashes to ashes
   - Dust to dust
5. Summary (*actualised core value*)
   - Certain of resurrection and eternal life

See *PowerPoint*

bulletproof

1. Indestructible; irrefutable, indisputable, beyond question, etc.
2. The kind of evidence Donald Rumsfeld said he had to 'demonstrate that there are *in fact* al-Qaeda in Iraq'. Moot, apocryphal, 'ain't necessarily so'.

> 'Defense Secretary Donald H. Rumsfeld said today that American intelligence had "*bulletproof*" evidence of links between al-Qaeda and the government of President Saddam Hussein of Iraq.'
>
> *New York Times*, September 2002

> 'We hold these things to be *bulletproof*.'

bump spaces

1. Study areas, internal cafés or utilities zones.
2. Meeting places. Pretentious spaces. Wank zones.

> '*Bump spaces*, whether they be open air relaxing or study areas, internal cafés or utilities zones, encourage contact. N@D is two buildings, each with a hollow core, but it is cross-hatched with gantries, bridges and walkways, drawing staff away from the typical insularity of a closed office environment. Campus MLC is a funky departure from a traditional financial services environment, one of the first colonists of the new terrain of workplaces . . .'
>
> *Bump spaces* 'encourage people to meet, to bump into one another; it will increase the chance for that flow of ideas'.
>
> *Australian Financial Review*, October 2004

> 'I'll be seeing you in all the old familiar *bump spaces* . . .'

bunker buster

1. U-28, laser-guided *smart bomb*, 'for *penetrating* hardened Iraqi command centres deep underground' with a 4,400-pound warhead.
2. Remark that cracks hardened centres of the brain. (E.g. Peter Costello saying he wanted Australia to be 'tolerant'. The remark *penetrated* a bunker containing hardened centres of intolerance.)

> 'It turned out to be a verbal *bunker buster*.'
>
> Peter Costello, July 2003

bush (the)

1. The country. Rural Australia. Not the city. Not Sydney. That with which all Australians should be in touch.
2. Birthplace of the noble bushman, mateship, the Drover's Wife, the kelpie, merino, koala, Archer, kangaroo, Don Bradman, 'wattle and bottle', Banjo Paterson, R.M. Williams, Slim Dusty, Crocodile Dundee, Captain Sturt, shearers and many other *icons* of *the bush*. Etc. A place where everyone is good, where *core values* come naturally and people don't need *consultants* to tell them what they are. Where real Australians live. Myth. Primal source of *Australian lifestyle*.
3. A *marketing* concept.
4. A political concept.
5. A dangerous place, hated by Henry Lawson; the dark side of the psyche, home to sociopaths, murderers, cannibals, etc. (Matthew Brady, Kelly Gang, Ivan Milat, Snowtown murderers, etc.). A place for incarcerating asylum seekers; exploding nuclear weapons, dumping nuclear weapons; dumping rubbish,

dumping car bodies, dumping human bodies. A dumping ground.

> 'I was talking to a lady in Rockhampton just after the OAM was announced and she said, "Remember Lee, not only is it an award for you, it's an award for *the bush*."'
>
> Lee Kernaghan, *HatTown Herald*

> 'Anyone can be good in *the bush*.'
>
> After Oscar Wilde

business processes

Processes requiring frequent *re-engineering*.

> '. . . we will need to renovate our *business processes* in all areas of operations'.
>
> Consultant to Queensland Studies Authority

business process re-engineering (BPR)

A form of *consultancy*. Management overhaul, frequently involving staff cuts.

> 'A fancy word for *process* redesign, *process* improvement or even streamlining workflow. The major idea is look at what you do, what needs to happen, and how to get there using less money and time, and satisfying your *customers* even more.'
>
> The Consultant's Consultant

> 'The American experience has shown that *BPR* has the potential to create *big step improvements* that can save millions — or be a mask for drastic *downsizing*.'
>
> www.growconnect.com.au

business touch-points

Something to do with *customer* experience.

> 'UCMS Solutions assists organisations to *deliver* the Customer Experience across their *business touch-points* and support their *Brand*. UCMS offers a diverse range of integrated *re-engineering* and operational services that will *focus* on transforming the end-to-end processes.'
>
> UCMS Solutions

buy-in

1. Support? Approval?
2. The point on which the murky world of *Human Resources* turns; an illusion peddled by *management* to pretend they care what their *reports* think about changes forced upon them. A term to indicate compliance, but not whether it is genuine or why it is granted. Employees *buy in* to changed '*behaviours*': sometimes they also *buy in* to humiliation, demotion and the sack.

> '*Communicating* the EDRM message to the rest of the organisation and gaining their *buy-in*.'
>
> From a conference: 'Planning, *implementing* and maintaining a seamless electronic document and record management *strategy*'

> 'All those who *buy-in* say "Aye"'.

café latte

1. Coffee made with steamed milk.
2. *Chattering class* or *elite* that drinks it, especially at tables on inner-suburban footpaths.

Not commoners, nor yet people of much substance. Pretentious, lazy, parasitic, opinionated, left-liberal caste, flaneurs, poseurs, Green voters. Never seen in your average chop house or suburban garden with *real people*.

> '*Café latte* set save economy.'
>
> *Australian Financial Review*, October 2003

See *chattering classes*, *elite*, etc.

calibrate

1. 'To check, adjust, or systematically standardise the graduations of a quantitative measuring instrument' (*American Heritage Dictionary*).
2. Fill in the details; correct me if I'm wrong; don't expect me to bother with all that shit, I've got a war on my hands.

> '*Calibrate me*, Dick.' 'Dick, *calibrate me*, if I'm wrong.'
>
> Donald Rumsfeld to Chairman of the
> Joint Chiefs of Staff

> 'We all make *miscalibrations*.'

call centre

A place where calls are 'attended to'. Attending to calls is *offshorable*: you may think the 'first available consultant' to attend your call is an Indian in Brisbane or Sydney, but he or she is more likely to be an Indian in New Delhi who works for a company that is not the one you thought you phoned but one you've never heard of. This is because attending to calls is not only *offshorable*, it is also outsourceable. But your call is no less important to them. Some people may find this disconcerting, but only those who think about it. You may be assured that it is in the interests of all *stakeholders*.

Please do not interrupt *call centre* workers: they will lose their place in the 'lawyer approved' script they are obliged by their employers to read. This script is non-negotiable and if they fail to follow it word for word they might be dismissed. Still we all need to have fun, and the worker can hardly be blamed if you say, 'How's the weather in Bangalore? Is Tendulkar still in?' Or: 'Talking to you reminds me of a great dhosa I had in Delhi in 1973.' Conversations with *call centre* workers are often better than those you have with your mother. Many *call centre* workers will talk with wit about George W. Bush, Nicole Kidman or *The God of Small Things*. Local *call centre* workers are in general less inclined to wander into these areas: they quickly develop a whining tone and treat you like a pest or an idiot. Remember, *call centre* workers are in a bind: they are not allowed to hang up on you, but they are marked down by their managers for taking too long. When they say that the company has made 'a commercial decision to charge fees for this category of transaction' the pickle is passed to you – do you let them know in brutal detail what you think about the weaselly 'commercial decision' and the egregious bloody outfit that made it, or do you pay the innocent underpaid person on the other end of the phone the kindness and respect working people deserve? Have a nice day.

'Should you ever need to page Premier Steve Bracks, chances are you'll have to speak to someone in Indonesia. And it's not just the Premier — calls made to the pagers of a string of Victorian MPs yesterday went to a telephone *call centre* in Jakarta.'

Age, October 2003

can-do department

1. A department which can get things done.
2. A department which can do what they like, whatever and whenever suits them, etc.
3. A wilful, capricious, stupid department, etc.
4. A whimsical department.

Can do like the Inquisition could, etc. Kafkaesque department.

'I *envisage* this *cultural change* will include *customer focus* . . . The Department of Immigration is in many respects a *can-do department* . . . the Government now wants the Department . . . to be a *can-do department in terms of* changing its own *culture* to be one that is *user-friendly* and has an open *culture* of *continuous improvement* . . . I'm confident that Mr Palmer's report will provide a strong basis for the department to *move forward* with the *challenges* ahead.'

Senator Amanda Vanstone *in terms of* the Australian Department of Immigration which has deported and locked up citizens who are Australian *in terms of* their citizenship and ill *in terms of* their health.

See *user-friendly*

cannibalise

1. To eat human flesh.
2. To break up one thing in order to repair another, to improve *productivity*, efficiency, or to make budget savings, etc., to a company, a department or division; a team; a *product*. Close relation to *reprioritisation*.

> 'The Shell Internet Fund, just one year old, and aiming to harness the Internet to *core* assets to create new *products* and services, has to prove its efforts won't eviscerate or *cannibalise* those of business development . . . Some ventures will bite back; outside ventures can grow up and compete with the *core*. Inside ventures may eat your current job by overtaking or redefining *core* businesses for the better.'
>
> Bain and Company, 2001

capability

1. The ability to do something.
2. Not entirely able; unable, incapable; once but no more; decrepit.

> 'We removed a declared enemy of America, who had the *capability* of producing *weapons of mass destruction* . . .'
>
> George W. Bush, July 2004

capability gap

Shortcoming; shortfall; failing; weakness; flaw; fault; defect; deficiency; unsoundness; inadequacy; ineptness or ineptitude; inefficiency; incompetence; maladroitness; ineptness; inability; incapacity; imperfection; oversight; lack; room for improvement; missing element; Achilles heel; limitation; chink in the armour. Blundering; blunderheaded; bungling; gauche; two left feet, too many cooks; too many chiefs, not enough Indians, etc. Too many drips, duffers, drunks, drug-addicts, inebriates, pedants, dimwits, imbeciles, bludgers, bureaucrats, oafs, cretins, ne'er do wells, lummoxes, lumpkins, hobbledehoys, etc. Too many rules, not enough common sense; all heat and very little light; too much red tape . . . etc.

Gap filled by *Business Process Re-engineering*; *downsizing, Neuro Linguistic Programming, Capacity Building, Behaviour Accountabilities Frameworks*, etc.

'A *Capability Manager manages* each of these. Below *Capability Managers*, Directors of Equipment *Capability* are responsible for identifying *capability gaps* in the equipment programme and for developing user requirements to fill them.'

UK Department of Defence

'And forgive us our *capability gaps* . . .'
('And deliver us a *portal* . . .')

capacity

What is 'built' to fill a *capability gap*.

'This project has been funded under the *capacity* building stream of the National Crime Prevention Programme. *Capacity* building involves the *short-term* (i.e. non recurrent) resourcing by the Federal Government of agencies, sectors, and jurisdictions in order to *enhance* their *long-term* ability to *achieve* crime and violence prevention *goals*.'

NSW Cannabis Diversion Intervention Program
for young offenders

'We are building the *capacity* of our *communities* so that *communities* can more effectively *manage change* and the only way *community capacity* building can be *sustainable* is if the people who live in the *community drive* it.'

Department of Human Services, South Australia

capacity release

Staff reduction. Pulling the plug on employees.

'Smithers, you're released!'

See *business process re-engineering, rightsizing, de-jobbing, decruitment, redeployment, performance management, excess staff situation, downsizing*

capture

1. To catch, imprison, confine, seize, trap, etc. To encapsulate, neatly define, etc. To take possession of the ball; grab, grasp. (Football).
2. To take captive information, including personal information, contact details, etc., for purposes of *networking*, sales, *leveraging*, data analysis, etc. To study, learn, commit to memory.

'This site will *capture* a series of information to help make the hiring process faster and easier for you and to *ensure* that you get the job that suits you best.'

Australian Customs Service

'This required a *level* of discipline and activity that was new to many of the group, including *capturing* data against measures for which they had taken *ownership*.'

Westpac

cascade, cascading the vision

'A series of structured *focus* groups was undertaken to *capture* the views of young people.'

Government document

'What did you *capture* at school today?'

See *make possession*

cascade, cascading the vision

1. (n) Torrent, waterfall, cataract; (v) To surge, gush, plunge; trickle, dribble, seep.
2. Flooding, saturating, soaking, wetting, drowning the whole organisation with your *vision*, ideas, fetish, etc. Not *trickling down*. *Change strategies* also are *cascaded*.

'Too often the *Vision* for the organisation goes no further than the CEO's office and organisations' foyers. *Cascading* the *Vision* through divisions, branches and other sub-units can be facilitated to create: *aligned Missions*, *Values* and *Visions* at all levels; a Steering Team process for *managing* the change program; a hit-list of barriers to improvement and opportunities for *change*.'

www.growconnect.com.au

'Start *cascading the vision*,
I'm leaving today . . .'

See *bottom up*; *one version of the truth*

casual (casualise, casualisation)

1. Informal; accidental; irregular; impermanent; nonchalant; relaxed and comfortable.

2. Part-time, poorly paid, insecure, poorly regulated employment. The worst jobs. Jobs consequent on 'creative destruction', *offshoring*, outsourcing, etc. Jobs in capital's great and necessary *churn*. Jobs of the 21st century. 28% of US workers. 25% of Australian.

> 'So why does Australia, which used to be known as the "Workers' Paradise", now have such a highly *casualised* workforce?'
>
> ABC, August 2003

catalyst

An *impactful* person or thing.

> 'The Australia Council has to *drive* improvements in the arts sector, by building the *capabilities* of artists and arts organisations . . . to *ensure* we are a *catalyst* for greater *impact* . . . by building a vital and more viable art sector, and *ensuring* that all Australians are *engaged* with and enriched by the arts . . .'
>
> Australia Council, December 2004

catastrophic success

A very quick military victory. (Pentagon 2003)

category management initiative

1. '*Category Management* is a retailer / supplier *process* of managing categories as *strategic* business units, producing *enhanced* business results by *focusing* on *delivering consumer value*.' (Dr Ecommerce)
2. *Initiative* that cannot be correlated specifically to job eliminations.

challenge

challenge

1. Call to fight; call into question; test of ability; objection.
2. Something you meet every day; humdrum; life itself. *Issue*, problem, task, hurdle, obstacle, water-jump, trial, injury, conundrum, paradox, poser, enigma, difficulty, question, job, things to do: defeat Osama bin Laden, end world poverty, change human nature, find cure for cancer, solve crossword, deal with problem on the back line, *enhance* tea and coffee-making facilities.
3. To have some physical, mental or environmental shortcoming is to be *challenged*; as in: 'vertically *challenged*' (short); 'fiscally *challenged*' (short of money); 'mentally *challenged*' (sandwich short of a picnic).

Problems or *issues* of an *ongoing* kind.

'DSD is a leading user of high performance computing equipment and the *dynamic* nature of our business requires rapid and *innovative* responses to *changing* and *challenging customer* requirements.'

Defence Signals Directorate

'The Agency does this through the use of collaborative and *consultative* processes with the aim of building *networks* and a collective approach to meeting the *challenges* and opportunities presented by the Internet and information economy. It aims to *add* further *value* . . .'

Government education online agency

See *ongoing*

challenger brand

A kind of university.

> 'This is to ensure that we consistently deliver *"on brand"* communication . . . we are aiming to be the *"challenger" brand* in the education market.'
>
> Victoria University

change

1. (n) Alteration, conversion, transformation, etc. (v. obsolete)
2. An *achieved outcome* driven by *drivers*. Something to be *managed*. A kind of *consultant*. (Also *sea change*.) *Reform*. See *transition (undergo a)*.

> 'A public inquiry into the effectiveness, efficiency and appropriateness of current assistance programs in meeting the Government's goal of *achieving* structural *change* and a more internationally *competitive* TCF sector by 2005, including a consideration of *outcomes* at the sub-sector level, and an assessment of the *long term* viability and opportunities of the TCF sector.'
>
> Productivity Commission

> 'The wind of *achieved outcomes* is blowing through this continent . . .'

change agent

Person who *changes* things; a team that *changes* things; consultancy that *changes* things; anyone or anything that causes, facilitates or assists *change*. E.g. Psychotherapist, God, hairdresser, etc.

'As the *Change Agent* there are two *issues*: First: you are on this *curve* yourself, so you had better deal with your own insecurities and inner demons. The second is that you have to deal with the various individual *curves*.'

> Val Larson & Mike Carnell, Developing Black Belt
> Change Agents

'A one day Change Leadership Workshop equips the *change agents* with project identification methods, *quality* techniques and *team* management *skills*.'

> www.growconnect.com.au

change agility

Item in a *skill set*. Nimble; *change* embracing *change*.

'Ms Larson has an MBA plus a second Masters in Organisational Development. She co-presents this simple, yet highly applicable *change* model with the intention that Black Belts add *change agility* to their *skill set*. Thus building nimble, *change embracing* cultures that are based on discipline, facts and data.'

> Developing Black Belt Change Agents

'A time to achieve *change agility*; and a time to achieve *change agility* not.'

change drivers

Causes of *change*: Globalisation, technology, competition, the economy, deregulation, etc. Causes of organisational change, such as information networking, *re-engineering*, *category management*, *capacity building*, etc.; leading to better service for *customers*, better *bottom line*, better *triple bottom line*, better *across the board* (except for the *dejobbed, downsized* and *re-engineered*).

> 'Provide authoritative advice to the Victorian government on skills and training matters by identifying:
> - major *change drivers impacting* on the sectors in the industry
> - enterprise and sector *strategies* to address the *impact* of the *strategies.*'
>
> Industry Training Board

> '*Change Drivers* for Teams: The large scale *drivers* leading organisations to use *teams* are much the same as the *drivers* producing *change* in other aspects of operations such as *downsizing*, decentralising, *re-engineering*, etc.'
>
> www.css.edu

> 'But the *change driver* was not in the wind,
> and after the wind an earthquake,;
> but the *change driver* was not in the earthquake . . .'

change management

1. *Managing change. Change* that requires managing, including multi-tasking.
2. A category of *consultant.* Money for jam, old rope, Magic Pudding, etc.

> 'Understand the process of *Change Management* and the skills required to successfully manage the *process*' (Trans. 'Learn the process of *change management* and learn the process of *change management*'?)
>
> Melbourne University Leadership & Professional Development Program

71

charisma

See *change*, *change drivers*, etc.

charisma

(Gk. 'Gift of grace') A magical attractiveness from which some leaders derive much of their authority. Bob Hawke, Ronald Reagan, Winston Churchill, Adolf Hitler, Bill Clinton and V. I. Lenin are said to have had *charisma*. John Howard, John Major, Neville Chamberlain, Bob Dole and George W. Bush are sometimes said to have had a '*charisma* bypass'.

High office can itself be 'charismatic' and bestow authority on an uncharismatic office-holder. The power of spin; the support of the Murdoch press; the size of Air Force One; the number of flags flying; the putting on of a military uniform and arriving by Black Hawk helicopter on a naval vessel called *Abraham Lincoln* can be effective substitutes for genuine *charisma*.

charisma enhancement™

A (trademark registered) course that will make you more magnetic. So people will love you, follow you, fear, obey, etc; achieve your goals for you; lift *KPIs,* etc.

> More *charisma* may be acquired in six days for less than $US2000.00 at *The Society of Neuro Linguistic Programming™*, or from Practitioners and Master Practitioners of NLP worldwide.

> 'What Are People Saying About Persuasion Engineering™ and Adventures For Everybody™ and *Charisma Enhancement*™ in Orlando 2003 exclusively with Richard Bandler & John La Valle.'

> www.purenlp.com

chattering classes

People of no account, no common sense, no fibre. First identified by Margaret Thatcher to refer to people who did not like her. People who believe there is such a thing as society. Non-battlers. People on government grants (Queen Elizabeth, etc.). Opinionated intellectuals esp. *bleeding heart* or *black armband* intellectuals, academics, bohemians, critics of prevailing views, etc. (Plato, Mill, Wittgenstein, etc.). Salon or *café latte* intellectuals (Christopher Marlowe, Samuel Johnson, etc.). Talkers not doers (Parkinson, Prince Charles, etc.). *Elites. Non-Anzacs.* Left-wingers, *liberals.*

The *chattering classes* do not include right-wing newspaper columnists, influential talkshow hosts or politicians from the main parties. Bob Ellis is a member of the *chattering classes*. Christopher Pearson is not a member of the *chattering classes*. David Marr is a member of the *chattering classes* (or on leave to them). Alan Jones is not a member of the *chattering classes*. Etc.

> 'Interest in Australia's cultural life is derided as the province of the privileged and the so-called *"chattering classes"*, alien to the real concerns of real Australians.'
>
> Senator John Faulkner, March 2004

> 'Meanwhile, of course, the *chattering classes* are getting bothered by the fact that Howard's wedge politics are succeeding so brilliantly with the great unwashed.'
>
> Crikey.com, October 2001

choice

1. Option, alternative; array, variety, etc.
2. Priceless virtue. What the *marketplace* offers. What must be maximised and made *flexible*. To the *marketplace* what equality was to socialism.

> 'To serve you better our *enhanced* billing system now comes in a *choice* of three styles of payment.'
>
> Telephone company

> 'With cash following *choice*, the schools, hospitals, surgeries and services that do more to a higher standard will earn more. Those that do not, will not.'
>
> Alan Milburn, British Labour Minister, 2004

chunk (and sequence)

Something a *consultant* does with information.

'You will gain the following benefits and skills:
· Chunk and sequence information for optimum digestion.'
Training Dynamics

churn

1. To agitate, stir, blend, roil. To produce by agitation, as with butter. To produce in a dull mechanical fashion ('The *churn* of stale words . . .' S. Beckett).
2. 'Creative destruction' in the capitalist economy. Necessary, inevitable and desirable phenomenon produced by *competition*. Primitive religion of free enterprise. 'Paradox of progress.' Means by which everyone grows richer and happier. ('The Great American Growth Machine. At its *core* are *consumers* and their endless list of *needs*, *wants* . . . Unlimited wants clash with the fundamental fact of limited resources . . .' W. Michael Cox.)
3. *Product churn* – selling more than the *customer* needs (or wants). Or selling the basic *product* (e.g. razors, printers) at a low price, and associated products (razor blades, printer cartridges) at an exorbitant one.
4. Customer *churn* – *churning* of *customers* from one business to another. (*Consultants* will tell you how to deal with it.)
5. Job *churn* – churning of employees. (*Consultants* deal with job *churns*, too.)

'As the UK distributor for Information Inventor, we address *churn* prediction and *customer management challenges* in record time, and with industry-leading accuracy.'

Oceans Blue Instant Intelligence

'Following a recent meeting between the ACA and the ACCC in respect of industry maintenance of the provision for a *customer* to retain his or her number and *churn* between carriage service providers of the same carrier.'

Australian Communications Authority

'And thus they joined the Rio Grande Valley's eight thousand other former inseam, watch-pocket, and waistband experts in what economists call capitalism's necessary *churn*.'

Katherine Boo, *New Yorker*, 18 July 2004

'We may lament the tragedies of the *churn*'s *downside*, but we shouldn't lose sight of its very powerful and important *upside*: it makes us better off. What's really going on is a healthy recycling.'

W. Michael Cox, Federal Reserve Bank, Dallas

circle of strength

A management term. It might derive from the ancient Druids. If not the Druids, the Elizabethans. If not the Elizabethans, possibly Tibetan Buddhism.

'The structure is based on the "*Circle of Strength*" model, deemed to be the most *appropriate* for the broad participation of multi-sectoral and diverse *stakeholders* such as is required to *drive* whole of region economic development.'

Sunraysia Mallee Economic Development Board

'The Circle . . . reveals the dynamic pattern various *behaviours* seem to invite within an interaction.'

Circles of Influence, Building Capacity Through Partnerships and Collaboration Conference, Canada

clear evidence

1. Evidence clearly seen. Proof. Unmistakable, unambiguous, *disambiguated*, definite, clear-cut, etc.
2. Somewhat hazy and indistinct. I think it was him, but the light wasn't very good; my glasses were fogged, etc.

'Facing *clear evidence* of peril, we cannot wait for the final proof – the smoking gun – that could come in the form of a mushroom cloud.'

President George W. Bush, 7 October 2002

See *imminent signs*, etc.

client

1. Company or individual; *customer*, buyer, patron, etc.
2. Patient, inmate, student, drug-addict, convicted felon, *job seekers*, pretty well everyone. Companies value their *client bases*, especially *client-focused* companies.

'We *commit* to the actions we take to *achieve* the best possible *outcomes* for our *clients*.'

Core DHS *Values*. Job description, Victorian Department of Human Services

'At CACI the *client* is . . . Number One! We are a *client-service*-oriented company. We are in business to provide *quality services* and *products* to our *clients*. Their *needs* are our opportunities. Our *goal* is complete *client* satisfaction. Once we have a *client*, our *goal* is to keep that *client* forever. Our "Ten Commandments" of *Client* Consulting are our continuing *road map* for service.'

> CACI mission statement (Operational Philosophy)

'1. Placing integrity and honesty above all else.
 2. Putting *clients* first'

> CACI's mission statement revised
> after certain events in Iraq

'*Clients* all, let us rejoice . . .'

'Friends, Romans, *clients*!'

See *customer*, *consumer*

client-centric

Centred on the *client / customer*. *Focused* on the *client*. Devoted to the *client*; committed to the *client*, etc. Aka *customer focus*.

'Our *client-centric* management philosophy ensures premium service worldwide, with the *client* management team closely aligned to *clients' strategic goals*.'

> Annual report

'Mad about the *client*,
It's pretty funny,
But I'm mad about the *client* . . .'

Client Infrastructure Representative (CIR)

Technician.

'The *Client Infrastructure Representative* will provide a wide variety of activities associated with installing, maintaining, servicing computer related products at the *client* site. The majority of activities will include Deskside support and break fix. They will respond within the negotiated SLA (Service Level Agreements) *timeframes*. They will provide technical support to *customers* in solving technical problems incurred in the installation or operation of company supported *products*. They must maintain a high degree of professionalism in actions, demeanor and dress.'

Diversity Work.com

'The Wichita Client Infrastructure Representative is still on the line.'

Glenn Campbell

closure

1. Finish, conclusion, completing the circle.
2. Notion deriving from Gestalt theory that 'completion' is a primary human *need* (or '*want*' that has grown into a *need*) replacing paradox, doubt, enigma, vagaries of fate, the essential unknown, the existential dilemma, the Book of Job, etc.

Without *closure* one can't 'move on'. Popular in *est* and other movements dedicated to *self-actualisation*. Also with legal profession.

> 'I done one thing today and that was for my children and grandchildren . . . I am pleading for someone to come forward to give them *closure* . . .'
>
> Widow of murdered criminal, Victor Pierce,
> March 2004

> 'Individuals have a need for *closure* . . . The need for *closure* has interesting *implications* for *marketers*.'
>
> Marketing textbook

coaling station

1. A port for re-fuelling ships.
2. A *strategic* presence; bridgehead, base, sphere of influence, client state, colony.

> 'Look back on the Philippines round the turn of the 20th century: they were a *coaling station* for the navy, and that allowed us to keep a great presence in the Pacific. That's what Iraq is for the next few decades: our *coaling station* that gives us great presence in the Middle East.'
>
> General Jay Garner, 21 February 2004

coalition of the willing

1. Coalition of the keen, eager, enthusiastic.
2. Coalition of the coerced, bribed, pragmatic, cynical, confused, sycophantic, compromised, bob each way.

Governments *willing* to support US-led invasion of Iraq, despite evidence that a majority of people in these countries were not willing.

'We now have a *coalition of the willing* that includes some thirty nations.'

Colin Powell, March 2003

cold-call

Phoning people out of the blue with the intention of turning them into *customers*; especially for financial *products*, insurance, real estate, including *senior living*, etc.

'[Frances] . . . had picked up on some new thinking about *cold-call strategies* in low-income ethnic concentrations, and had discovered she had useful intelligence of her own to put into play about structuring earnest-money proffers so that the buyer offered full price up-front, but was protected right to closing, and could get out without a scratch in case of buyer's remorse.'

Richard Ford, 'Abyss' in *A Multitude of Sins*

collateral damage

1. Damage to collateral.
2. Damage to innocent people.

Also colloquially in politics, business, sport, personal relationships.

'Broadly defined, *collateral damage* is unintentional damage or incidental damage affecting facilities, equipment or *personnel* occurring as a result of military actions directed against *targeted* enemy forces or facilities. Such damage can occur to friendly, neutral, and even enemy forces.'

USAF Intelligence Targeting Guide, 1998

colourful

History, if it is worth mentioning at all, is always *colourful*. Some people have a *colourful* past.

> 'Lithgow today is shaped by a *colourful history*, *challenged* by ongoing technological and cultural development and, most importantly, surrounded by nature.'
>
> Lithgow tourism website

> 'QUT is a leading Australian university with a *colourful history* dating back to the beginning of technical and teacher education in Queensland when the Brisbane School of Arts was established in 1849.'
>
> Queensland University of Technology

> 'Previous to venturing on his long and successful career with CSIRO, Noel had a *colourful history*.'
>
> Stored Grain Research Laboratory, CSIRO

columnist

A pedlar of predictable opinions.

See *commentariat*

commentariat

Columnists in general (considered *holistically*). The opinionated *media*. An *elite*.

> 'Some of the *commentariat* may also be beginning to grasp the fact that a sizeable proportion of women actually

want to be with their child during the formative first few years . . .'

commit, committed, commitment

1. (i) (v) To pledge, vow, dedicate, warrant, assure; believe; hold dear; swear fealty to; determine; say you'll do it; etc. (ii) (n) Dedication, allegiance, loyalty, attachment, obligation, promise, vow, responsibility, determination, resolution, etc. (iii) (adj) A person or organisation determined upon doing something or believing in something. ('Esso is *committed* to the environment.' 'I am *committed* to leaving my wife for you.' Etc.) According to *marketing strategy*, most people have a *commitment* to a *lifestyle*.
2. (i) For sure . . . not. Of course . . . maybe. In all likelihood. Can't see why not . . . probably, depending on the circumstance. Intend to passionately. *Non-core*. (ii) Wouldn't say it if we didn't mean it, would we? It's in the *mission statement*, after all, (iii) *Absolutely* . . . in the present *context*.

'What counts is total *commitment*.'

J.P. Sartre, 1946

'We are really *committed* to rounding up the militias operating outside the law.'

First Vice President of Sudan, August 2004

'It should come as no surprise that the foundations of the sixth largest bank and one of the largest general insurers in

Australia are built on the *commitment* and *skills* of all our
employees.'

Suncorp job advertisement

'The *commitment* to Australia is the one thing needed to be a
true Australian.'

Bob Hawke

'It is rather for us to be here *committed* to the great *commitment* remaining before us — that from these honoured dead
we may take increased *commitment* to that *commitment* for which
they gave the last full measure of *commitment* — that we here
highly *commit* that these dead shall not have *committed* in vain
— that this nation, under God, shall have a new *commitment*
to freedom — and that government *committed* to the people,
by the people, for the people, shall not perish from the
earth.'

'Do you, Jason Birdwhistle, *commit* to Shannon . . .?'

commodities

1. A useful thing or a thing that can be made useful.
2. A primary (rather than a manufactured) article for
trading, such as coal, canola, teak, pork bellies, goose
feathers, etc.
3. Anything that can be sold. On the internet one may
buy from 'Commodities Ltd': Fibre Optic 15-inch
witches; pumpkin decorating kits; Thanksgiving giftable
treats; etc.
4. Any want that through advertising and *marketing*
can be turned into a *need*, or vice versa. Ditto things

such as the 15-inch witch you neither wanted nor
needed until they told you about it.
5. Anything.

The value of commodities depends on (i) their scarcity;
(ii) the demand for them; (iii) the advertising campaign;
(iv) the capacity of consumers to turn them into fetishes.

> 'Since 1921, at least, there has never been a better buying
> *opportunity in terms* of the CRB 17 *commodity* basket.'
>
> Zeal Research Intelligence Consulting

> 'DSD *Commodities* has a great selection of Silk Plants, Trees,
> Etched Glass Decals and much more.'

> 'And out of the ground made the Lord God to grow
> every*commodity* that is pleasant to the sight, and good for food.'

common sense

1. 'Received wisdom or opinion'. '*Common sense*
approach' – not theoretical or fanciful. *Battler
philosophy*; *ordinary Australians*, true Australians, real
Australians. Not *un-Australians*. Not exclusive thought
or language. Not politically correct. Plain, unadorned,
genuine. Not fancy or obscure. Unsophisticated but
sound. Appropriate. 'Every man thinks he is well-
supplied with it' (Descartes).
2. Populism. Tyranny of the majority. Anti-
intellectualism, slumming, appealing to prejudice,
stupidity, etc. Common justification for cruelty.
Glorified pragmatism.

'I am an optimist about reconciliation because I believe in the decency, tolerance, generosity and *common sense* of *the Australian people*.'

John Howard, 1997

'My view on issues is based on *common sense*, and my experience as a mother of four children, as a sole parent, and as a businesswoman running a fish and chip shop.'

Pauline Hanson, Maiden Speech, 1996

communicated

1. Conveyed, imparted, passed on.
2. Ineffectively conveyed. *Communicated*, not.

'Now, if there were doubts about the underlying intelligence . . . those doubts were not *communicated* to the President, the Vice President or to me.'

Condoleezza Rice on Iraq seeking uranium from Niger

communications

1. Passing and receiving of messages.
2. Means by which messages are passed and received.
3. The messages.
4. Common category of (influencing) *skills*.
5. An industry.
6. Subject of study.

'And he said unto them, What manner of *communications* are these that ye have one to another, as ye walk, and are sad? Be not deceived: Evil *communications* corrupt good manners.'

1 Corinthians 15.33

'*Key* to your success will be your persistent approach with the energy to work in a relationship-driven environment where your influencing and *communication skills* have been heightened.'

See *dialogue*, *global village*, *calibrate* (me)

community

The word recommends itself to politicians and corporations wishing to suggest a shared purpose where one may not exist (e.g. 'the intelligence *community*'); that one is *in touch* with ordinary people and '*community* attitudes' (as in: 'Put something back into the *community*'; 'Respect the wishes of the *community*'); or that one is kindly and *context sensitive* and remembers what the *consultants* said about *corporate social responsibility (CSR)*.

Among the various *communities* alleged to exist: the business *community*, the regional *community*, rural *community*, European *community*, international *community*, global *community*, arts *community*, church, bird, legal, racing and film *community*; *community* of practice.

When something tragic or unusual happens in them, *communities* are said to be 'reeling'.

community values

Values that politicians and land developers say exist in *communities*. Great place to bring up children, etc. Being in touch with *community values* is often the same thing as getting *communities* into your particular tent.

See *context sensitive / common sense*

company-centric

Peculiar to or typical of the company, especially in-efficiencies, follies, rituals, etc. As in: 'We know it's *company-centric* to ask you to do it, but we don't have a forklift.'

> 'The emerging reality forces us to re-examine the tradi-tional system of *company-centric value creation* that has served us so well over the past 100 years. We now need a new *frame of reference* for *value creation*. The answer, we believe, lies in a different premise centered on *co-creation of value*. It begins with the changing role of the *consumer* in the industrial system.'
>
> 'How to put your *customers* to work', CIO.com.au

> 'And was Jerusalem builded here? Amongst these dark *company-centric* mills.'

compassionate conservatism

From (i) compassionate – kind, understanding, forgiving and (ii) conservative – defender of the established order; reactionary, every man for himself, let them eat cake, make 'em pay, break their arses, etc.

Kinder, gentler, greener, altruistic conservatism. *Bleeding heart* conservatism; *liberalism;* conservatism with a human face – there is such a thing as society after all. Faith-based, pro-life, *community values* conservatism. ('. . . to put conservative values and conservative ideas into the thick of the fight for justice.' George W. Bush)

'I call my philosophy and approach "*compassionate conservatism*". It is compassionate to actively help our fellow citizens in need. It is conservative to insist on responsibility and on results. And with this hopeful approach, we can make a real difference in people's lives.'

President George W. Bush, April 2002

'Certainly on social issues I would be seen pretty much as a conservative — I hope a thought-through conservative and a *compassionate conservative*, whose conservatism arises out of a genuine concern for people and their *wellbeing*.'

John Anderson, Deputy Prime Minister, April 2001

competencies

Capabilities, abilities, expertises, aptitudes, attainments, proficiencies, *skills*, smarts, nouses, ablenesses, adeptnesses, dexterities, facilities, prowesses, artistries, workmanships, endowments, finesses, flairs, etc.

'The *Key Competencies* are a set of seven generic *competencies* that people need for effective participation in the workforce. The *Key Competencies* provide an excellent structure for the development of life-long, generic and transferable skills: as well as a framework for the development of more specific industry and enterprise *competencies*.'

Victorian Education Department

'Thy *competencies* and thy glory.'

competition

1. Contest; rivalry. The opposition in a commercial struggle.

2. A universal good. That which is energising, *empowering*, *enhancing*, *innovating*, creating, freeing, emboldening, *achieving*, deregulating, *big-step improving*, *capacity building*, enlarging, internationalising, *globalising*, *challenging*, *changing*, increasing, *aspirationalising*, *skilling*, *continuously improving*, *diversifying*, *offshoring*, *dejobbing*, *downsizing*, etc. (NB. A certain amount of *watch-dogging* is required to *ensure* that it's working.)

'. . . a necessary condition for *consumer* benefit is effective *competition* in the market. A well-functioning *market empowers consumers* . . . *Competition* energises, to the benefit of *consumers*, companies already operating in the *marketplace*.'

Allan Fels, 2002

competitive advantage

Whatever – labour costs, technology, skills, brand-name, monopoly – gives a company an advantage over its competitors. A large *competitive advantage* is called a *sustainable competitive advantage*. Cities, communities, sporting clubs, scout packs, etc., often refer in their *mission statements* to *competitive advantages* and their desire to *leverage* them.

Applied to nations it is called a 'national advantage'.

Related to but not the same as 'comparative advantage', which is an ingenious theory of international trade devised in the early nineteenth century by Ricardo and only understood by *economists*.

'We're a People Developer Company. In today's new knowledge economy, people are the *strategic competitive advantage*.'

KK Women's and Children's Hospital, Singapore

competitive environment

1. Free market; free enterprise; capitalism.
2. An environment for growing businesses, profits, jobs, etc.

'They're demanding more than the *competitive environment* will admit.'

CEO Borders Group, US

concrete (set in)

Fixed permanently; enduring; ironclad; indelible; everlasting; unending. Unchanging and unchangeable. Immovable. Invariable. Stuck, etc.

'As a pre-emptive measure which recognises that this *issue* is not going to go away. We . . . believe that there are three ways we can go, but this is not *set in concrete*.'

Consultancy

'He that believeth on me hath life *set in concrete*.'

conscious

A kind of CEO.

'The *Conscious* CEO can have an incredibly expansive influence on an organisation, and can bring a balanced integration of organisation *vision, strategic* and operational realities. The only difference between a *Conscious*, Unconscious and Anti-conscious CEO is the choice they make.'

Association Management

consensus

1. General agreement, consent, accord.
2. Agreement sufficient to move on.
3. What governments say they have from the people at large. What gives them a *mandate*. When they don't have it they show *leadership* and strength by ignoring its absence – not driven by opinion polls, not populist, etc.

'. . . something in which no one believes and to which no one objects.'

Margaret Thatcher

consistent

1. Conforming to a principle.
2. Conforming to one's purposes.
3. *On message.*

'The use of armed force against Iraq is *consistent* with the United States and other countries continuing to take the necessary actions against international terrorists and terrorist organisations, including those nations, organisations or persons who planned, authorised, committed, or aided the terrorist attacks that occurred on September 11, 2001.'

President George W. Bush to US Senate,
18 March 2003

'But in a circumstance where one of the other countries captured the prisoners and transferred those prisoners to the other, let's say Americans captured prisoners and transferred those prisoners to Britons, then the Americans would have retained some overall responsibility for the welfare of those prisoners, although the management of those prisoners would be handled by the British, *consistent* with the Geneva Conventions.'

Alexander Downer, ABC, 2004

consultant(s)

Alternative to school-teaching and unemployment. What the *dejobbed*, *rightsized* and *decruited* become. Something to do after politics or sport. *Lifestyle* incorporated. The plague-rats of managerialism.

'So that said, you can get *consulting* work knowing very little, as long as you can do what the *client* is paying you to do, and do it well.'

The Consultant's Consultant

'Get thee to a *consultancy*.'

consultation

1. Meeting, *dialogue*, workshop, seminar, weekend retreat, *team-building* exercise, etc., with a *consultant* or firm of *consultants*.
2. Telephone call with same.
3. Redistribution of revenue, often from public to private. *Outsourced input*.

consume

'The symposium and internal *consultation* will inform the nature of the documentation and processes for the proposed external *consultation*. The following are dates and times for internal *consultation* that will be facilitated by either Donna or I [sic].'

Consultant to the Queensland Studies Authority

consume

Live.

'*Consume* fast, die young.'

'*Consume* and let *consume*.'

consumer

1. (Lit. one who eats.) Buyer, user, victim.
2. Shoppers, *customers*, home-buyers, users of services, taxpayers and ratepayers, subscribers, those who attend the arts and games, *clients*, depositors, readers, patients, students, recipients of charity and government services and financial benefits, the needy, etc. Citizens of the post-modern. A person of *choice*. People in all their many aspects, etc. (As in: 'each *consumer* has a unique *personality*' – *marketing* textbook.) People with '*lifestyle* characteristics' that marketing can 'segment' and '*target*'. Humans. *Consumer* opinion – what a *consumer* believes about *consuming*; what opinions they are able to form while *consuming*.

'The *Community* Development Project (CDP) seeks to *enhance* the *capacity* of the *community* sector (non-government organi-sations and individual *consumers* of mental health services and their carers) to undertake the advocacy work through increasing knowledge and strengthening *skills* within the mental health *community* sector.'

Department of Health and Human Services

'The *consumers* of mental health services have taken over the asylum.'

See *customer*, *client*

consumer choice

A tautology.

consumer durables

An oxymoron.

consumer needs

Human wants when *marketing* has finished with them.

'Human *needs* — *consumer needs* — are the basis of all modern *marketing*.'

Marketing textbook

contestability

1. What should exist in a *competitive environment*. Whatever can be contested.
2. *Choice*.

> 'Value for money requires *contestability* and choice in the provision of government services.'
>
> Victorian Department of Treasury and Finance

> '*Contestability* means *customers* can choose their energy retailer.'
>
> Energex

context sensitive

1. Sensitive to context.
2. Sensitive to *communities*, environments, the *issues*, politics, etc. Engineering, design, advertising, development, etc., that does not spoil or deface the local environment or offend *community values,* and may even *enhance* them. *Consulting* with the *community* to win its approval for development. (*Context-sensitive* grammar is concerned with computers and does not involve opening *dialogues*.)

> '*Context Sensitive* Design: Roadway Design that is Responsive to Local *Community Values*.'

> 'The aim of the project is to develop *context sensitive* models that can be used by the tourism industry to *engage the community* and vice versa.'
>
> CRC for Sustainable Tourism, Canberra

continuous improvement

Unbroken, uninterrupted, unending, ceaseless, incessant, unrelenting, constant, non-stop, unremitting,

24/7, endless, unrelieved, perpetual, everlasting, permanent, week-in week-out, interminable improvement.

'How we do our work:
- Adapting to both a changing world environment and evolving *customer* needs
- Accepting *accountability* for our actions
- *Continuous improvement* in all that we do.'

CIA mission statement

'Policy *Engagement* forums are held to enable VET practitioners and policy makers to engage in constructive debate about how to *continuously improve* the policy *underpinning* the national training system, based on learning from both practice and theory.'

www.reframingthefuture

'. . . ford every stream,
Continuously improve, till you *achieve* your dream.'

control technique

1. Not torture.
2. A form of Human Resources activity.

'It's not torture. Pyramids can be used as a *control technique* . . . Don't cheerleaders all over America form pyramids six to eight times a year?'

Defence lawyer at Abu Ghraib court martial

See *blunt force trauma* (and other *control techniques*)

core

1. The centre, heart or truth of something. The innermost part. The bit containing the seeds (*core policy, core commitment, core strategy, core* beliefs, etc.). The essential thing.
2. *Key.* (As in: *key* policy, *key commitment, key strategy, key* beliefs, etc.)

> '*Core* of my heart, my country!
> Her pitiless blue sky . . .'
>
> > Dorothea Mackellar

> 'The *commitment* I made not to introduce a GST was not a *core* promise, but a *non-core* promise.'
>
> > After John Howard

> 'Although he may not be the man some
> girls think of as handsome,
> To my heart he carries the *core*'
>
> > After George Gershwin

core business / core business activities

The business done best by the business (cf. 'The business of America is business'). The *core business* of Kentucky Fried Chicken is frying chicken: *core business activities* include killing, plucking and cooking chickens. Making *aircraft* would be *non-core business* for KFC.

> 'We now effectively deliver the *core business activities* of the three previous bodies.'
>
> > Development of 2004-06 Strategic Plan

core learning outcomes ('nested')

Key learning outcome (nested)

'Judgments and reports about progress on *continua* also include the aspects of literacy and numeracy described by the early years Diagnostic Net and the sequence of *"nested" core learning outcomes* in *key learning area* syllabuses.'

Queensland Studies Authority

core promise

1. The main promise, the big one, the heart of the matter, the non-negotiable promise, the deal-breaker, the one to which we are *absolutely committed*. *Key* promise. Not *non-core*. The one that might be kept.

'What won't you concede? What are your *core issues*? What are your *core promises*?'

Journalist (to Shadow Minister), Channel 7, June 2004

core values

Refer to the company *mission statement* (usually located in the reception area). World's best; *continuous improvement* cornerstones; excellence in poultry, earth moving equipment, interrogation, etc. Deep respect for people, oxen, poultry, all living things, etc. Integrity, probity, profit, etc. *Customer-focused*, etc. Often discovered when setting the *vision*.

corporate citizens

Limited liability citizens.

> 'Last August, in a corner of south Texas where local news-
> papers still call businesses *corporate citizens* . . .'
> *New Yorker*, March 2004

corporate communications

Influencing, *supporting*, communicating, *enhancing*,
influencing, etc. Whatever one makes of this.

> 'The mission of the *Corporate Communications Unit* is: To
> influence and support our *internal clients* to *communicate*
> effectively about the services they provide in order to
> *enhance community* perceptions of the council's activities and
> positively influence *community behaviours*.'
> City of Port Phillip, job description

corporate oversight system

1. How corporates see.
2. How they fail to see – through an oversight.

> 'People are understandably frustrated and angry at what
> they see as a lack of corporate *transparency* and *accountability* and
> a breakdown in the *corporate oversight system*.'
> Bank chairman

corporate social responsibility (CSR)

1. A stalking horse for an anti-corporate *agenda*.
2. A stalking horse for a pro-corporate *agenda*.

3. Decent behaviour.
4. A sham.

> '*CSR* involves a *commitment* to contribute to the economic, environmental and social *sustainability* of *communities* through the on-going *engagement* of *stakeholders*, the active participation of *communities impacted* by company activities and the public reporting of company policies and performance in the economic, environmental and social *arenas*.'
>
> www.benchmarks.org

cost factor

How much it's going to cost.

> 'Tony Eastley: Mr Mansfield, what is it and how much is it going to cost?
> Bob Mansfield: The *cost factor* hasn't been ascertained *at this point in time* Tony.'
>
> ABC radio, May 2004

cost-effective communication vehicle

1. Advertisement.
2. Alan Jones (according to Telstra).

course complete

Having completed the course.

> 'If you are not *Course Complete* when you expected to be, you should contact us or your local TAFE campus.'
>
> TAFE NSW Hunter Institute

courtesy fence

> 'And Storky's Hope broke his off hind leg and did not *course complete.*'

courtesy fence

See *energised fence*

covering

1. To report, survey, work, etc. an area, *event*, *issue*, etc. (As in: 'I cover the waterfront'; 'I'm *covering* the story', etc.)
2. To believe everything someone says even if it's unlikely or plain stupid so long as it's front page copy and sells. As in: 'My job isn't to assess the government's information and be an independent intelligence analyst myself. My job is to tell readers of the *New York Times* what the government thought about Iraq's arsenal' (Judith Miller).

> 'I've been *covering* Chalabi for about ten years. He has provided most of the front page exclusives on WMD to our paper.'
>
> Internal *New York Times* email from
> Judith Miller

critical success factors

Key success factors. *Key* factors for success. Factors for success. Reasons for success. Requirements. What is needed. '*Key* areas of activity in which favourable results are necessary for a company to reach its goal.'

crystal ball

1. (n) Fortune-telling tool (risk analysis and conjecture).
2. (n) Management tool (risk analysis and conjecture).
3. (v) To extrapolate from the figures. (As in: 'I'll just
crystal ball it.') Aka: stochastic optimisation.

> 'Day 1 of *Crystal Ball* for Six Sigma uses *hands-on* instruction
> and real-world case studies to teach students the basics of
> Monte Carlo simulation . . .'
>
> Decisioneering

cultural relativism

Belief that there are no objective moral truths (e.g. Thou
shalt not kill). Belief that one culture or society is as good
as another (e.g. Saudi Arabia and United States). Forgiveness and understanding that have gone too far. Too
context sensitive to possess *moral clarity*.

> '. . . theory espoused by out-of-touch leftist, *elitist*
> academics who have no concept of America's founding
> principles and who are disappointed over the *outcome* of the
> Cold War.'
>
> New Federalist Paper No. 12

culture

1. The sum total of learned beliefs, values, and customs
that serve to regulate the behaviour of members of a
particular society.
2. 'The sum total of learned beliefs, values, and
customs that serve to regulate the *consumer* behaviour
of members of a particular society.'

(Leon G. Schiffman and Leslie Lazar Kanuk, *Consumer Behaviour*)
3. The foundation of an organisation, such as an international corporation, a taxation office or a football club.
4. The foundation *in terms of the values* of an organisation.

'. . . if *culture* is the foundation of the organisation, morale is the daily energy and enthusiasm engendered by *embracing* new winds of *challenge* and opportunity brought by each day.'
Jeff Floyd, *Australian Chief Executive*, October 2002

'This knowledge, coupled with effective management, good training, sound information systems and a team *culture* can generate exceptional power.'
Easy HR

'When I hear the word *culture*, I reach for my gun.'
Hermann Goering attrib.

'When I hear the words popular *culture*, I reach for my popgun.'
Jim Davidson

See *self-harm*

curves

Rational subgroup.

'It is the individual *curves* (think of it as a *rational subgroup*) that will determine the group *curve* (the overall *process capability*).'
Val Larson & Mike Carnell, Developing Black Belt Change Agents

customer

Hospital patient, resident of nursing home or mental asylum, university student, library user, airline passenger. *Consumer*, *client*. Satisfied *customer*. *Target customer*. Victim. Prisoner, enemy detainee, taxpayer (see *Chief Knowledge Officer*), subject of interrogation by private contractor, recipient of social welfare services, recipient of intelligence, person on whom every excellent organisation is *focused*.

> 'What we stand for:
> * Intelligence that adds substantial *value* to the management of crises, the conduct of war, and the development of policy.
> * Objectivity in the substance of intelligence, a deep *commitment* to the *customer* in its forms and timing.'
>
> CIA Vision, Mission and Values

> 'Details of the *strategies* to be *implemented* to *ensure* that service *delivery* is *customer focused*, taking into account patient's rights and the nature of the *core services* of the hospital.'
>
> Victorian Department of Human Services,
> Performance Standards (cleaning)

> 'There is a tide in the affairs of *customers*, which, taken at the flood, leads on to fortune.'

customer-centric

Focused on the customer. But wait, there's more! *Focus* with *strategy*, *commitment*, *alignment*, etc. Very like *client-centric*.

customer-facing member services team

'A truly *customer-centric* organisation will have a *strategy* that conspicuously reflects a *commitment* to *addressing* what our *customers* are telling us, i.e. it is about getting what we say and *commit* to doing *aligned* with what we actually do and *ensuring* that this incorporates *customer requirements*.'

Chief Customer Service Officer, *PowerPoint Presentation* at Centrelink, *'Future Directions'* Conference, 2004

customer-facing member services team

Not facing away from customers.

'Instead of the old departments and compartments, we are going for a *customer-facing member services team* and we needed technology to allow us to cope with the calls coming in.'

Scouts Australia

customer service

1. Ongoing practice of serving *customers* once the *marketing* has got them into your tent. *Client* service. *Consumer* service. Punter service. Joe Six Pack service, etc.
2. Say it often enough and they might believe you mean it.

'Contribute to *team* function during events so procedures are adhered to and a high level of *customer service* is attained.'

Personnel advertisement, Groundsperson: *key* duties

customer service representative

Will be with you shortly.

customer studios

Interviewing rooms at the Commonwealth Bank of Australia.

cut and run

1. Naval term; to cut the cable and run before the wind. To depart quickly.
2. Abandon (to chaos, civil war, etc.); act in a cowardly fashion; commit treachery; faithlessness; desertion; folly; play into hands of terrorists; act in an *anti-American*, *un-Australian* way. Much admired military strategy employed at Gallipoli 1915 and Dunkirk 1940.

> 'We will not *cut and run* from Iraq.'
>
> George W. Bush, November 2003

> 'This is not the time to *cut and run.*'
>
> John Howard, Alexander Downer et al., April 2004

See *Anzac*

cutting edge

Leading edge. Where innovation occurs. No self-respecting company would be anywhere else. Often appears in *mission statements*.

See *state of the art*

Dd

daisy cutter (military)

Massive Ordnance Air Blast. Designed to clear jungle (hence 'daisies') in Vietnam, used as an anti-personnel (hence 'daisies') weapon in Afghanistan and both Gulf wars. Also used as an 'intimidation weapon because of its very large lethal radius . . . combined with flash and sound visible at long distances'.

> 'The BLU-82B/C-130 weapon system, nicknamed Commando Vault in Vietnam and *daisy cutter* in Afghanistan, is a high altitude *delivery* of 15,000 pound conventional bomb . . .'
>
> FAS Military Analysis Network

damaging energy exchange

An accident.

> 'Occupational Health and Safety Management and Law 1G. Historical and contemporary models of accident and injury causation. The nature of safety hazards and the concept of *damaging energy exchange*.'
>
> University of South Australia

> 'This course considers the spine under a variety of models, e.g., biomechanical. The time distribution of the *damaging energy exchange processes* are [sic] also considered.'
>
> Managing Back Damage and Pain Course

dead-enders

1. People caught in an impasse? Or slums? No-hopers. ('Dead end: Of or characteristic of the slums or life in

the slums.' *American Heritage Dictionary*)
2. *Pockets* of Iraqi resistance said (first by Donald
Rumsfeld) to be fanatically loyal to Saddam and
prepared to fight to the end.

> 'US intelligence officials split the difference and suggested
> that Baathist *dead-enders* had hired foreign jihadists (or,
> possibly, local fanatics) to drive the suicide vehicles.'
>
> *Newsweek*, 2003

> 'Surely, John, you don't wish to blame certain communist
> *dead-enders* in Vietnam for the carnage?'
>
> Mark Hand, www.pressaction.com

See *cultural relativism*

debris event

Debris from occurrence or incident. What happens to be
debris. A happening with debris. Whatever's going down
with debris. There were up to twenty *debris events* across
western US before Mission Control in Houston realised
what was happening to the *Challenger*. There was a
debris flow event at Hummingbird Creek, British
Columbia, in 1997. *Debris flood events* and underwater
debris events have also been recorded.

> 'If that is confirmed by the independent investigation team,
> it would mean that, contrary to initial shuttle program
> analysis, the tank *debris event* at launch played a *key role* in the
> root cause of the accident.'
>
> Report on the *Challenger* Space Shuttle Disaster
> (*Event*)

> 'When beggars die, there are no *debris events* seen . . .'

decant

1. To pour fluid, esp. wine, to another vessel.
2. To move people to another room.

'We recently refurbished our office, and most staff were moved from different parts of the building into one central space. However at no stage was it referred to as "moving", "relocating" or even "shifting". We were "*decanted*". The temporary space you went to while waiting for your new desk was "*the decanting room*". This was at all times discussed with a straight face.'

Company victim

'So Moses *decanted* Israel from the Red Sea, and they went into the *decanting land* of Shur.'

decent-minded (Australians, South Australians, West Australians, Texans, etc.)

1. Not dirty-minded or disposed to vileness, indelicacy, impropriety, treachery, loutishness or appalling acts of violence, etc.
2. Like me, like us.

'But they were condemned by all *decent-minded* Victorians and by the Victorian Government, especially through the Premier.'

Victorian Office of Multicultural Affairs

deconflicted, deconfliction

1. Elimination of possible conflict or danger – in airspace, broadcasting, drug investigations, etc.
2. Elimination of an enemy force (US military).

'Time Sensitive Targets were *deconflicted* in a matter of minutes using a Theater-wide Joint Fires Coordination Information System.'

Lt. Gen. William S. Wallace, US Army

decruited / decruitment

Policy or state of dismissal. Productivity improvement. Employed no longer, *downsized*, *rightsized*, *rationalised*; *terminated*, given the heave-ho, sacked, fired – essentially.

'That's why Schmitt "*decruits*" marginal producers – he essentially fires them – and replaces them with top producers, often from the very companies that take in the salespeople he's let go. Schmitt says his "*decruitment*" program helps land top producers. "Word gets around, and they like what they hear." In short, they want to be where the slackers aren't.'

Today's Realtor

See *business process re-engineering*, *involuntary career event*

dedicated

1. Set apart for some purpose.
2. Committed to an action, creed, vocation, person, team, principle, proposition (e.g. '. . . a new nation, conceived in Liberty, and *dedicated* to the proposition that all men are created equal.' Lincoln, Gettysburg Address).

Organisations *commit* themselves to being *dedicated* to whatever it is they do, and to the processes, *strategic plans* and *implementation strategies* by which they do it. They are *dedicated* to their customers, their *stakeholders*, their *bottom line* and to *going forwards*. Sometimes they *dedicate* themselves to being *committed* to these things.

'Southcorp is *committed* to being a *dedicated* and leading premium winemaker with a portfolio of brands and wines that range from the contemporary to the *iconic* . . .'
Southcorp media release, 2004

'It creates time for learning-area *dedicated* teaching.'
English curriculum, Department of Education, Tasmania

'The author was assigned a *dedicated* Senior Media Strategist to *strategise* his book with the media.'

deemed (by myself)

(v) Thought. Decided.

'It is however *deemed* by myself as the project manager that to give the Department and this project the best chance of

overall success the system fundamentals need to meet the *known* business requirements and produce expected *outcomes.*'
                          SAP Upgrade and Improvements Project

'I *deem*, therefore I am.'

defrag

As one *defrags* one's hard drive, one *defrags* one's mind or nervous system. Relax, chill out, wind down.

'I'm going home to *defrag* in front of the box.'

degraded

1. Reduced in rank, character or reputation. Lowered in value.
2. Debauched, debased.
3. Killed, wounded, rendered dead or incapable, *lit up*, 'softened up', *taken out*, exploded, 'pureed' (by e.g. *daisy cutters*), etc. As, for instance, Stalin *degraded* millions. Hiroshima was *degraded*, etc.
4. Attrited.

'We know that overall each of those remaining four divisions have been significantly *attrited* to this point, significantly *degraded.*'
                          Major General Stanley McChrystal,
                          US Joint Chiefs of Staff, April 2003

'I mean I think, over the last eighteen months, they have been *degraded* as an organisation, to use a phrase.'
                          Alexander Downer, May 2003

'An Iraqi division has been *degraded* by 70%.'

New York Review of Books, May 2003

'The King is *degraded*! Long live the King!'

'You're a long time *degraded*.'

'You wouldn't be *degraded* for quids.'

deliver

1. To send successfully, take to, hand over; set free; assist at the birth; make good on an obligation or promise.
2. To teach or instruct (as in: *deliver training packages* or *trainings*), modify behaviour in another. To *implement*. Some people (and racehorses, greyhounds, ferrets, etc.) never *deliver* on their promise, talent, etc.

'. . . her experience with direct investments enable [sic] her to *deliver* insight into this area.'

Consultancy promotion

'Through this initiative we are working to *deliver* the evolution in how we interact with you.'

Bank promotion

'And more, much more than this,
I *delivered* it my way.'

deliverables

That which can / should be *delivered*. *Key deliverables* are the most important ones.

'*Communicating* major *deliverables* and activities to all *key stake-holders.*'

Victorian Department of Human Services

demotivated / demotivating

Suffering a loss of motivation. Jaded, crushed, stuffing knocked out, rug pulled from under, etc. Depression, ennui. (As in: 'She was *demotivated* by the news that her *skill sets* needed *enhancing.*')

'It is much more difficult to know what *demotivates* people. Of course, rotten behaviour, unfairness, disregard for the basic rights and humanities all add up to serious *demotivation.*'

John Bittleston, May 2003

'We are *demotivated.*'

Sergeant Chris Grisham
military intelligence office, Iraq

deplane

Get off the plane. (US)

'We are waiting on Customs to provide us with authorisation to *deplane.*'

Pilot

c.f. deboat, debicycle, depot.

detention centre

Prison.

dialogue

(n) Discussion, conversation, exchange of ideas. (As in: Plato's *Dialogues*.) *Dialogues* are 'cultivated' or 'entered into'. We 'open the way' to them. They are 'fruitful', 'constructive', 'creative' or 'useful'.

(v) To talk, converse, discuss, chat; phone, email, fax. (As in: 'Let's *dialogue* on Wednesday.' 'We should *dialogue* with Harold asap.' 'We've been *dialoguing* for months but he hasn't *delivered*.')

'. . . encourage *dialogue* among *key* government, corporate and academic institutions in Canada, the United States.'

'This will expand our already extensive web of bilateral and multilateral *strategic dialogues* to include these *key players* in the *global* security *environment*.'

Alexander Downer, February 2002

'Now, in my own circumstances at home, Janine and I have a non-stop *dialogue* about work and family . . . Millions of Australian families are engaged in this kind of *dialogue* every night.'

Mark Latham, February 2004

'We have *dialogued* enough.'

Trinity Communications, 2004

'You *dialoguin'* to me?'

Robert de Niro, *Change Driver*

direct reports

People. Underlings, folk of lower rank, privilege, status.

> 'A major goal of the program is to help managers to become
> emotional coaches for their *direct reports*.'
>> Consortium for Research on Emotional
>> Intelligence Organisations

> 'The *direct reports* are hungry.'
> 'Then let them eat cake.'

> '*Direct reports* who need *direct reports*,
> Are the luckiest *direct reports* in the world.'

dirty bomb

Not a 'precision' weapon. Not *low yield* or *smart*. One
that does not *limit collateral damage*. A *dead-ender's* sort
of bomb.

> 'It is unlikely, but not impossible, that al-Qaeda has
> obtained a nuclear weapon, security experts said in a
> Reuters article. More probable is that the organisation
> would develop a "*dirty bomb*" that would spread radioactive
> material over a limited area.'
>> Reuters, 21 March 2004

disclosure (poor)

Failure to tell the truth, the whole truth, etc. Misstatements, lying, dissembling, deceiving, dodging, weaving,
hiding, etc. A failure of *transparency*. *Unaccountable
behaviours*.

disconnect

> 'After a number of record corporate collapses, *poor disclosure practices* and some highly questionable *behaviour* by a few, who can blame them?'
>
> Bank chairman

disconnect

1. (v) To cut off; to break or end a connection.
2. (n) The state of being dissimilar, not the same. As in, 'There's a *disconnect* in the figures.' 'There's a *disconnect* between our *outcomes* and our *core goals*.' 'We need to do something about the *disconnect* – Nigel, can you *recontextualise* it?'

> 'What a *disconnect* a day makes.'

discuss / discussions

1. To talk about.
2. To bury, sideline, etc. (As in: Those are all part of the *discussions* that are going on now, and those *discussions* are underway.)

Discussions are full and frank, fruitful and encouraging. Our leaders 'welcome' them, and 'look forward' to them.

If a journalist asks a difficult question about some difficult matter, the correct answer is, 'Look, I mean, I've *discussed* that issue in the past and I'm not going to dwell on it. It's time to move on.'

See *the past*; *dialogue, workshop*

discussant

One who discusses.

> 'The panel sessions will involve panel members and discus-
> sants.'
>
> Conference brief

disposition

A cause of post-traumatic stress disorder in Iranian 6-year-olds.

> 'A lot of psychiatric disorders arise because you have a *dis-position* to them.'
>
> Phillip Ruddock on Shayan Badries, a disturbed
> 6-year-old *detainee*. ABC, August 2001

See *it, self-harm.*

distance mode

As you would when you're a long way away.

> 'While a majority of young people will typically attend two
> or more schools, some will learn in *distance mode*.'
>
> Queensland Department of Education

> 'A long time ago, in a galaxy in *distance mode*.'

diversity / diverse

1. Variety, assortment, mixture, polyglot, disparate, varied, mixed, etc. Not uniform or homogenous.

2. Universal good – especially when it is 'rich, multicultural diversity'.

> 'Cr Davidson said the Shire valued the *diversity* of its people and their ability to live harmoniously with one another.'
> Surf Coast Shire Community Newsletter

dog whistling

As dogs respond to whistles pitched so high that humans cannot hear them, in politics a *dog whistle* is a message pitched in a way that only some voters recognise it. Racist voters, for instance. Form of wedge politics.

> 'Federal Labor accused the Prime Minister of "retreating to the *dog whistle*" – on one hand rejecting [Pauline Hanson's] views, on the other saying he understood why some people would agree with her.'
> *Sydney Morning Herald*, August 2003

> 'So it is back to *dog whistle* politics again: *dog whistle* and wedge. This is the only feasible explanation for Howard's extraordinary attack on state schools as too "politically correct" and "values neutral". It was a not-so-coded message to his constituency of former Hansonistas . . .'
> Mike Carlton, *Sydney Morning Herald*, January 2004

See *we*

dormantising

To make as if asleep, esp. *customers*, while you close their accounts. As with the Woolwich Building Society, UK, that closed rarely used accounts without the account holders' knowledge.

'The Big *Dormantise*'

'. . . and our little lives are rounded with a *dormantising* event.'

'Now I *dormantise* myself, I pray the Lord my soul to keep.'

dotted line

An invisible power exercised by one person over another in a workplace, team or department. As, 'There's a *dotted line* to him.'

downside

1. Bottom, lower, under side. Not the higher side.
2. What comes with an upside, and often as a consequence of it; the depressing bit that you have to put up with. Disadvantage, drawback, shortcoming, flaw, flipside, bad side, bad part, part to be regretted, hitch, snag, deficiency, defect, imperfection, weakness, impediment, encumbrance, hindrance, fly in the ointment, sting in the tail, bummer, bad news, downer, etc. (NB. Some things are all *downside*.)

'We may lament the tragedies of the *churn*'s *downside*, but we shouldn't lose sight of its very powerful and important upside: it makes us better off. What's really going on is a healthy recycling.'

W. Michael Cox, Federal Reserve Bank, Dallas

'What's the *downside*?'

'What do you want to hear first, the upside or the *downside*?'

'The *downside* is — you'll have to pay tax on the upside.'

downsize / downsizing

To make smaller, diminish, reduce, especially the number of your employees.

> 'This is not an evacuation, just a further *downsizing*, and the security situation in the country remains under constant review.'
>
> UN spokesman, 2003

See *business process re-engineering*, *rightsizing*, *de-jobbing*, *decruitment*

dreamful attraction

Initial stage of *self-actualisation*.

> 'Just the other day, a kid stopped me and told me that he wanted to be like me. That is *dreamful attraction*.'
>
> Shaquille O'Neill, US basketballer

drill down

To 'focus in'. One *drills down* through a data base to find the information one needs. More generally in management speak, to seek and sometimes find more information or knowledge; as for example, Newton *drilled down* to discover gravity, Bach the fugue, etc.

> 'Nevertheless, when the group came together for a first *Strategy Review* meeting, they were able to assess the progress that had been made toward objectives, identify and *drill down* on road blocks and develop *short to medium term* solutions.'
>
> Westpac

driver – key, core, critical, etc.

1. Someone or something that drives; or, as with a golf club, is used for driving.
2. The most important forces or factors for *change* or growth in a business, department, economy, school, hospital, football team, etc. Hence also *change drivers*. Talent, effort, *productivity improvements, enhanced skill sets*, teamwork, *international benchmarking*, loyalty and accounting processes that focus on *outcomes*, are all *key* (or *core*) *drivers* at various times.

Blind faith, greed, jealousy, favouritism, luck, bribery, covetousness, sociopathy, fawning, social aspirations, the primitive urge to win at all costs and performance-based salary packages including allocations of shares are not called *key drivers*. Nor are sabotage, murder, etc.

> *'Commitment* and discretionary effort as *key drivers* of *competitive advantage.'*
>
> Corporate document

> 'The most contested value *driver* in the knowledge economy is the new real estate of intellectual property.'
>
> Terry Cutler, *Making Australia a Knowledge Economy*

> 'Infirm of purpose! Give me the *drivers!*'

> 'May the *key drivers* be with you.'

ducks in a row

Well-prepared, set up, ready to proceed logically, efficiently. Sorted.

'Show the world you have all your *ducks in a row* — purchase the GAYducks T-shirt for $20.'

GAYducks.org

dumb bomb

Stupid bomb. Not a smart one.

'The Joint Direct Attack Munition, or J-DAM, is a kit that converts "*dumb bombs*" into *smart* ones.'

Fred Kaplan, *Boston Globe*, February 1998

See *smart bomb, dirty bomb*

duress

1. Constraint by threat. Illegal coercion.
2. Attempting to influence Australia's immigration policy by throwing one's children into the sea. Act of the political imagination.

'More disturbingly, a number of children have been thrown overboard, again with the intention of putting us under *duress*.'

Philip Ruddock, ABC, October 2001

Ee

earnings accretive

Profitable.

> 'It is an effective use of the Group's capital and will be immediately *earnings accretive*.'
>
> Lend Lease, January 2004

> 'For what is a man's *earnings accretion*, if he shall gain the whole world and lose his own soul?'

economic rationalism, economic rationalist, economic rationalists

Economic theory. (No longer required.)

economic refugees

Second order refugees; ones without a legitimate claim on our sympathy; ones with enough money to pay a 'people smuggler'; refugees who have made a *lifestyle decision* to leave Iraq, Afghanistan, etc., as if they had the same rights as white South Africans and Zimbabweans to make *lifestyle decisions*; refugees who are not fit.

See *queue jumper*

editorial integrity

1. Editorial integrity.
2. Refusal to sell to a documentary-maker frequently aired film footage of government ministers without

written approval from the ministers to the filmmaker. The right of politicians to censor the public record. Breach of the ABC Charter.

> 'When licensing program material, the ABC will ensure that the *editorial integrity* of the material is protected.'
>
> ABC to *Media Watch*, July 2004

efficiency gain

Anything that makes an organisation, process, country, television antenna, can opener, prime mover, racehorse, netball team or golf club more efficient (i.e. more effective, economical, easy to use, higher ratio of *output* to *input*, etc.) Anything from a robot to a new photocopier, to a new game plan, to a bit of *downsizing* – anything – may be responsible for an *efficiency gain*. '*Enhanced* efficiencies' is another popular way of putting it. 'Productivity gain' is similar, but implies *dejobbing*.

> 'They exclude dynamic *efficiency gains*, including *synergies* with microeconomic and labour *market reforms*, and do not take full account of the *impact* of removing non-tariff barriers.'
>
> Department of Foreign Affairs and Trade

eight behaviours (the)

'Non-traditional *behaviours*' characteristic of *web organisation*.

> 'Managers and Coordinators are expected to take a *leadership* role in developing their staff to *implement* a series of

non-traditional *behaviours* based on an understanding that service *delivery* in an ever-changing world is complex . . .'

Leadership@City of Port Phillip

See *behaviours*

elite

1. Small privileged group; elevated in rank, status, power, wealth, celebrity, skill, accomplishment, etc. Pick of the crop, crème de la crème, the best.
2. People lacking the homely virtues, *common sense*, self-interest, modesty, *aspirations*, etc.; dull-wittedness, ignorance, prejudice, bigotry, unreason, etc. Non-*aspirationals*; non-*battlers*; non-*Anzacs*, etc. People of narrow or arcane views. Wrong people.

The most wealthy, powerful and elevated are rarely of the *elite*. Rupert Murdoch is not of the *elite*. *Elite* sportsmen and *elite* sportswomen are not of the elite. (It would be like saying talkshow hosts are members of the *chattering classes*.)

'Much of what passes for quality on British television is no more than a reflection of the narrow *elite* which controls it and has always thought that its tastes were synonymous with quality.'

Rupert Murdoch, 1990

'The Toyota Extreme Superbull Bullriding Series will not only become a part of the Great Western Hotels' entertainment program . . . but more importantly, will continue the great tradition of *elite* Bullriding and rodeo events being showcased in Central Queensland.'

HatTown Herald, July 2004

elite (liberal)

> 'I just think it's time to retire the "*liberal elite*" label, which, for the past 25 years, has been deployed to denounce anyone to the left of Colin Powell. Thus, last winter, the ultra-elite right-wing Club for Growth dismissed followers of Howard Dean as a "tax-hiking, government-expanding, latte-drinking, sushi-eating, Volvo-driving, *New York Times*-reading, body-piercing, Hollywood-loving, left-wing freak show."'
>
> Barbara Ehrenreich, *New York Times*, July 2004

> '"Miss Troutman has been very successful in raising money from Martin Sheen and other members of Hollywood's *liberal elite* who support a pro-gay, anti-gun, pro-abortion agenda," said Hayes' spokesman Jonathan Felts.'
>
> CNN, July 2004

> 'I thought that was a particularly patronising, condescending, and dare I say, *elitist* article.'
>
> John Howard, *Daily Telegraph*, January 2004

embedded (journalist)

1. *Deconflicted* journalist. Journalist assigned to military unit during war (Iraq 2003), or to police or paramilitary unit during civil disturbance (Florida 2004), rather as the disciples were to Jesus but with less chance of escape. Irresistible to media proprietors and news editors.
2. In bed with, bedded, seduced. Owned, made a prostitute or whore, etc. A 'brilliant, persuasive conspiracy to control the images coming out of the battlefield . . .'
3. Not 'unilaterals'.

> 'The only journalists they wanted inside the country were those "*embedded*" with the coalition forces, carefully chosen by the Pentagon and placed with various units on the battle-field. The rest of us, registered as "unilaterals," were to be kept in Kuwait, and taken out on organised day-trips, until they declared the countryside was safe, or to use their expression, until it was "benign."'
>
> Paul Workman, CBC TV

embedded (values)

Corporate values strongly held; whole of government / company / department values; values deep in the *culture*; values understood across the *totality*, in the DNA, *Neuro-Linguistically Programmed* values; values near as dammit programmed into human nature; as values are to the Amish, *embedded* values are to the organisation; rusted on; rusted in; rusted up, etc.

> 'The ability of an organisation to meet daily *challenges* with enthusiasm, supported by its *embedded values*, is what deter-mines outstanding performance.'
>
> Jeff Floyd, *Australian Chief Executive*, October 2002

embrace

1. To hug, hold, cuddle, squeeze. As in: '*Embrace* me, my sweet embraceable you / *Embrace* me, you irreplaceable you' (George and Ira Gershwin).
2. To include; take on, take up.
3. A metaphysical, quasi-religious act of submission to abstract principles, mundane tasks, *core values*, diversity, *key behaviours*, *mission statements*, *consultants*, whatever you're told to do.

> '*Embrace* selling, *customer* care and the careful use of our "resources" . . .'
>
> Kettering, (UK) coffee dispenser company
> mission statement

> 'Ten unique destinations sharing an ideal spanning five decades — elegance without pretense, *embracing* and *enhancing* spectacular surroundings.'
>
> Rock Resorts (The Difference is Legendary) advertisement

emergent learning

Not your ordinary learning.

> '*Emergent learning* is a group *engaging* in a cycle of alternating anticipation-reflect planning with periods of intentional *action*. The learning *emerges* and gets *captured* in the course of *doing* your work. This kind of learning directly *impacts action* and effectiveness in both the *short and long term*.'
>
> Signet Consulting Group

emotional blackmail

1. Manipulation of people and events by appeal to their most subjective responses, such as love, fear, prejudice, dislike of emotional blackmail, etc.
2. Extortion of money or other items of value, including freedom, safety and votes, by this method.

> '*Quite frankly*, Alan, I don't want in this country people who are prepared, if those reports are true, to throw their children overboard. And that kind of *emotional blackmail* is very distressing.'
>
> John Howard, PM, October 2001

emotional intelligence (emotional competence, EQ)

1. Empathy and self-awareness.
2. A *(key) competency* – or set of *competencies*.
3. A global industry 'teaching' these *competencies* to business 'schools, homes and organisations'.

Emotional intelligence is by one definition: 'The mental ability we are born with which gives us our emotional sensitivity and our potential for emotional learning management skills which can help us maximise our *long-term* health, happiness and survival.' (S. Hein, March 2004)

Also aids in selling life insurance: Financial advisers at American Express who had undertaken the Emotional Competence Training Program 'grew their businesses by 18.1% compared to 16.2% for those whose managers were untrained'.

emotional release

What *torture lite* provides for the torturer. There is evidence to support this theory, and also evidence that suggests there is more to it than this.

> 'You know, these people are being fired at every day. I'm talking about people having a good time, these people. You ever heard of *emotional release*?'
>
> Rush Limbaugh, 2004

empower, empowered, empowering, empowerment

Key goal of all organisations. Employees are *empowered* when they *take ownership*, usually by becoming *competent*. Customers are *empowered* by *choice*, shareholders by profit, dividends etc. Thus is the *triple bottom line empowered*. (See *ducks in a row*.)

We are all *empowered* by employment, education, a win at the races, a new set of spectacles or teeth, etc. Some are *empowered* by God; others are *disempowered* by Him. Faith *empowers*: the loss of it can *empower* equally. Ditto Reason. Hitler and Stalin were both *empowered* by 'transforming unwanted beliefs into beliefs that *empowered* them'. An *est* word.

> '*Transform* unwanted beliefs to beliefs that *empower* you.'
>
> Neuro Linguistic Programming

> 'To reach and influence the world by building a large Bible-based church, changing *mindsets* and *empowering* people to lead and *impact* in every sphere of life.'
>
> Hillsong Church Mission Statement

> '*Empower* thy sheep.'

enactor

Not unlike *enabler* and *facilitator*, but more of an *implementer*. NOT a ratifier, authoriser, legislator, etc. An institutor. One who does it.

> 'While teachers in schools are the major planners and *enactors of curriculum programs*, there are other "*curriculum planners*" and "*educators*".'
>
> Queensland Department of Education

132

'And more, much more than this,
I *enacted* it my way.'

endeavour, endeavoured, endeavouring

Never say 'try'. As in: 'We shall *endeavour* to answer your call as soon as possible.' 'Just bear with me, and I'll *endeavour* to find out.' 'If at first you don't succeed, *endeavour*, *endeavour* and *endeavour* again.'

end of the day (at)

1. Dusk, evening, nightfall.
2. When all's said and done; after all; in the end. The gist of it; what really matters; the nub of it. When you boil it down, separate the wheat from the chaff, the sheep from the goats, etc. The truth, however unpalatable. At *the end of the day* 'our little life is rounded with a sleep'.

> '*Look, at the end of the day* I know that they had [weapons] programs, there's no doubt about that.'
> Alexander Downer, ABC radio, January 2004

> 'Now *look, at the end of the day, look*, people can make up their own minds about this, but John Howard and I are as one in our passionate concern . . .'
> Alexander Downer, 3AW, June 2004

> 'And *look, at the end of the day* . . .'
> Alexander Downer, 2GB, March 2004

> 'I think, *at the end of the day* . . .'
> Alexander Downer, *Australian*, June 2004

end of the spectrum (demand)

'But *look, at the end of the day . . .'*
>> Alexander Downer, *Sydney Morning Herald*, July 2004

'*At the end of the day . . . at the end of the day . . . look, at the end of the day.'*
>> Alexander Downer

end of the spectrum (demand)

Not the *supply* end of it.

Other reported ends of the spectrum include: long, short, low, lower, low skills, upper, top, bottom, wide, narrow, other, another, one, high, opposite, quality, private, most serious, multimedia-left and libertarian-right.

'However, support at the *demand end of the spectrum* has the potential to provide multiplier benefits for artists which grants alone cannot provide.'
>> Australia Council

end-to-end

A form of business *process* review that 'simplifies, standardises and consolidates a company's *processes* and practices'. Front to back? Back to front? *Back-ended going forwards*.

'Under the Veraison program the Company will undertake *end-to-end* business *process* reviews in order to simplify, etc. . . . current *processes* . . . etc.'
>> Southcorp media release, 2004

end-user experience

The experience of a user at or in the end?

'To support the *"end-user experience"* by *continual improvement* in the Centre's policies, procedures and service *delivery* in response to the University's needs.'
> *Key Result* Area 4, *Strategic Plan* 2005–2008,
> Centre for *Flexible* Learning (*Building Partnerships* for Success*), Macquarie University, Sydney

'Waiter! There's a fly in my *end-user* experience!'

enemy prisoner of war

1. Prisoner of war.
2. Not a prisoner of war.

Until 1991 it was assumed that any person taken prisoner in war was a prisoner of war. The UN laid down certain conventions relating to the proper treatment of such people. During the Gulf War the US decided that the assumption was not an *appropriate* one. It is possible that they have a similar and not unrelated view of the conventions.

energised fence

Description of 9000 volt fence on plan of Baxter Detention Centre, South Australia.

'No, it is not an electric fence . . . It is an *energised fence*.'
> Deputy Secretary, Department of Immigration

energy

1. Necessary for *outcomes*.
2. A possible use for men.

> 'EOWA's Women in Management Tools Module 5 – Increased *energy* for improving employment *outcomes* for women can be obtained by *engaging* a broad range of men as EO partners.'
>
> Equal Opportunity for Women in the
> *Workplace* Agency (EOWA)

engage

To *engage* in *dialogue* (discuss); *engage* with ideas (think); *engage* the enemy (fight); *engage* with another country (trade); engage the reader, student, audience, client, etc.; *engage* people (interest, entertain, amuse, occupy, get involved, absorb, engross, divert, charm, persuade, enlist, employ, captivate, fascinate, intrigue, excite, involve, seduce, please, delight, satisfy, get onside, keep onside, *capture*, rope in, bring over, intimidate, con, fool, trick, win, flatter, deceive, bamboozle, fob, inveigle into, dupe, hoodwink, gull, beguile, bluff, play for a sucker, cozen, gouge, swindle, dazzle, mesmerise, sign up, get on board, get in the tent, bag, etc.; get onside, *buy-in*, make one of the *ducks in a row*, etc. Get singing to the same tune, attending workshops, speaking the same language, reading off the same page, etc.).

> '[Our] approach to *change management consultancy* is *underpinned* by *Appreciative Inquiry* that is an inclusive method to *engage* people *impacted* by *change* (*stakeholders, clients* and *staff*) in the *process* of *strategic planning* so as to *achieve* socially *sustainable outcomes*.'
>
> Consultancy document

enhance, enhanced, enhancement

To improve, increase, grow, streamline, beautify, strengthen, lengthen, tighten, loosen where necessary or desirable; make go faster; *implement* an *efficiency-gain*; brighten, whiten, lighten; make hairier, scarier, lairier, etc. Make more violent or serene. There is nothing that cannot be *enhanced*. *Enhance* your penis, your garden, your prospects, your retirement, breasts, *lifestyle*, chances, medical cover, relationships, froth with a 'froth enhancer', (Qantas Inflight advertisement).

'Puffing Billy is *strategically* important to the Yarra Valley and Dandenong Ranges region as it is one of the region's most significant drawcards. The railway has a very high visitor recognition, and is one of the key "*attractors*" that drives *visitation* to the region.

'The Facilities *Enhancement* Project aims to maintain and further develop the facilities and services of the Puffing Billy railway as a significant *world-class* tourist attraction in the lead-up to the Commonwealth Games. It *focuses* on the *high priority* capital works identified in the ETRB *strategic* plan.'

Victorian Government

'The University of Wollongong will *enhance* its position as a research institution with an international reputation for high *quality*, student-centred undergraduate and graduate education.'

University of Wollongong's vision

'AusAid explored design and *implement* models for project design to *enhance* recipient government involvement in project preparation. This model [sic] proved to be expensive and inefficient.'

Company document

'Be *enhanced* and *enhance*, and *enhance* the earth, and *enhance* it.'

Genesis 1.28

'Go ahead, *enhance* my day.'

enhanced behavioural analysis

See above.

'. . . *enhanced behavioural analysis* techniques and reporting structures'.

Child-care centre

enhanced interrogation techniques

Improved, expanded, sexed-up interrogation techniques. *Torture lite*. Sensory deprivation. Humiliation. Infliction of pain and fear. Torture.

'The "*enhanced interrogation techniques*," as the CIA calls them, include feigned drowning.'

Nat Hentoff, *Village Voice*, 2 July 2004

ensure

To make sure, make certain, confirm, warrant, certify, guarantee, assure, verify. Put beyond doubt. To *commit* to *implement commitment*. To *proactively oversight delivery*. Etc.

'We will *ensure* that our program *team* is fully acquainted with
AusAid's *quality* in *implementation tools*. A suite of *quality* assessment *tools* used by AusAid will be adopted and adapted by
the program *team* to *ensure* that *outsourced* activity can be
effectively *managed*, monitored and assessed.'

Company document

See *tools*

Enterprise Capability Group

Strategic Capability Group

'The *Enterprise Capability Group* is responsible for the identification and definition of *strategic capabilities* for Centrelink's
future. (Location in this team will last approximately six
months whereby the position will be transferred to the
Enterprise Program Office.)'

Centrelink

entrepreneur

1. Capitalist.
2. Astronaut.

'I want to thank the astronauts who are with us, the coura-
geous spacial *entrepreneurs* who set such a wonderful example
for the young of our country.'

George W. Bush, January 2004

envision / envisioning / re-envisioning

1. To imagine, picture, conceive, conjure, dream up,
think up, visualise, fancy, see in the mind's eye.

2. *Envision* structurally: to see beneath the surface in your *vision.*
3. Future *envisioning*: to have a *vision going forwards.*
4. *Re-envisioning*: when it is no longer a clear or agreed *vision*; when *focus* has been lost and must be regained, etc.
5. *Envisioning* process: the way it is done.

> 'Coming together to *re-envision* the Ph.D. to meet the societal needs of the 21st Century.'
>
> University of Washington, Graduate School

> '*Envision* there's no heaven,
> it's easy if you try . . .
> *Envision* all the people . . .'

est

Popular variety of Large Group Awareness Training founded by Werner Erhard (John Rosenberg) in San Francisco in 1971. Related to Zen, Dianetics, Scientology, Abraham Maslow, Carl Rogers, Dale Carnegie, Napoleon Hill, gestalt, etc. 'A hodgepodge of philosophical bits and pieces culled from the carcasses of existential philosophy' (Robert Todd, *The Skeptic's Dictionary*).

est's prominent place in the 'Human Potential' market – reprogramming people to meet their potential – made it a significant influence on *human resources (HR)* and New Age thinking more generally. The US Secretary of Defense, Donald Rumsfeld, sometimes speaks in *est*-like ways (see *known knowns*). A source of much organisational jargon relating to *self-actualisation*, including *empower*.

Neuro Linguistic Programming and *Landmark Forum / Landmark Education Corporation* (founded by John Rosenberg's brother, Harry) *training* are later influential offshoots.

See *known knowns*

established relationship

1. Relationship.
2. Not a relationship; more of a suggestion of a relationship.

> 'Saddam Hussein . . . also had an *established relationship* to al-Qaeda, providing training to al-Qaeda members in the areas of poisons, gases and making conventional bombs.'
>
> Richard Cheney, October 2003

See *known knowns*

establish order

1. To make peace, provide security, get things sorted, put *ducks in a row*, etc.
2. To annihilate opponents. To incite disorder.

> 'The failure to *establish order* was the prime mistake, from which all other problems flow.'
>
> David Brooks, *New York Times*, April 2004

> 'As we *establish order* and justice in Iraq, we also continue to pursue WMD.'
>
> George W. Bush, June 2003

evaluate

What must be done to *outcomes*.

See *high level thinking*

event

What happened. Happening. Weather *event*, severe weather *event*, rain *event*, environmental *event*; hiring *event* ('*Strategies* for responding to hiring *events*'), literary *event*, publishing *event*, *debris event*, etc. Taxable *event* – *event* with a tax consequence. Macrosuede Sofa *Event* – furniture sale *event*.

When thirteen Chinese inmates at Villawood detention centre slashed their wrists in June 2005, it was called 'an organised self-harm *event*'.

> '*In terms of* the rain that fell in a very short time, it's a one-in-100-year type of *event*.'
>
> Bureau of Meteorology

> 'Severe weather *events*.'
>
> Bureau of Meteorology

> 'The department has been informed that one or both of the dams partially failed during a recent rain *event*.'
>
> Michigan Department of Environmental Quality

> 'In fact we had four *events* of thunderstorms compared to our normal one *event* in January.'
> Adelaide Weather Bureau spokesman, ABC, February 2005

> 'And God said, let there be a light *event*; and there was a light *event*.'

'Come on baby, light my fire *event.*'

'Singing in the rain *event*', etc.

evidence

1. Confirmation, substantiation, examples going to show, signs, data, facts.
2. Something you have to recognise piles up.

Interviewer: 'Is there any intelligence that Saddam Hussein has any ties to September 11?'
Donald Rumsfeld: 'You have to recognise the *evidence* piles up.'

September 2002

evil (axis of)

1. (n) Wickedness, something morally bad or wrong. Possessed by Satan.
2. Foreign policy proposed in Deuteronomy 22 to 'put *evil* away from among you', mainly by stoning evildoers to death. 'See I have set before thee this day, life and good, death and *evil*.' Also Judges 20, where it is said of the followers of Benjamin that they knew not that *evil* was near them and were amazed when 'they saw that *evil* was come upon them'.

Word used by President Bush more than 300 times since 11 September 2001.

'*Axis of evil*'. '. . . monumental fight between good and *evil*. Good will prevail.' 'Today we saw *evil*.' 'Our responsibility is

clear . . . to rid the world of *evil*.' '. . . defeat the *evil* doers.'
Etc.

President George W. Bush 2001 / 2002

excellence

What we are all *committed* to *achieving*.

'The *energy* and enthusiasm that our employees bring to the workplace creates an *exciting* place to work with a constant striving for *excellence*.'

Titan Corporation (Abu Ghraib and Guantanamo Bay
interrogation contractors)

'The 2003 NSW Training Awards recognise and celebrate *excellence* in the NSW vocational education and training sector.'

TAFE NSW News

St Martins in the Field, which for 800 years provided charity to London's poor and homeless, now provides "*excellence* in hospitality".

excellent

1. Good, happy, well, all right, cool, *vibrant*, etc.
(As in: How are you? *Excellent*.)
2. Of a high standard, pleasing, satisfactory, just the ticket, what the doctor ordered, fun, satisfying, thrilling, knock-out, full on, awesome, to the max, gratifying, cool, *vibrant*, etc. (As in: How was the meeting, report, soufflé, concert, match, date, massage, cocktail, joint, workshop, facilitator, brainstorming session, strategic implementation plan, facelift, repositioning, colonic irrigation, etc.? *Excellent*.)

Mr Burns: 'Smithers, who is that hooved fellow?'
Smithers: 'Ah, that's the Prince of Darkness, sir.'
Mr Burns: '*Excellent.*'

excess staff situation

See *redeployment, performance manage out, business process re-engineering, rightsizing, downsizing, de-jobbing, decruitment, excess staff situation,* etc.

exciting

Stimulating, stirring, inspiring, exhilarating, titillating, thrilling, etc. (As in: '*exciting* new knitting patterns'; '*exciting* investment opportunity'; 'Victorian classic in *exciting* location'.)

Whatever is new is also *exciting* – *exciting* new era; *exciting* new offer; *exciting* new discovery; *exciting* new business opportunity, new development, new housing development, new retail development; *exciting* new *lifestyle*; new photos; new recipes; new competitions; *exciting* future, *exciting* past; *exciting* gardens; *exciting* possibility; 'a more *exciting* animated you', etc.

'Please enter our website and choose from the *exciting* New Zealand bed & breakfast properties available throughout New Zealand.'

Selections NZ

'To grasp and understand the Estonian sound is to go on an *exciting* voyage of discovery.'

Kasbah.com

'As a member of the Titan *team*, you will be exposed to the most *exciting* career adventures situated on the *cutting edge* of technology.'

Titan Corporation (US military security and
intelligence contractors)

exit

1. To leave.
2. To sell off assets; get out from under; flit; *cut and run*.

'The *exit* process is expected to be largely completed by the end of the 2004 calendar year.'

Annual report

'Love me, or *exit* me.'

exiting employee

An employee who is leaving. A fleeing employee. A *migrating* employee. One who can bear it no longer. One who has been driven out by boredom, poor wages, oppressive or incompetent managers insufferable jargon or a new vocational calling such as politics or religion. One attracted to viticulture or free range poultry. One who is entering the *churn* or becoming *vanilla*. One who has been headhunted. One who has been encouraged to go, or given no choice. An employee with a bad *attitude* or an inappropriate *mindset*: one for whom the company *culture* is not a good fit. An employee who was not prepared to do the company thing, who did not *grow* with the company, who did not *embrace* its *core values*, did not *sign off* on them or did not *buy-in*. One who did not sign the *Personal Business Commitment* (*PBC*). One who cannot stand the *mission statement* any longer. One who has been asked to write a new *mission statement*. One who has decided to get a life. A redundant employee. A *downsized* or *re-engineered in terms of business process* person. Etc.

'It is company policy to conduct an *Exit* Interview with all staff *exiting* [the company]. The purpose of the *Exit* Interview is to provide the *exiting employee* with an opportunity to pass on suggestions for improvement in company policies and practices, those of their department and managerial practices, to enable the company to consider and *implement* improvements.

'*Exit* Interviews are conducted by a member of the Executive team and *feedback* is forwarded onto the *exiting employee's* manager, his or her manager, the applicable member of the Executive *team*, *HR* and the Managing Director. *Exiting employees* may elect to disclose information to all of these people, in which case it will be recorded on this form, or to only disclose information to the interviewer, in which case it will not be recorded.'

'*Exit* thee to a nunnery!'

exit strategy

1. Plan for leaving. To cut your losses. Fly the coop. Get out while you still can. Flit. Midnight flit. Leave

town. Leave by the fire escape. Take a holiday. Do a
runner. Vamoose. Bolt.
2. *Cut and run.* Leave in the lurch. Give comfort to
terrorists. Do something disastrous and *un-Australian.*
Not the Australian way.

> 'The government has no *exit strategy.*'
>
> Mark Latham, 2004

> 'Fifty *exit strategies in terms of* your lover.'

> 'Love me, or *implement* an *exit strategy.*'

See *cut and run*

expand

To enlarge, stretch, etc. Can be substituted for both *enhance*
and *grow.* (As in: 'In line with our *enhanced operational
footprint* we are *committed* to *expand* pickling operations
by 15 per cent.' Or: 'We are *committed* to *expanding* our
operational *footprint* in line with a forecast 15 per cent
growth outcome in our pickling operations.' Etc.) *Expand*
is preferred to *increase.*

> 'Dr Switkowski also hopes to *expand* Telstra's *footprint* in Asia
> over the next four years . . .'
>
> *Age*, January 2004

> 'In the future, an increasing amount of Australia's
> international education activity will take place overseas.

Diversification in overseas activity will be *facilitated* by profiling Australia's *innovation capabilities*, building partnerships to *expand access* to overseas education and *innovation* systems, protecting Australia's reputation as a *quality* provider, and encouraging trade liberalisation.'

Media release, Brendan Nelson, October 2003

expectation–reality mismatch

Mistake, error, cock-up, botch, triumph of hope over reason; delusion; con job, scam, or triumph of hype over reason.

'The overriding *issue* is the *expectation-reality mismatch* . . . The war was supposed to be quick. We were supposed to be greeted as liberators. It was to pay for itself with oil revenues. And we were supposed to find chemical and biological weapons.'

Retired Air Force Col., Sam Gardiner

'Those who don't learn from an *expectation-reality mismatch* are condemned to relive it.'

'To have an *expectation-reality mismatch* is human, to forgive divine.'

explanation

1. The reason(s) why; the causes of an *event;* an argument or
case.

2. Story, narrative; *spin*, *takeout*; contextualisation; way out, over or through; *exit strategy*.

'As a *shareholder*, you deserve an *explanation* as to how this situation arose.'

Annual report

Ff

facilitate, facilitator

(v) To make possible, easy or convenient; make happen; help, assist, lend a hand, aid; organise, marshall, direct, encourage, conduct, etc.

(n) Master of ceremonies, *catalyst*, group leader, discussion leader, teacher, *team* builder, *consensus* builder, problem solver, supervisor, adviser, instructor, guide, trainer, salesperson, motivator, coach, *refocuser*, *empowering* agent, mediator, guru, poobah, Rasputin, Svengali, *change manager*, *process* re-engineer, *process* improver, spruiker, carpetbagger, evangelist ('Veriditas Labyrinth *Facilitator* Training: *facilitating* the labyrinth is a spiritual path'); undercover agent, diplomat, linkman, go between, Machiavel, *consultant*, etc.

'*Facilitate* the creation of *mission, vision* and *value statements*.'

'Dale is a *facilitator* of energetic exchanges in self acceptance, belief identification, meditation, dreams / dream interpretation, trans-focal exchanges . . .'

intuitivefacilitating.com

'When other *facilitators* fail,
and comforts flee,
facilitate of the *facilitatorless*,
O abide with me.'

fair go

Mythical. (Aust.) cf. bunyip.

family values / family

Universal political mantra. Hitler recommended *family values* to the German people. *Family values* are 'simple' and 'enduring' values, such as love, togetherness, harmony, security, etc. Families provide 'secure nurturing environments'. Family *trusts* are for nurturing family assets. George W. Bush comes from the Bush *family* which nurtured him into great wealth and the US Presidency after he gave up drinking. The Bin Laden *family* nurtured Osama. Other *families* include the Suharto *family*, the Holy Family, the Typical *family* and the Corleone *family*.

> '. . . the simple, enduring *values* – love, *family* togetherness, sharing and *mateship*.'
>
> John Howard, Christmas Message

> 'I suppose three important things certainly come to my mind that we want to say thank you. The first would be our *family*. Your *family*, my *family* – which is composed of an immediate *family* of a wife and three children, a larger *family* with grandparents and aunts and uncles. We all have our *family*, whichever that may be . . . The very beginnings of civilisation, the very beginnings of this country, goes back to the *family*.'
>
> US Vice President Dan Quayle

fast track

Short cut to *achievement of agreed outcomes*.

fears

(n) Fears are held – always. Phobias, concerns, worries, anxieties, etc., are not held. Fear, including 'grave fear', is not held; but 'grave *fears* are held for the future of our disease-ravaged native frog species . . .' *Sunday Star Times*, April 2002
(v) Dreads, worries, thinks. Is alarmed, worried, disquieted, discomforted, concerned by; nervous, anxious, uneasy, apprehensive, wondering about; terrified, afraid, frightened, scared, unsure, uncertain of.

'Russia *fears* US oil companies will take over world's second-biggest reserves.'

Independent, September 2002

'US intelligence *fears* Iran duped hawks into Iraq war.'

Guardian, May 2004

'Pope *fears* Bush is antichrist.'

New Catholic Times, May 2003

feedback

Response; calls, cards and letters. Talk, abuse, boos, barracking, cat-calls, back-turning, pants-dropping, walkouts. Praise, tributes, congratulations, acclaim, commendations, applause. Information, criticism, analysis.
Feedback is always welcome, wanted, useful – especially constructive or positive *feedback*. *Feedback* sometimes forms a loop.

fenestration

'The 100 or so managers who attended were very positive in their *feedback* and appreciative of his style and genuine *commitment* to his subject.'

Report on presentation by former
Burger King CEO

'And that's OK as long as you go back, debrief and determine what worked well in the process and what could be done differently, so you're supporting a *continuous improvement* and *feedback loop*.'

Kristin J. Arnold

'There is no such thing as failure. There is only *feedback*.'

Dale Kirkby, Neuro Linguistic Programmer

fenestration

Town planners' word for windows.

'A fenestration of opportunity.'

fire prevention

Question of *commitment* and *behaviour*.

'Your vulnerability largely depends on your knowledge of, and *commitment* to, *fire prevention* and survival preparedness, and your likely behaviour during a wildfire *event*.'

Surf Coast Shire Community Newsletter,
November 2004

first scan attractiveness

Positive first impressions?

> 'This *process* involves the following steps: *strategic alignment* with the *vision* on where to take the company, competitive *differentiation*, *first scan attractiveness* of the idea, feasibility organisational *capabilities* to execute cross-department inclusion, consistency of *process*, *buy-in* to *output*.'
>
> Report provided by consultants
> Booz Allan Hamilton

> 'Where both deliberate, the love is slight: Who ever loved, that loved not at *first scan attractiveness*?'
>
> Marlowe

flagpole

1. A pole on which a flag is flown.
2. *Run it up the flagpole (and see if anyone salutes)*. To put forward a plan and see what the response is. Take soundings. Test the water. Throw something into the ring. Throw it at the wall and see if it sticks. Something to do at a *brainstorming* session, *workshop*, *think tank*, etc. Popular *marketing* cliché – put it out there and see what the punters think.

> '"Exactly," said Bruce Buchanan, a political scientist at the University of Texas at Austin. "*Run it up the flagpole and see who salutes*."'
>
> *Houston Chronicle*, July 2004

'We'll run it up the flagpole and see who salutes that booger.'

Texas House Speaker, Gib Lewis

flank environment

Pseudo-military. Adjacent departments; departments with whom we work; associated departments, others, who or what is on one's flanks.

Huey, Dewey and Louie are Donald's *flank environment*. Abbott is Costello's, etc.

'The two departments (EZ and DET) are our *flank environment.'*

Queensland Studies Authority

flexible, flexibility

1. Supple, malleable, bendy, tractable, plastic, pliable, amenable; plenty of whip in it; movable, adjustable, adaptable, *agile*, embraceable, changeable; whatever you want to make it, bob each way; open to interpretation, ad hoc; not *set in concrete*; offering *customer choice*. What every company must *enhance*. *Flexible* working hours, employment practices, goals, *product* offerings, etc. Labour market *flexibility*.
2. No job security.

Organisations must *achieve flexibility* without losing *focus* or *commitment*. They do this through *focusing* on a *commitment* to *flexibility*.

'*Flexibility underpins* this model.'

Annual report

'Passion for entertainment *products* and a *flexible work ethic* is required.'

'*Flexibility* – reviewing, developing and distributing studies, *products* and services *flexibly* in response to altered circumstances and government policies, without diminishing the centrality of the *values* and principles of the Queensland Studies Framework.'

Queensland Studies Framework

focus

(v) To concentrate on. Not to be distracted. Purposefully attend to in the appropriate way: e.g. *focus* on the soufflé: cooking it; *focus* on the garden: weeding, fertilising, cultivating; *focus* on the children: feeding, comforting, educating, clothing, reading to, etc.
In business the *focus* is on *goals*, *core issues*, *key objectives*, *main game*, etc.
(n) That on which one *focuses* ('maintaining a strong *focus* on *core* business is the *key* to success' . . . etc.).
(adj) *Focused* – single-minded, resisting all distraction, switched-on, fired-up, pumped, come to play, etc. ('I was really *focused* today' – swimming, netball, high jumping, etc.)

'An *output* management *focus* by departments.'

Victorian Department of Treasury and Finance

'Clear direction allows organisational *alignment*, and a *focus* on the *achievement* of *goals*.'

Gracedale Private Nursing Home

'We must *focus* on our garden.'

Voltaire

'*Focus* on the lilies, how they grow.'

fora

Archaic plural of forum. Meetings, conventions, gatherings, conferences, weekend retreats, etc. Sometimes 'foras'.

'In my capacity as Branch President I thought it *appropriate* to attend a number of *fora* in the south of France.'

foreign

Depends what you mean by *foreign*. Mexicans are *foreign*, but Mexico is not.

'I've been talking to Vincente Fox, the new president of Mexico . . . so we'll not depend on *foreign* oil.'

George W. Bush, Boston, October 2000

foreseeable future

Depends where you are looking and how far you can see.

'We have no plans for that eventuality in the *foreseeable future*.'

forum shopper

Muslim refugee, *queue jumper, unauthorised arrival, illegal,* etc., who wishes to live in Australia rather than a camp or a less democratic and prosperous country. Not the sort of person we want . . . etc.

forward-looking

1. Looking forward. *Focused* on the future, *focused going forwards*. Distinguishes an individual or organisation from backward-looking rivals.
2. Not historical facts.

'Statements contained in this news release that are not historical facts are *forward-looking* statements within the meaning of Section 27A of the Securities Act of 1933 and Section 21E of the Securities Exchange Act of 1934. Examples of such *forward-looking* statements include, but are not limited to, the statements by Gene Ray [CEO].These statements are subject to risks and uncertainties that could cause actual results to differ materially from those set forth in or implied by *forward-looking* statements.'

Titan Corporation, statement by CEO, 7 May 2004

for your convenience

'*For your convenience*, the cabin will be pressurised.'

Heard on a Virgin flight from Brisbane to Sydney

'*For your convenience*, wings have been fitted to this plane.'

freedom

1. The condition of being free. Liberty. Not slavery.
2. A universal gift of divine origin.

'You see, *freedom* is not America's gift to the world; *freedom* is the Almighty God's gift to every man and woman in this world.'

George W. Bush, January 2003

'God who gave us life gave us liberty . . . these liberties are the Gift of God.'

Thomas Jefferson, 1781

'. . . all efforts to remove the recognition of God from the minds of the people should be viewed upon [sic] as efforts to remove our liberties.'

William Federer, 2004

free enterprise system of government

From (i) government: system of public administration and authority, etc., and (ii) free enterprise: private enterprise, market economy, business, etc.

System of government that serves, defends, advocates free enterprise; is open to influence by free enterprise; or is one and the same thing as the free enterprise economic system. Not the Westminster system. Not the communist system. Not the Australian system. The US system: as commonly described by US citizens (e.g. Lyndon Baines Johnson: 'our great free enterprise system of government', October 1964).

'My dedication to Northwood and the "Northwood Idea" comes from my belief that the American *free enterprise system of government*, although not perfect, has brought the greatest good to the greatest number of people. I have dedicated by business career to helping *clients* participate in this system.'

Venita VanCaspel Harris, Northwood University, Texas

'Since the primary purpose for the existence of the school is a spiritual ministry, evangelistic efforts are made to bring all students to a saving knowledge of Jesus Christ so that the teaching of spiritual truths may have a firm foundation. We believe the traditional system of education educates the mind and builds character. It teaches the value of living and encourages achievement under a *free enterprise system of government*.'

Mt Carmel Christian Academy,
Philosophy and Statement of Purpose, Virginia

'The business of America is the *free enterprise system of government*.'

free world (It's a)

A phrase.

'It's a *free world* – to use a phrase.'

Alexander Downer, 22 April 2004

fresh

1. Not stale – as in *f*. air, *f*. water, *f*. pineapple.
2. Now also new, unused, unspoiled, different, unique, first, atypical – *f*. news, *f*. software, *f*. music, *f*. patents, *f*. address, *f*. choice, etc.
3. Meaningless, as in 'My*fresh*baby.com: the only complete solution for making all natural baby food at home.'

'Abbas wins *fresh* truce commitment.'

BBC

'Papa's got a *Fresh* Bag.'

James Brown

'Have you met Darren's *fresh* wife?'

frictional unemployment

The unemployment of people between jobs. What comes of 'people following their hearts and dreams' (US economist). *Frictional* job-seeking.

As in: Are you unemployed? Only *frictionally*.

> 'That would suggest an unemployment rate of 1-2% allowing for some short-term *frictional* unemployment when people change jobs.'
>
> BBC, October 1999

friendly fire

A form of *collateral damage* in which people on your side are the collateral. According to The American War Library, 39% of US casualties in Vietnam and 49% in the first Gulf War were caused by *friendly fire*.

Relatives of *friendly fire* victims may find it difficult to achieve *closure*.

> 'American pilots in Afghanistan, blamed for a series of "*friendly fire*" incidents and devastating erroneous attacks on innocent civilians, were routinely provided with amphetamines to tackle fatigue and help them fly longer hours. Pilots were allowed to "self-regulate" their own doses and kept the drugs in their cockpits.'
>
> *Independent*, UK, 3 August 2002

front of mind

Not the back. In mind. On one's mind. Don't forget. *Focused* on. (As in: 'Let's keep it *front of mind*.')

fully job network eligible job seekers

Unemployed persons.

> 'This table refers only to *Fully Job Network Eligible Job Seekers* aged between 18-49 years in receipt of Youth or Newstart Allowance.'
>
> Department of Employment and Workplace Relations

functionality

It works (*in terms* of its *functionality*).

future directions

Common name for conference, seminar, retreat, *brainstorming*, *networking* session, *PowerPoint presentation*, etc. *Strategic planning*.
An opportunity to be *forward-looking*, to reflect on where we've been and where we're going, where we are *at this point* on the continuum, *in time*, *time period*, etc., and where we want to be in two years' / months' time. Etc.

See *going forwards*

Gg

game plan

From American football, now also Australian football. (Likewise flooding, zoning off, zone defence, etc.) Belief common in sport, politics, business (and possibly war) that success depends on an 'agreed' *strategy* or plan that everyone must 'stick to'. Increasingly common in everyday language.

> 'Don't be a loser — stick to God's *game plan*.'
>
> Sign, Catholic Church, Terang Vic.

> 'They lost because they didn't stick to the *game plan*.'

> 'They won because they had a *game plan* and they stuck to it.'

> '. . . to love, cherish and to stick to the *game plan*, till death us do part.'

gate (mutual obligation)

1. An opening in a fence or wall; a movable barrier. 'Strait is the gate, and narrow is the way, which leadeth unto life, and few there be that find it.' The gates of Paradise. 'Wide is the gate and broad is the way, that leadeth to destruction.' The gates of hell. Etc.
2. 'A *job seeker*'s MO *gate* is 6 months after his or her allowance start date. If the *job seeker* has not commenced in an activity 6 weeks after the 6-month point (i.e. at 7½ months), they can be compelled to participate in an activity with a CWC (Community Work Coordinator).'

'Mutual Obligation: To compel a *job seeker* to commence in an MO activity with a CWC check that the *job seeker* is on the full rate of Youth or Newstart Allowance (on the Registration Other tab), is aged 18-49 years and has been on allowance for more than 7½ months. Check the *job seeker's* PfWA and confirm on the Referral and Placement tab that the *job seeker* is not participating in an approved activity and has a current ISmo referral.'

Department of Employment and Workplace Relations document for Job Network Services

gender equity outcomes

Outcomes in the area of gender equity.

'A *focus* on *outcomes targets* without an emphasis on improved employment practices will not *deliver* support from men and will not result in *sustainable* changes in organisations to improve *gender equity outcomes.*'

Equal Opportunity for Women in the Workplace Agency (EOWA)

geographies

More than one geography; or, as in the following case, 'region'.

'Central to that *goal* is the ability to *source* fruit from diverse *geographies* . . .'

Southcorp media release, 2004

giftedness

Gifts? Possessed of gifts? One who has been *gifted* gifts?

> 'Vertical timetabling structures will provide boys with *giftedness* in particular subjects with the opportunity to pursue these studies ahead of time.'
>
> Independent School, Victoria

> Beware of Greeks *gifting giftedness*.

gifting

1. Giving with a view to profiting, marketing or reducing tax.
2. A kind of pyramid scheme. Note: *Re-gifting* is the practice of giving to others the unwanted gifts one has received.

> 'It is better to *gift* than to receive.'

> '*Gift* it to me, baby.'

global bulge bracket pedigree

Global bulge bracket: a full range of investment services in all major international markets. The *pedigree* is elusive.

> 'DB has transformed to a lean, aggressive, focused universal bank with a *global bulge bracket pedigree*. How in your opinion can DB maintain this status in such a competitive market?'
>
> Question asked of a Deutsche Bank job applicant.

globalisation

1. International economic integration through liberalised trade and technology that allows rapid flow of information and goods.
2. An unstoppable force already of inestimable benefit to billions of people and with the potential to enrich everyone.
3. '. . . the imposition on the entire world of the neo-liberal tyranny of the market and undisputed rule of the economy and of economic powers, within which the United States occupies a dominant position' (Pierre Bourdieu).
4. An ideal of shared wealth, limitless *innovation*, world government and no more war.
5. Another word for corporate greed, exploitation and destruction (particularly of the environment).

It depends on your point of view, but also on where you live.

global player

Player in the big league. *Aspirational* in the little league.

'Austrade's view of making Australia a serious *global player* in information and communications technologies is a *holistic* one.'

Executive General Manager,
Australian Operations, Austrade

global village

The half of the globe that is on the phone.

'The new electronic interdependence recreates the world in the image of a *global village*.'

Marshall McLuhan, 1962

goals matrix

Key performance indicators drawn up scientifically as a table with columns containing *goals*, such as 'reducing through-life costs and *timeframes*', '*aligning* operational requirements with *core strategy*', 'continuous attitude surveys', etc. There are learning *goals matrixes*; program *goals matrixes*; *strategic goals matrixes* – pretty well anything can be done this way.

'We have used the following simple assessment system in the *matrix*:

T   the Action meets (or improves on) the Objective
o   the Action has no impact on the Objective
na   the Objective is not relevant to the Action
X   the Action does not meet (or has a negative impact on) the Objective
?   the impact of the Action on the Objective is uncertain.'

'The *goals achievement matrix* is shown in Figure K-1. The labelling of the actions is in accordance with how they are numbered in Volume I Section 6 of the Plan.'

Sinclair, Knight, Merz (*consultants*), transport, parking and access plan for Centennial Park

going forwards

1. Advancing, progressing, moving onwards, pressing on.
2. In future, the future, *at this point in time* in the
future (As in: 'Excuse me, can you tell me the time
going forwards?'); going on (ongoing). In the existential
or evolutionary moment; not going backwards.
A cousin of *continuous improvement*.
3. Now; in the future; *at this point / moment in time*
between where you are and where you are going,
between the past and the *agreed outcomes* (As in: 'Romeo
Romeo, wherefore art thou, *going forwards*, Romeo?')
4. Not looking backwards; not mired in the past; not
regressive; *forward-looking*; progressively speaking; on
the curve, *in terms of the strategy / game plan*, etc.
Aware of life's unpredictability and the relentless
passage of time.

'. . . *implementation going forwards*'

'. . . *achieving* our *goals going forwards*'

'Where are we now in *ball-park terms going forwards?*'

See *move on, forward looking*

go live

(v, n) To begin, start, commence, press the switch, ignite,
make it happen, *implement* the *action plan*, *implement*
anything, etc. (As in: 'Ready, set, *go live!*')

'DEAL – manufacturer certificates *go live* for registrable and
listable therapeutic device applications.'

Department of Health and Ageing

> 'At *Go-Live* the final transfer of knowledge and *ownership* will occur between the consultants and the *internal resources.*'
>
> SAP consultants

> 'And the Spirit of God moved upon the face of the waters. And God said, Let us *go live.*'

See *migrate, roll-out*

go the extra mile

To try harder, make a special effort, go out of one's way to help, work weekends, extend credit, offer discount, don't make a complete bastard of yourself, Good Samaritan, etc.

> '82% of Americans Looking for Hassle-Free Clothes That *Go the Extra Mile.*'
>
> Nanotechnology information site

> 'Will instinctively know when and how to *"go the extra mile."*'
>
> Advertisement for Relationship Development Manager

governance

The manner and means by which one is governed. The character and structure of administration. Where the power lies; where the checks on power are; to whom or what the powerful are *accountable.*

> 'The report recommends that the current TAFE *governance* model be retained but that the *governance* practices within the framework as a whole and within individual Institutions could

be *enhanced*. Therefore, to enable participants within the TAFE framework to fully *embrace best practice* corporate *governance* . . .'

TAFE Governance Review

'The presentation will discuss the *key issues*, barriers, *challenges* and implications that can be drawn out of the conference for *capacity* development for Indigenous *governance* in the NT as well as *key* principles for *best practice* that have been identified. These should inform the way in which *capacity building* for *governance* is carried out.'

NT Building Effective Indigenous
Governance Conference

grandmother test

Test that assumes grandmother thinks any kind of *mission statement* is worth the trouble of writing it.

'Consider using the *"grandmother test"* on your *mission statement* – would your grandmother understand what your company is about if she read your *mission statement*?'

e–Business Plan tutorial

great / greatness

Excellent, good, pleasing, profitable, internationally competitive, whatever. Anything exceptional. Anything one likes. Any improvement. Anyone or anything it suits to flatter or inflate.

'Give me the opportunity to develop *greatness*.'

Advertisement for a Principal Marketing Strategist

'. . . all past and present Olympic representatives of our *great* nation . . . So there is *great* symbolism about this event in this

171

building . . . how magnificently generous you have again been in a *great* national cause . . . We are, as everybody knows, *great* lovers of sport . . . this nation arguably has had its *greatest* sporting successes . . . And all of it is, in a sense, but a *great* national preparation . . . to see his *great* enthusiasm to do *great* things for his country . . . and the *great* decency of all of the Australian people . . . I want to wish every one of them the *greatest* of success . . . It will be our *greatest* sporting event ever. It will be a *great* world event. It will do *great* credit to our nation and the support that you are demonstrating tonight will deliver a *great* deal of that reality.'

John Howard, September 2002

greenwashing

Making your company look greener or more *sustainable* than it is. A response to the *stakeholder challenge*. Superficial or mock green.

'The same companies that are being *targeted* by NGOs and indigenous *communities* for their negative environmental and social *impacts* are the leaders in espousing *triple bottom line* principles and it remains to be seen whether this approach can *deliver* real benefits to *communities* or becomes a more sophisticated form of *greenwashing*.'

Subhabrata Bobby Banerjee, Contesting Corporate Citizenship

grief

1. Deep mental anguish, profound sorrow and desolation caused by loss for which there may be no consolation (e.g. Psalm 77 or '. . . grief flieth to it', Bacon, *Of Death*).

2. Upset, unhappiness, sadness. Anything requiring consolation; or *grief* counselling to *achieve*, *closure* or *moving on*.
3. A public spectacle. An advertising bonanza.

group think

The mentality of groups: individually intelligent people make collectively bad decisions. Alleged examples include the Bay of Pigs invasion, Vietnam War and the invasion of Iraq. The Soviet Union's invasion of Afghanistan was probably another example of *group think*. The Soviet Union was another one. The disasters caused by *group think* in matters of state have so far not discouraged *management*'s obsession with groups and *teams*.

> 'This *group think* caused the *community* to interpret ambiguous evidence such as the procurement of dual use technology to mean Iraq had an active weapons program. It is clear that this *group think* also extended to our allies . . .'
>
> Senate Intelligence Committee, July 2004

grow

Enlarge, expand, increase, augment, multiply, add to, improve, develop, etc.

Businesses *grow*. (As in: '*Grow* the business'). They *grow* by *growing* their *customer* or *client bases*, their relationships, *product*, etc. Economies *grow*. People who become more mature, personable, varied in their interests, etc., are said to *grow*.

growing the client base

'Andrew leads a talented and highly *focused* management *team* who will aggressively *grow* Chimes wholesale business.'

iiNet media release

'Financial security is essential to *grow* our influence and build an even stronger organisation for all Australians.'

South Australian Liberal Party

growing the client base

To attract, win, increase, enlarge, *enhance*, build, sign up, get more – clients, customers, punters, mugs, etc.

'Due to company growth this dynamic IT company is looking for a Business Development Manager to join them and help in *growing their client base*.'

Personnel advertisement

'Be fruitful,
and multiply thy *client base*.'

growth

Outcome of growing something: daffodil, economy, business, market share, etc.

'The economy expanded by just 0.2 per cent in the March quarter – about one-sixth of the revised 1.3 per cent *growth* recorded in the previous quarter, and substantially below economists' expectations.'

Sydney Morning Herald, June 2004

'A closer examination of the economic data, however, revealed the continuing split in the economy: while the domestic sector was growing strongly, the external sector was a net drag on *growth*. As housing comes off the boil, and the rural economy rebounds, that dynamic is changing, leading to more balanced *growth* in 2004.'

'After almost three years of flat *growth*, the US and world economies are looking up.'

ANZ Bank, June/July 2004

growth trajectory

A sort of escalator, like, you know, that children need to get on early, you know, in terms of literacy, like.

'. . . some children are not getting on to a *growth trajectory* as early as they should *in terms of* literacy.'

Chair of the Australian Government's National Literacy
Review, *Sydney Morning Herald*, December 2004

'The Nips are on a *Growth Trajectory*.'

Hh

hands on

(adj) Human supervision, the personal touch, *implementation* with a human face. (As in: 'Brian is very *hands on in terms of* his approach.)
(n) The condition of being *hands on*. An operation conducted in this way. Some religions are very *hands on* in their approach.

> 'SMEDB's support and assistance for the emerging mineral sands industry will be clearly demonstrated by leading the mineral sands Murray Basin delegation to meet with Federal Ministers and Heads of Department in Canberra in late August, as well as through the continued *hands on*, across industry, government and education providers working relationship provided by SMEDB *dedicated* mineral sands project officer Helena Howe.'
>
> Sunraysia Mallee Economic Development Board

> 'After spending some *hands on* time with the Proactive Multi-Channel Customer Service Version, I found it to be a good *tool* for enabling *customer* self-service features and managing interactions.'
>
> IDG News Service

hard yards

Hard work.

> 'When he's not putting in the *hard yards*, Ries is hitting the books and working his way through a degree in business management.'
>
> Hawthorn Football Club website

'And the suggestion that Australia, having done the *hard yards*, can now take a rest is wrong. We have to continue to do the *hard yards*.'

Peter Costello, October 2000

harmonization

The creation of (i) harmony; or, as some say, (ii) lockstep.

'The Participants ("Participants") of the Exploratory Meeting of Interested Parties Concerning the Future of Substantive Patent Law *Harmonization*, held February 3–4, 2005 in Alexandria, Virginia, wishing to promote and *facilitate* progress on certain *key issues* under consideration in the World Intellectual Property Organization (WIPO) . . .'

IP (Intellectual Property) Australia

harvest

1. To gather up a crop, etc. The procedure before threshing. Often accompanied by rituals of thanksgiving, celebrations, sacrifice to fertility gods, etc.
2. Something to do with balancing managerial *risk-taking*.

'*Network* and participate in *think tanks* and *harvest* ideas to learn practically about the balancing of the managerial *risk–taking*, entrepreneurial energy and high *capability*, with monitoring, so that management direction is *aligned* with the interest of those who have entrusted their resources to the organisation and to the interest of other *stakeholders*.'

Governance seminar, Benchmarking Partnerships

See *capture*

heads up

To tell you. To let you know. To inform, give you the lowdown, etc. As in, '. . . just thought I'd place a call to give you a *heads up* on what's been happening at the recent meeting . . .'

health reasons

1. Reasons of health.
2. Reasons of state.
3. Reasons of *downsizing*.

> 'They killed my son and they did not permit me to be there to see the coffin. They said it was for *health reasons,* and . . . they did not want the public to see it and they did not want the newspapers there.'
>
> Soldier's mother, Independent, 24 April 2004

help desk

1. A person with some expertise in computers, IT, etc.
2. A person capable of asking, 'Is it switched on? Have you tried rebooting it?'
3. Not a desk. Not helpful.

> 'When you work at a *help desk*, there's often a time limit, and you can get in trouble for spending too much time with one caller. Sometimes techs are given scripts that they must follow even though the scripts might not have all of the solutions. A tech might know the solution to the problem, but management won't allow him or her to use that solution

because it might interfere with other software functionality, thus increasing the company's liability.'

> Confessions of a help desk tech, CNN, August 2003

high impact deal

A good deal.

'This is accomplished through the *penetration*, development and expansion of the *vertical market segment* and *strategic* close of *high impact deals* . . .'

> Personnel advertisement

high level thinking

Thinking which produces writing like this:

'1. Assessment will be *holistic*.
Just as the *skills* and *processes* are not compartmentalised in the creation *process*, the evaluation of *outcomes* will occur against a background of understanding that separation of *outcomes* into discrete components is subordinate to the evaluation of the total *process* as a comprehensive *outcome*. Put simply, "As a whole, what happened?"'

> Greenwood Senior High School, WA

high payoff target

HVTs with a payoff.

'*High payoff targets* are those *high-value targets*, identified through wargaming, which must be acquired and successfully attacked for the success of the friendly commander's mission. Also called HPT.'

US military glossary

high priority environment

Not just any kind of environment.

'Oh those ideas I think are very, very complex and we need scientific *input* and obviously a *high priority environment* in consideration of those, so I wouldn't say yes or no, it needs a *common sense* approach involving all elements of *input*, government, farmers from the rural area, scientists, and coming up with an answer that's best for the nation.'

Bob Mansfield, ABC radio, May 2004

high value

1. Valuable. More valuable. Extremely valuable.
2. Value added: *customers*, *consumers*, crops, jobs, *managers*, *products*, *knowledge objects*, purchase orders, insurance, fluorine compounds, people, etc.

'The women, however, are kept in another part of the prison, cell block IA, together with nineteen *high value* male detainees.'

Guardian, 20 May 2004

'Seize the opportunity to *grow* your top line and beat your competitors through delivering *high value* to *customers* . . . By adopting PA's more aggressive "*High Value* to Customer" *strategy*, businesses can seize the opportunity to *grow* their top line and beat their competitors. To succeed, this *"High Value to Customer"* approach (we call this HV2C) requires the business to adopt solutions that integrate knowledge and experience from across the organisation.'

PA Consulting Group

high value targets (HVTs)

Whatever and whomever is called a High Value Target is a High Value Target.

'A target the enemy commander requires for the successful completion of the mission. The loss of *high value targets* would be expected to seriously *degrade* important enemy functions throughout the friendly commander's area of interest. Also called HVT.'

US military glossary

'"Our attitude and actions have been the same since September 11 *in terms of* getting *high value targets* off the street, and that doesn't change because of an election," says National Security Council spokesman Sean McCormack.'

New Republic, 19 July 2004

'Musharraf did not name the al-Qaeda figure believed to be surrounded, referring to him as a *"high value target."*'

CNN, March 2004

hire

1. (v) To employ, obtain a service for money.
2. (n) A person hired.

'*On-boarding* accelerates *a hire's* progress by reducing the transition time between his or her starting date and full
productivity.'

Development Dimensions International

'*Decruit* those *hires*!'

'*Hires* of the world, unite!'

1. Story of events. Study and interpretation of past
events. '. . . a tableau of crimes' (Voltaire); '. . . a
nightmare from which I am trying to awake' (Joyce).
Whatever is past, gone, obsolete, dead and buried.
(As in: 'She's *history*.' 'He's in "the dustbin of
history".')
2. A weapon for defending oneself and attacking
others. A movable feast. Whatever it suits one to make
of it. Calling of pedants. Rubbish, humbug, baloney,
'. . . a distillation of rumour' (Carlyle);
'. . . more or less bunk' (Ford).
3. Story that repeats itself: '. . . the first time as tragedy,
the second as farce' (Marx).
4. Story which, if we do not learn it, we are
'condemned to relive' (Santayana).
5. Story of which all citizens should be proud.
Heritage. That which made us, inspires us, enriches,
informs and guides us.
6. Judge. '*History* will judge me kindly'; '. . . stand
before the bar of *history*', etc.
7. Second refuge of the scoundrel.

'Now there are some who like to re-write *history* – revisionist historians is what I like to call them.'

George W. Bush, June 2003

'Australians are free to be proud of their country and heritage.'

John Howard, Draft Preamble to Constitution

'. . . *history* is on our side. We will bury you.'

Nikita Krushchev, 1958

holism, holistic approach

1. Thesis that wholes in general are more than the sums of their parts (Gk. *Holos* – whole, complete); organicism. 2. Taking account of more than one part. Not partial or fragmentary, therefore yielding superior conclusions. Not inadequate. As *holistic* medicine might treat the liver to cure a sore ankle, a *holistic approach* in business will try to cure a sales downturn by overhauling the *communications department*.

'The Queensland Studies Framework *is learner-centred* . . . People construct deep understandings about particular phenomena, as well as broad transference and applications of knowledge from one aspect of their lives to other aspects. This *holism* and *synergy* contributes to learning coherence and learning rigour and is a continuous activity throughout life.'

Queensland Studies Authority

'All of me, why not take me *holistically*?
Can't you see, I'm no good without you.'

183

homicide bomber

Suicide bomber *rebranded*.

> 'Hamas, the organisation behind many *homicide bombings*, appears to have been sensing the change in public opinion.'
>
> Fox News

honest

1. Honest.
2. *Honest* in the *context* of the situation at a particular *point in time* that is not necessarily the same as this one. (As in: 'There's no way a GST will ever be part of our policy. Never ever.' John Howard, May 1995). *Honest* about the first part of the question; honest in all but a few non-essential details; *honest* to the *core*, but not the *non-core*; honest in a way that might have misled a few boneheads among the general public; misleading in a way for which I can't be blamed; pretty *honest*; not entirely honest, but impeccably intentioned; *honest* on the basis of the evidence that was given me by highly professional, but ultimately very human, accountants, officers of the department, etc.; to *misspeak*; we couldn't find a Bible on which to swear.
3. Ironic – as in: '*Honest* John'.

> 'Everything that I said was based on the advice of the defence department. I did not set out to *mislead* anybody.'
>
> John Howard, June 2004

> 'Well I, to be *honest* with you, I think I owe the public and the, and my own integrity for that matter, an element here

of, of just facing up to the facts as I see them. I have an enormous amount of information on this issue. I have spent a lot of time with the Americans and others talking it through . . . I'm saying that there is a very high risk of war, of course there is, and we've been very frank with the Australian public about that and, *look*, I just owe it to people to be *honest* with them as I see the situation.'

Alexander Downer, *AM*, August 2003

hopefully

Buoyantly, optimistically, rosily; prospectively, expectantly. I / we / they hope. I hope so. With hope. In the hope that. With luck. With a bit of luck. Here's luck. If we're lucky. God willing. With every confident expectation. With hope in our hearts. Here's looking up your kilt. Here's mud in your eye. Touch wood, etc. Barring accident. Hope, hoping, hopeful. (As in: I hope we can meet – *hopefully* we can *dialogue*. Hoping to hear from you – *hopefully* we can *touch base*. I am hopeful – *hopefully*.)

'I've got a twinge in the groin but *hopefully* I'll be all right next week.'

'Hope springs eternal, *hopefully*.'

horizontalise

Reconceptualise to the horizontal.

'Using an Actor-Network Theory approach, data was collected from the film and TV production industry of Sydney to show that if we "*horizontalise*" our conceptualisation of the creative industries we find that there is a multiplicity of topologies which simply cannot be restricted, constrained or limited to the preconceived meta-narratives of conventional creative industries research.'

> Re-conceptualising the Creative Industries:
> The Horizontalisation of the Film and TV industry in
> Sydney, University of Technology Sydney

'Would you *horizontalise* with me in a field of stone?'

'Where a mother *horizontalised* her baby
In a manger for his bed.'

horizontal service delivery platform

One of those.

'CONTENT AUDITOR: Ericsson will provide ongoing services for the development and deployment of content-based mobile services on a new, *horizontal service delivery platform*.'

> Seek.com.au, December 2004

how's your day been so far?

1. How's your day been so far?
2. As if I care.

Customer: 'I would like to buy a pair of size 34 underpants, please.'
Shop assistant: *'Great. How's your day been so far?'*

Customer: 'Hello. I want to complain about the telephone service.'
Calcutta call centre: *'Excellent. How's your day been so far*, sir? Please hold the line.'

See *shortly, call centre*

human capital management

Managing staff.

> 'Combining the expertise of our industry-*leading practice partners* and associates with our *holistic* approach and the creation and *implementation* of *best practice resources*, positions JML Australia at the forefront of *human capital management* in Australia.'
>
> JML Australia

> Cf. Human cattle management: 'The primary advantage of spaying is the guaranteed nonpregnant status of the heifer and *marketability* as such. Pregnancy in feeder heifers is costly, primarily in the feedlot and when slaughtered.'
>
> Stocker Management, Kansas State University

human resources (HR)

1. Personnel (aka ED – Employee Development). People working in the *knowledge economy*, i.e. *most* people. Managing them, inc. recruiting and *decruiting* them. *Enhancing* their *skills*, *competencies* etc. *Harvesting* their minds for *value adding* in the organisation. Lucrative field for *consultants*.
2. Management tool for coercing and manipulating staff and controlling their thought and behaviour. *Downsizing implement*. (See *re-engineering* etc.)

> 'The university is reviewing *human resource* policies to *ensure* that such policies are updated to be consistent and appropriately linked, unambiguous, written in plain English and do not contain unnecessary detail. A clear *strategy* for *communication*

of the policies will form an integral part of the *implementation* process.'

University of New England policy review document

'Mercer's new *HR* Effectiveness Monitor survey can show the degree to which your *HR* function is *transforming* from a task-oriented, administrative back office to a front-line, *strategic* powerhouse for today's *leading-edge* organisations.'

HR consultant

'Easy HR Pty Ltd is able to provide a cost-effective and *value adding* consulting service. People represent the real "heart" of any organisation. Easy HR can help you to harness the power of your people by assisting you *manage* your team more effectively.'

Easy HR

'The human potential movement . . . offers us a new organizing principle in psychology, sociology, law and politics — one based on empathic liberation and trust.'

The Politics of *Trust Network*:
Inspiring a *New Human Agenda*

See *knowledge management, re-engineering*

hunting where the ducks are

Campaigning among those who might vote for you, and not among those who won't. Attributed to 1964 Republican presidential candidate, Barry Goldwater, who figured that as black Americans would never vote Republican, it was better to ignore them and go after the white vote.

Modern polling makes it easier to distinguish ducks from non-ducks. By this means politics is made a little more scientific, but it also might have the effect of making it sound 'like a series of signals meant for somebody else' (Joan Didion, *Political Fictions*).

Ii

icon

1. Image or representation, usually of a saint or other sacred Christian personage (e.g. 'A few weeks ago, the Holy Father communicated to the patriarch of Moscow his wish to give to the Russian Orthodox Church the sacred *icon* of the Lady of Kazan.')
2. Computer symbol.
3. Any well-known footballer or cricketer, the Big Pineapple, the Crocodile Man, Uluru, Sydney Opera House, Dame Edna Everage, Sir Les Paterson, Germaine Greer, the Dog on the Tucker Box, Gough Whitlam, Malcolm Fraser, Bert Newton, Blue Hills, The Man from Snowy River, Breaker Morant, Nicole Kidman, Lindy Chamberlain, the gum tree, the wattle, the cypress, the galah, the crocodile, the kangaroo, the koala, the sulphur-crested cockatoo, magpie, crow, *Anzac*, ANZUS, wattle, etc. Any well-known person or thing. There are business *icons* ('Business *icon* shares her story'), sporting *icons*, cultural *icons* (Les Murray, Roy and HG, Little Pattie, Clive James, etc.), food *icons* (meat pie, pie floater, Big Mac, vegemite, chump chops, Foster's Lager, etc.), environmental *icons*, feminist *icons*, political *icons*. Anything that's been around for a while. Anything dinkum (e.g. 'Lee Kernaghan, Country Music *Icon*').
4. Anything or anyone you say. (Make your own list.)

'Accounts Payable Clerk for Australian *Icon*.
Our client is an Australian *icon* and market leader. They are currently looking for an accounts payable clerk.'

Job advertisement

'New Minister Welcomed by Wine Industry *Icon*.'

Ballandean Estate Wines press release

'When we show an Aussie *icon*, we have done so in a way that has never been seen before.'

Consultancy to Australian Tourism Commission

icon (destinational)

One simply must go.

'. . . QM2 has achieved the status of a *destinational icon*.'

ABC *Limelight* magazine, December 2004

iconic

1. Having the status of an *icon*.
2. Not contemporary (unless a contemporary *icon*).
Something old and important.

'Southcorp is *committed* to being a dedicated and leading premium winemaker with a portfolio of brands and wines that range from the contemporary to the *iconic* . . .'

Southcorp media release, 2004

identification, monitoring and reporting

1. Keeping a watch on things. Being a *watchdog*.
2. Being *accountable* and *transparent*.

'Processes for *Governance*: what methods are established to enable *identification, monitoring, reporting* and subsequent actions in respect of *risk management*, evaluation and response to risks, risk policies and *strategies*.'

Governance seminar

illegal immigrant / illegals

Here is another way of putting it:

> 'Notice what *strategies* you are using now, identify where these are not *achieving* the desired result, and gain *strategies* that will enable you to do something else. (*Change* current habits and patterns.)'
>
> Melbourne University Leadership & Professional Development Program

illegal immigrant / illegals

Refugees seeking sanctuary in Australia under the protection of international law, namely the UN Convention on Refugees. People who are not in breach of any law, until one is devised to make them so.

> 'The Australian public has been blitzed for the past week with the story of whether or not the *illegals* threw their children overboard. Most people couldn't give a hoot over a relatively minor incident that occurred four months ago.'
>
> *Australian,* 17 February 2002

immediate

1. *Imminent*, about to happen. Clear and present – now.
2. The sort of word journalists put in one's mouth.

> 'Well, you're the – you and a few other critics are the only people I've heard use the phrase "*immediate* threat". I didn't. The President didn't. And it's become kind of folklore that that's – what happened.'
>
> Donald Rumsfeld

'No terrorist state poses a greater or more *immediate* threat to the security of our people and the stability of the world than the *regime* of Saddam Hussein in Iraq.'

Donald Rumsfeld

See *imminent*, *misspeak*, *signs*, etc.

imminent

1. About to happen; just round the corner; clear and present danger; coming right up.
2. A threat of which the public must be made aware without delay; a threat requiring a pre-emptive strike; whatever we damn well say it is; *shock and awe*, etc. Condition of pre-emption; requiring pre-emptive attack.
3. Not ever going to happen.

'. . . some have argued that the nuclear threat from Iraq is not *imminent*, that Saddam is at least five to seven years away from having nuclear weapons. I would not be so certain.'

Donald Rumsfeld

'For centuries, international law recognised that nations need not suffer an attack before they can lawfully take action to defend themselves against forces that present an *imminent* danger of attack.'

White House White Paper, September 2002

Journalist: 'Is North Korea an *imminent* threat to the US?'
President Bush: 'You know, that's an operative word . . .'

William Safire, *International Herald Tribune*,
February 2004

See *immediate*

impact

(v) To effect, influence, bear upon, sway, persuade, win over, inspire, engage, convince, brainwash, earbash, control, change, stimulate, make them understand, make them repent, penetrate their minds, blow their minds, sell, make them listen, convert, bend, mindfuck, exhilarate, impress, affect, move, excite, rouse, stir, transport, move, inflame, ravish, seduce, overwhelm, fire, shock, arouse, impassion, anger, depress, soothe, stir, infect, lay them in the aisles, bore them stiff, etc. Whatever has been affected has been *impacted*.
(n) An effect, consequence, result, etc.

'In particular the *impact* of our respective roles and responsibilities are [sic] clearly highlighted in the survey results.'
Victorian Department of Human Services

'A great deal has been written about the factors *impacting* the performance of Lend Lease.'

Annual report

'Modern audiences are sophisticated, educated, and saturated with messages so to *impact* them requires new speaking *skills*.'
Business Seminars Australia

'*empowering* people to lead and *impact* in every sphere of life.'
Hillsong Church *Mission Statement*

'Theirs not to make reply,
Theirs not to reason why,
Theirs but to make an *impact*.'

impactful

Full of impact. Having an impact.

'I am *impactful*: What I do makes a difference in the lives of others.'

Steven R. Covey,
The 7 Habits of Highly Effective People

'And the way we cover that *issue* of the water grid is probably a hundred year plan, but we've got a five point plan, some of which is immediately *impactful* . . .'

Bob Mansfield, ABC radio, May 2004

'More *impactful* than a locomotive.'

implement, implementation

To put into effect, action, practice, operation, service. Carry out. Get it up and going. Get it running, moving. Bring about. Apply. Start, kick start. Initiate. Activate. Maintain. Institute. Proceed with. Do.

'Adhere and *implement* ethical standards.'

Consultancy document

'A clear *strategy* for communication of the policies will form an integral part of the *implementation* process.'

University of New England

'Thy kingdom come; thy will be *implemented*.'

'*Implement* it to me one more time.'

implementable

Can be done.

> 'There are a lot of *implement*, immediately *implementable* things
> that can be done . . .'
>
> Bob Mansfield, ABC radio, May 2004

> 'Call me *implementable*.'

inappropriate behaviour

Riots, self-mutilation, attempted suicide, hunger strikes,
etc., by refugees held in Australian detention centres.
'Moral blackmail' (to which we will not submit); 'antics'
(Philip Ruddock); behaviour that will not achieve the
desired *outcomes*.

'*Evil*' behaviour – see *queue jumper*, *un-Australian*

incomplete success

A success with a little way to go; success in progress;
success *going forwards*, in future *iterations*, *scenarios*,
etc. Success not entirely *implemented*. Mission sort of
accomplished.

> 'His great, if *incomplete, success* in Iraq may be many things, but
> it's not a triumph of the military reforms he rightly
> championed.'
>
> *Wall Street Journal* on Donald Rumsfeld, 12 April 2003

increasingly competitive marketplace

Marketplace. Marketplace made competitive by government intervention.

See *downsizing*, *rightsizing*, etc.

indication / indicator

Sign, symptom.

> 'I've not seen any *indication* that would lead me to believe I would say that.'
>
> Donald Rumsfeld, September 2003

influencer

A person of influence.

> 'There are of course many ways to learn, and as leaders and *influencers* of the future we need to *ensure* that these ways are employed in the most effective manner when working with others.'
>
> University of Melbourne, Leadership and
> Professional Development Program

information needs identifier

1. One of those.
2. INI.

> 'The *information needs identifier (INI)* would discover, as a bye-product [sic], several ideas, *tools*, methods and techniques of satisfying *clients* . . .'
>
> Knowledge Management

initiative

1. First step in a process; the initial step. To set out to
resolve or confront a situation or problem. To show
some gumption, spirit, get up and go, etc. Something
one seizes. A plan of action.
2. Any step. Anything done or proposed. The
organisation established to do it. (e.g. Proliferation
Security *Initiative*, Depression *Initiative*, Urban
Stormwater *Initiative*, Hugo Mutation Databox
Initiative, Western Australian Herbicide Resistance
Initiative – WAHRI.) Many *initiatives* are *strategic*.

> 'Cost reduction *initiatives* to derive $88 million per annum
> in sustainable pre-tax operating savings.'
>
> Annual report

> 'In the beginning was an *initiative*.'

> 'Heaven and Earth Creation *Initiative*.'

innovate, innovative, innovation

1. (v) To introduce, create something new. (n) 'A totally
new product, new service, or new practice' (*consumer
behaviour*).
2. Universal desideratum; self-evidently desirable and
superior; what every *consumer* wants, what every
business needs.

> '*Innovation* and Creativity *tools*, techniques and training to
> build a greater *innovation* competency to help organisations
> develop more *innovative strategies*.'
>
> www.thinksmart.com

'. . . capturing the value of newness'.

New South Wales Innovation Council

See *state of the art, cutting edge*

input

1. (n) Contribution, help, advice, offering, suggestion, something put in.
   (v) To put something in.
2. An idea, remark, song, joke; a design for a new fighter aircraft or hairclip, or an actual fighter aircraft or hairclip; everything that goes in is an *input*.

'In March 2003, a second round of staff *workshops* will be held for staff to *input* to and confirm the QSA *Strategic* Plan 2004-2006.'

Change Management consultancy

'SMS . . .: communicating via mobile phones by *inputting* a text message using the phone keys.'

Australian Competition and Consumer Commission

'I am the Alpha and the Omega, the *input* and the *outcome*, inputteth the Lord.'

'And on the seventh day God ended his *inputs*.'

See *output*

in-service education

A kind-of education strategy.

'*In-service education* is an ongoing thought-out school-based *strategy* co-operatively conceived and professionally executed

integrate (integrated / integration)

to co-ordinate and exploit the in-built and developmental dimensions to comply with the well-known definition of the creativity of the school, geared towards self-renewal but not ignoring extra-mural influences.'

Resolved at a meeting with the Standing Committee for
In-service Education, Queensland

integrate (integrated / integration)

To put together; combine; amalgamate.

'Rapid *integration* of the vertical structure' is alleged to heighten efficiency and even make things 'seamless'. Integration of this kind is related to *involuntary career events*.

'. . . parking *integrated* with the streetscape and pedestrians'.
Surf Coast Shire Community Newsletter,
November 2003

'Birds of a feather flock *integrated*.'

intelligent product

1. Product that has '(i) a unique identity (ii) can *communicate* with its environment (iii) retains data about itself (iv) deploys a language (v) participates in decisions about its own destiny'.
2. Can of soup with a barcode on it.

'Talking about the "skin", the aesthetic aspect of IZZI has a fundamental role, as a simple *intelligent product* she has a pleasant face, she smiles, she assures you that she will do the best for you!'

Electrolux dishwasher

interactive opportunity

Opportunity to *communicate* in an exciting, fuelled kind of way.

> 'As 2003 draws to a close, PTW Interiors is delighted to announce to our friends and *clients* a range of new *communications initiatives*. First and foremost, our new web presence at . . . will provide us with an ongoing, *interactive opportunity* to stay in touch with the thinking that motivates us in our continuing collaboration with you . . . We approach 2004 with a great deal of enthusiasm, fuelled by the *energy* inherent in our many projects and excited by the new ways we are exploring to *communicate* our ideas and *processes* to our *clients*.'
>
> PTW Interiors

interconnectedness

1. 'Everything connects.'
2. Sort of like, you know, it's amazing, weird.

> '"Spirit of Learning" encourages the integration of all dimensions of ourselves whilst understanding our essential *interconnectedness* with each other and our environment.'
>
> ReaLearning *Innovative Consultancy*

interface

(n) Relationship, relations, point of contact, where organisations meet, etc.
(v) To deal with, communicate with; talk to, write to, fax, ring up, have a drink with, meet (with).

interlock

'Results-oriented, *customer-centric* professional seeking to *leverage* experience with multiple *implementations* to help organisations exploit the benefits of Siebel and CRM. Adept at *facilitating* user sessions, defining new *processes*, documenting business requirements, evaluating *change* requests, *capturing* and *prioritising* bugs . . . Easily *interfaces* with users, executives, development *team*, and partners.'

Resume

interlock

1. To talk, converse, discuss, speak, yarn, chat, communicate, have a confab. Oral *interface*. *Engage* in verbal terms. *Dialogue* with a *discussant*.
2. To coordinate, or work cooperatively. As in, 'Bruce, you had better *interlock* with Melisande on the furry boot deal.'

'I will *interlock* with my wife to see if I can come to dinner tomorrow night.'

in terms of

1. For.
2. About.
3. Nothing.

'They're moving things around the different baskets, but it will be the end game *in terms of* putting numbers in square brackets *in terms of* tariff reductions, if there's significant requests on time frames *in terms of* phase-in.'

Mark Vaile, Deputy Prime Minister, Canberra Times
6 December 2003

'For *in terms of lifestyle* we've got the germs of
A ripper concept to think *in terms of*.'

> Sir Les Paterson, *In Terms of My Natural Life*

'*In terms of* rain falling in a short period this was a once in a
hundred years *event*.'

> Bureau of Meteorology

'He said of his father, "He is the wrong father to appeal to for
advice. The wrong father to go to, to appeal to *in terms of* strength."
And then he said, "There's a higher Father that I appeal to."'

> President George W. Bush, conversation with
> Bob Woodward

'Werriwa has very much a prestige element to it *in terms of* the
number of former incumbents to this position.'

> The new Labor candidate for Werriwa, NSW

'Much Ado *in terms of* Nothing.'

internal clients

Staff, students, patients, inmates, residents, etc.

'To influence and support our *internal clients* to *communicate*
effectively . . .'

> City of Port Phillip, job description

'The benefits of Cleaner Production and Eco-efficiency
will be promoted to *internal clients* (college staff and students)
and to the wider *community*, including contractors that
provide services to and for the College.'

> Action Plan for WA Central TAFE

internal / external environments

Inside and out.

> 'Reporting to the director, the role *facilitates* the work of the
> *HR* functions, *continuously improves strategies* and procedures,
> whilst *interfacing* the *internal* and *external environments*.'
> Manager, Administration — Monash University, Melbourne

internal resources

Staff, employees, *internal clients*, etc.

> 'At *Go-Live*, the final transfer of knowledge and ownership
> will occur between the *consultants* and the *internal resources*.'
> SAP consultants

interrogate

A military word of increasingly uncertain meaning, not
to be confused with *interview* or *debrief*. 'One is a voluntary act, and one is under a certain amount of duress or
coercion' (Senator Robert Hill, Minister for Defence).

A study of the recent record establishes at least two
definitions.

1. Something that Australian military personnel do: 'A
very major job remains to *interrogate* those who have
information on Iraqi *WMD*' (Senator Robert Hill).
2. Something that Australian military personnel do not
'do', as in: 'Australia does not *interrogate* prisoners'

(Senator R. Hill). 'The whole purpose, right from day one when we sent ISG to Iraq, they went under written orders that they were not permitted to participate in *interrogation*' (Senator Hill).

Even some *interrogators* do not properly understand the word. Rod Barton, a member of the ISG, believed he had taken part in *interrogations* of '*high-value detainees*' at Camp Cropper near Baghdad until the Australian Defence Department told him, 'We regard that you did *interviews* and not *interrogations*.' Punching and other forms of *blunt force trauma*, and keeping *detainees* in solitary confinement with hessian bags over their heads for two days before the *interview* has no bearing on the definition. For this reason we must assume that the detainee who died of head injuries at Camp Cropper had been *interviewed* to death.

interview

A voluntary, sometimes fatal act.

See *interrogation*, *blunt force trauma*, *control technique*

involuntary career event

1. An unemployment *event*.
2. ICE. Hence – to be *iced* is to be sacked. (cf. Mafia 'ice' – to kill.)

Also known as *involuntary career transition*. See *downsized*, *rightsized*, *dejobbed*, etc.

involved

Of a possibly dodgy, mysterious or dark nature, though of course one would not like to cast aspersions when one is not privy to all the facts; but notwithstanding the foregoing it is nonetheless distinctly possible that not everything to which we are not privy is as innocent or benign as it may seem and we would be foolish indeed to assume the bona fides and good character of those of whom we speak.

> 'I'm not privy to the issues *involved*, but in weighing up any approach in relation to these matters, you have to look at the conduct of the people *involved*, and that includes the party who's making the claims.'
>
> Phillip Ruddock, ABC, 23 May 2005

irrefutable

1. Beyond doubt or dispute; watertight; incontrovertible; only the mischievous, treacherous or unreasoning could deny it.
2. Maybe so / maybe not.

> '[It is] hard to imagine how anyone could doubt Iraq possesses *weapons of mass destruction*.'
>
> *Washington Post* in an editorial headline, 'Irrefutable', after Colin Powell's presentation to the United Nations

> 'The things that you're li'ble
> to read in the Bible
> are *irrefutable*.'

issue

1. The matter to be resolved.
2. Any argument, difficulty, injury, bone to pick,
sore spot, difference of opinion (faith-based or rational),
complaint or *problem* existing between one party and
another, or in one single entity. Whatever is going on
between people or organisations. One can have an *issue*
with anyone or anything, including life itself.

> 'Facilitated *workshop* on practical solutions and the way forward
> regarding your *issues* in Senior Executive *Leadership*.'
>
> > Benchmarking Partnerships, Senior Executive
> > *Leadership* workshop

> 'Denis has had some major *issues* with neck problems.'
>
> > Fox Footy Channel, April 2004

> 'To be or not to be; that is the *issue*.'

it

Personal pronoun.

> [The post-traumatic stress disorder of 6-year-old Shayan
> Badries, an Iranian detainee in Australia, may be due to the
> fact that] *it* 'is not the natural child of the mother, *it* is a
> stepson.' . . . 'I understand *it* receives food and liquids.' . . .
> 'We are working at getting the child into an environment in
> which *its* condition can be *managed*.'
>
> > Phillip Ruddock, Minister for Immigration,
> > ABC, August 2001

See *self harm*, *disposition*

iteration

1. What is said or performed again. What repeats.
2. Mathematics – an algorithmic technique. Computer science – 'The solution is obtained by *iteration*.'
3. Business (especially closed loop *marketing*) – several can create a *time crunch*.

'If several *iterations* were required, the cycle could create a *time crunch*.'

DM Review

'Planning can be a painful annual process that staggers through multiple *iteration* and reviews before it is finally approved.'

Montgomery Research

'*Iteration* drives emergence.'

Sigma Consulting Group

'The *iteration* that hath been, it is the *iteration* that shall be.'
Ecclesiastes, King James *iteration*

Jj

job seeker

1. An unemployed person. A person who has been *rightsized* or experienced an *involuntary career event*. A *churned* person. A person on the dole, including one who has passed through the *'Mutual Obligation' (MO)* *'Gate'* and is no longer deserving of support without returning something to the *community*. ('A *job seeker*'s MO gate is 6 months after their allowance start date', Commonwealth Department of Employment and Workplace Relations.)
2. A *client* earning $167.00 per week.

'The mobile phone, as the small piece of hardware that is available to the *job seeker*, is part of a much bigger fabric under the Active Participation Model to bring together a greater range of opportunities that are helping more *job seekers* get into work faster.'

Australian Senate Estimates

Kk

key

1. (n) Something to open a lock; a means of access or control; pitch or tonality, etc.
2. (adj) *Initiatives*, decisions, *inputs, outputs, outcomes, focus, issues, players, priorities, stakeholders*, etc. are *key* whenever they are not *core*. (As in: 'There are two *key* issues *going forwards*.')

Crucial, critical, vital, decisive, necessary, indispensable, influential, dominant, all-pervading, principal, main, essential, splendid, primary, most important, substantial, significant, crucial, *colourful*, educative, noteworthy, effective, productive, popular, etc. Chief, foremost, paramount, pre-eminent, etc. Of consequence, etc. *Core*.

> 'To stay informed of the views and expectations of *key stakeholders* and interested *communities*, the department has formed *key partnerships* with interested *communities* and *accountabilities*.'
> New South Wales Department of Women

> 'The Australian *brand* voice is *key*.'
> Consultancy to Australian Tourist Commission

> 'He is *key* for us *going forwards*.'
> Ricky Ponting

See *core*

key attractor

Important attractor that drives things.

> '. . . a *key attractor* that drives *visitation* to the region.'
> Victorian Government

210

'How, like a moth, the simple maid
Still plays about the *key attractor!*'

key deliverable

The sort of *deliverable* on which much depends.

'Examining new *performance management* / measurement
models that will be emerging to change the *key deliverables* of
the finance professional in a new technology world.'

Conference brochure

'Some of the objectives for this *initiative* include:
Developing and coordinating the three discrete *key service
processes:* Planning, Financial Intermediaries and Support
and Communicating major *deliverables* and activities to all
stakeholders.'

Department of Human Services' Individualised Planning
and Support *Growth* Funding *Initiative* 2003–04

'So Moses went down unto the people,
and spoke unto them *key deliverables.*'

key differentiators

Not any old *differentiator*, but a *key* one.

Key differentiators are:
1. Corpgroove *workshops* and conference breakers are individually tailored to each *client* to *ensure* the day or session
output is *aligned* with their objectives
2. Research and consulting precedes each event to *ensure* an
educated *delivery* of the commercial content on the day.
3. The *workshop* days are 2/3rds commercial content and the

remainder drumming for fun and reinforcement of the commercial *messages*.

Corpgroove, Sydney

'He could not tell the *key differentiators* between fact and fiction.'

key enabler

Important person, process, force, policy, idea, piece of technology etc. to help us reach our *agreed outcomes*. *Key facilitator*.

'The development of an Individualised Planning and Support approach is a *key enabler* of the *priority strategy* that aims to reorient disability supports.'

Victorian Department of Human Services

'There came *key enablers* from the east to Jerusalem.'

key indicators

Signs, markers, measures – *key* ones.

'Toby's Individual Student Profile shows that he is *achieving* all the *key indicators* of Phase B on the Writing Developmental Continuum. He is also mapped as *achieving* Writing *key indicators* C1, C2, C3, C4 and C5. Although Toby is not yet operating in Phase C, he will not need to undertake the Writing validation task because he is already achieving both C2 and C5, which are part of the validation sub-set of *indicators* for Writing.' (i.e. Toby does not write well, but he is improving.)

Sample student report, Queensland Studies Authority

See *learning continua*

key learning needs

What you want to learn.

> 'Please advise your *key learning needs* from the *workshop*, so that we can advise the speakers.'
>
> Consultant's spiel

> 'Ask, and it shall be given you. Advise your *key learning need* and ye shall find.'

key objectives

Objectives – *outcomes driven.*

> 'The *key objectives* for AusAid support is *outcomes driven* with a strong *focus* on improved *governance*.'
>
> Company document

key performance indicator (KPI)

Quantifiable measures of an organisation's success. E.g., a business might agree that turnover is a *KPI*; a school that the number of students graduating is the measure; a poultry farm, the number of birds killed and dressed; a hospital, the number of patients sent home in better health than they were enjoying when admitted.

> 'The total discharge compliance score is based on the number of medical records for which all four *key performance indicators* are complied with. For some patients, e.g. same day patients, they will only be able to comply with a maximum of 2 PI's. Where an *indicator* is determined to be "not applicable" then, for the purposes of the audit, it will be deemed to

having [sic] *achieved* compliance. In all cases, if compliance were *achieved* to all relevant *indicators*, then that would mean that the Total Discharge Compliance Score is *achieved*.' (i.e. You can go home tomorrow.)

Victorian Department of Human Services

key stakeholders

Shareholders, staff, *customers*. *Key* people holding stakes. Hierarchies within these groups.

People responsible for *key stakeholders* come from *stakeholder relations*.

knee-jerk reaction

1. An impulsive reaction. Decision taken without necessary reflection, or the services of a *consultant*.
2. Inappropriately decisive reaction.
3. Decisive reaction.
4. Reaction. (President Bush upon being told that a second aeroplane had hit the World Trade Centre.)

'*Knee-jerk reactions* with long-term consequences in transient conditions is no way to run a country . . .'

Submission to Isle of Man's Treasury, 2004

know

1. To apprehend with certainty; regard as true beyond doubt; possess knowledge.
2. To have a kind of reason to believe; or a reason to believe what one would like to believe, or cannot

persuade others to believe without a reason. (As in: 'We *know* they have biological and chemical weapons . . . And we also have reason to believe they're pursuing the acquisition of nuclear weapons' Vice President Cheney, 17 March 2003.)

3. To have no doubts, even if your intelligence officials tell you they have them and that you should have them too. To pretend, *spin*, deceive, invent, con, dissemble, *re-brand*, *lie*, etc.

4. To surmise. To assert on the basis of faith; because it sounds good, or because you're stupid enough to believe it.

'We do *know* that there have been shipments going into . . . Iraq . . . of aluminum tubes that . . . are only really suited for nuclear weapons programs, centrifuge programs.'

Condoleezza Rice, 8 September 2002

'And we *know* that for our blessed nation, the best days lie ahead.'

George W. Bush, July 2004

'We *know* where they are. They're in the area around Tikrit and Baghdad and east, west, south and north somewhat.'

Donald Rumsfeld, 30 March 2003

cf. 'If it was so, it might be; and if it were so, it would be: but as it isn't, it ain't.'

Lewis Carroll, *Through the Looking Glass*

knowledge

1. What is known. E.g. how babies are made; varieties of experience; why birds sing; when Caesar crossed the

Rubicon; how to make porridge; if Anna Karenina was ever truly happy; what in the world has no answer.
2. *Key product. Key input.* What is known in the company. What is known in the hospital, school, etc. What needs to be managed.

> 'It is *knowledge* which is the *key product* and the *key input* of the global economy. And *knowledge* . . . can move in a second.'
>
> Martin Carnoy, Global Progress
> Commission

> 'A little *key product* is a dangerous thing.'

> '*Key input* thyself.'

knowledge entity

An entity known to *knowledge managers.*

> 'Any *knowledge entity* is incomplete if it does not cultivate a *dialogue* between the members of the community of practice to advance the defining and refining of a socially constructed *process.*'
>
> The Brint Institute, The Knowledge
> Creating Company™

knowledge management (KM)

1. Managing an organisation's intellectual capital; rounding up (*harvesting*), capturing and sharing the skills and experience of its employees to increase productivity and innovation.
2. A common species of *consultant – knowledge managers.*
3. Virus.

'Our ignorance exceeds our *knowledge* where *issues* of motivation and *commitment* of *knowledge* workers are concerning in the context of *knowledge management systems* (KMS) *implementation*.'

Syracuse University School of Management

'Here's how we like to pretend *knowledge management* got started: Analysts, *consultants* and managers noticed that there was this really important type of information that was going unmanaged. So we called it "*knowledge*" and set about managing it.'

Dr Dave Weinberger, Harvard University

knowledge officer (Chief)

1. Officer chiefly of knowledge.
2. Officer of chief knowledge.
3. Official knowledge chief.

'Chief Knowledge Officer.
The Australian Tax Office (ATO) employs around 20,000 people across the country, and manages in excess of 11 million *customers* through its nationwide network of offices and *call centres* . . . In essence, this represents an outstanding opportunity to create and build a *holistic knowledge management* function in one of Australia's significant, *customer focused* organisations.'

Job advertisement, ATO

known knowns

1. Things we *know* we *know*.
2. Things we *know* we made up.
3. Things we forgot we made up.
4. Things we forgot we *knew*.

'As we know, there are *known knowns*. There are things we know we know. We also know there are *known* unknowns. That is to say we know there are some things we do not know. But there are also unknown unknowns, the ones we don't know we don't know.'

Donald Rumsfeld

'The more you know the more you don't know. It's what you don't know you don't know.'

Werner Erhard (founder of *est*)

Ll

Landmark Forum / Landmark Education Corporation

Californian New Age descendant of *est*. Influential in management and education, especially in *human resources* and *knowledge management*.

> '*Landmark* is dedicated to *empowering* people in generating unlimited possibilities and *making a difference*. Our work provides limitless opportunities for *growth* and development for individuals, relationships, *families*, communities, businesses, institutions and society as a whole. Well being, self-expression, *accountability* and integrity are the tenets upon which we stand. This stand leads to our extraordinary *customer*, assistant and employee satisfaction.'
>
> Landmark Education Charter

large group awareness training

'Human Potential' training developed in the US in the 1970s. The philosophical principles vary, but Napoleon Hill, *Think and Grow Rich*, appears to be seminal: Every achievement begins with a *plan*. *Plans* call for *implementation*. What you think is what you do. Therefore banish negative thoughts, visualise objectives, think positive, talk positive (even if it's poppycock). 'I'm here to *make a difference*', may derive from this philosophy.

See *est, Neuro Linguistic Programming, Landmark Forum, known knowns*

leadership

1. Art or fact of leading.
2. Essential to every organisation and community.
3. In politics, synonym for 'out of touch'.

> 'It is an interactive *workshop* about the techniques and rela-
> tionships of *leadership* and has at its *core*, the critical question:
> "How much control do I exercise over this person in these
> circumstances."'
>
> Consultant

leadership initiative

Doing something.

> 'Creating McDonald's Animal Welfare Council — the
> industry's first independent board of academic and animal
> protection experts. The Council has led to additional
> *leadership initiatives* for the well-being of cattle, poultry and
> hogs.'
>
> McDonald's Corporate Social Responsibility

> 'Come now therefore, and I will send thee unto Pharaoh,
> that thou mayest take additional *leadership initiatives*.'

leadership role

1. *Leadership*.
2. The kind of *leadership* that needs a *strategic
framework* to *underpin* it.

'It is serving as a *strategic framework* to underpin the Australian Government's *leadership role* in encouraging the development of *appropriate* economic and social policies.'

Australian Government Department
of Health and Ageing

leading edge

Cutting edge. The technology frontier. Nothing quite like it in the history of the world.

'We are expert coaches, trainers and *facilitators*, who *achieve* results for our *clients* by the *consistent* application of universal and timeless principles, combined with the use of *leading edge* learning technologies.'

Wilfred Jarvis Institute

See *state of the art*

learned

How things are *known*.

'The British government has *learned* that Saddam Hussein recently sought *significant* quantities of uranium from Africa.'

President George W. Bush, 28 January 2003

learner-centred

Centred on the learner; *focused* on the learner; *learner-centric*; *about* learners. Concerned with students.

Learning and learners are at the heart of it – as one would expect with a 'Studies Framework'. So why bother saying it?

> 'The Queensland Studies Framework is *learner–centred*.'
>> Queensland Education Department

learning coherence

Not the incoherent *learning* you get without *holism* and *synergy*. (As in, perhaps: 'Rarely is the question asked: Is our children learning?', President George W. Bush.)

> 'This *holism* and *synergy* contributes to *learning coherence* and learning rigour and is a continuous activity throughout life.'
>> Queensland Education Department

learning continua

1. Two or more continuums, i.e. (i) a set of points on a line (ii) a set of real numbers.
2. Learning *going forwards*.
3. Human production line.

> 'The objective of the e-legacy *learning continua* is to meet the *challenge* of perpetual modernness required by employers in the months and years to come.'
>> Professor Howard A. Kanter
>> DePaul University, Chicago

> 'For *learning* that is planned for from descriptions of *learning continua* such as in the early and middle years of *learning*, judgements can be made about the *learner's* progress along those *learning continua*.'
>> Queensland Studies Authority

'Where did you get to on the *learning continua* at school today, Barry?'

learning environment

Classroom; schoolroom; room where teaching and learning occur.

'Each seminar incorporates brain research, current learning *strategies*, team concepts and techniques, as well as effective uses of technology to improve *learning environments.*'

Langford International Inc. Seminars
aka Learning *climate*

'I warned you, Barry! Stand in the corner of the *learning environment!*'

learning outcomes (achieved, achieving)

Results, marks, consequences. What has been learned. What is done to primary, high school and tertiary students. *Achieving implementation success* with a minor.

'How will you know if you have *achieved* the *learning outcomes*? List the evidence you will use to measure the *achievement* of your *learning outcomes.*'

Sponsored Independent Learning Contract

'A measure of *learning outcomes* requires learners to complete tasks, which demonstrate that they have achieved the standards specified in the learning outcomes.'

University of Melbourne
Assessing *Learning Outcomes* and Providing *Feedback*

See *KPIs*

learning reinforcement tool

1. A *tool*, method, device, contrivance etc. to make the learning stick, e.g. rote, repetition, use of examples, abuse, threats, corporal punishment, as in: 'To teach him a lesson he would never forget, the teacher gave Jeffrey 10 strokes of the cane.'
2. Drumming (corporate), as in: 'There are many corporate drumming troops and they do great work however we are corporate *workshop facilitation* specialists using drumming as a *learning reinforcement tool* in a similar vein to the techniques used in *accelerated learning environments*' (Corpgroove, Sydney).

'Spare the *learning reinforcement tool* and spoil the child.'

level

1. Height, watermark, benchmark, etc. Low, medium and high level; especially high, but things frequently 'sink to a new level'. Pinnacle, acme, zenith, peak, apex, summit, farthest reaches, top. Performance *level*, emotional *level*, educational *level*, literacy *level*, enjoyment *levels*, etc. Footballers, racehorses and businesses when they improve are said to have 'gone to another *level*'. Sometimes they have 'ratcheted up' or 'ramped up' to another *level*.
2. State or category of being or doing. A place – of sorts.

'And to ensure the highest *level* of service, cabin crew are exclusively *dedicated* to Business Class . . .'

Qantas promotion

'It's all about service at a personal *level*.'

Qantas promotion

'What a swell party, at the enjoyment *level*.'

level playing field

cf. Tooth Fairy, Yeti, Min Min Lights, etc.

leverage

Advantage, bargaining chip, whatever gives power over others. A company might *leverage* its *brand*, reputation, assets – anything. To succeed in business one might *leverage* intelligence, experience, scandalous rumours, sexual allure, sense of humour, ability at karaoke, golf, etc.

'We have *leveraged* different mediums and different angles (using film, art, poetry, photography, sound) to *re-frame* and three-dimensionalise *iconic* Australia.'

Consultancy to Australian Tourism Commission

'They give back what they know, *leveraging* their diverse talents and scarce time.'

Greg Ferguson, Mercury Development

'*Leverage* international mindset (lived in five countries).'

Employment profile 'Career Objectives'

'For what is a man profited, if he shall gain the whole world by *leveraging* his own soul.'

leveraging off

A form of *leveraging* suited to opportunities.

> 'I *implemented* the development and *enhancement* to the functionality of the existing geographic information and mapping systems by *leveraging off* opportunities within inter-agency *initiatives.*'
>
> Job application

liberate, liberated, liberating, liberation

1. To set free.
2. To conquer. To make a *coaling station* of.

> 'The *liberation* of Iraq is a crucial advance in the campaign against terror. We've removed an *ally* of al-Qaeda.'
>
> President George W. Bush, 1 May 2003

See *coaling station*

lie

1. (n) Untruth told with the intention of deceiving. False witness. (v) To deceive deliberately.
2. (n) Matter of emphasis. (v) *Miscalibrate* the emphasis, *misspeak*; make a *non-core* promise, etc.

> 'We were not *lying*. It was just a matter of emphasis.'
>
> US Official on WMD as the justification for invading Iraq, April 2003

> 'Thou shalt not bear false emphasis against thy neighbour.'
> (9th *Commitment*)

life-broad, life-deep

Not life-high.

> 'Learning is life-long, *life-broad* and *life-deep*.'
>> Queensland Education Department

lifestyle

1. A *marketing* term for Life. ('In the midst of *lifestyle* we are in death' – hence *Lifestyle* Funerals, Geelong, Victoria. 'He had a short *lifestyle* but a happy one.') Something to be *segmented* and *targeted*. *Aspirational* life.
2. Anything that occurs on a patio.
3. Something to which one has a *commitment*, even a passionate *commitment*. *Enhanced lifestyle*, etc.

> 'Mode of living as identified by a person's activities, interests and opinions (AIO).'
>> Marketing textbook definition

> '*Personality* and *self-concept* are reflected in *lifestyle*.'
>> Marketing textbook

> 'Greater love hath no man than this; that he lay down his *lifestyle* for his friends.'

> '. . . The Resurrection of the body. And the *lifestyle* everlasting. Amen.'

See *Australian lifestyle*

lifestyle choice

1. Selection of one brand over another.
2. Selection of Australia over tyranny, persecution, death, famine, etc.

> 'In the main, people who have sought to come to Australia and make asylum claims do not come from a situation of persecution; they come from a situation of safety and security . . . They may not be able to go back to their country of origin but they are making a *lifestyle choice*.'
>
> Philip Ruddock, January 2002

light up / lit up

(US military) To shoot dead.

> 'We fired some warning shots. They didn't slow down. So we *lit them up*.
> Q: *Lit up*? You mean you fired machine guns?
> A: Right. Every car that we *lit up* we were expecting ammunition to go off. But we never heard any.'

> 'With us being trigger happy, we didn't really give this guy much of a chance. We *lit him up* pretty good.'
>
> Discharged US Marine

> 'Thou shalt not *light up*.'

> 'Caesar, now be still
> I *lit thee up* with not half so good a will.'

linkage

A link or links. (cf. *signage*)

> 'Recent improvements *implemented* and their *impacts* will be raised, along with *linkage* of *Governance* and *Risk Management* through *Business Excellence.*'
>
> Governance seminar, Benchmarking Partnerships

> 'This *linkage* will strengthen government's *strategic* and fiscal control.'
>
> Victorian Department of Treasury and Finance

live

1. To be alive; feel, see, hear, breathe, laugh, weep, etc. To have / get a life. *Live* life to the full; *live* it up; *live* a life, etc. 'Come *live* with me, and be my love / And we shall all the pleasures prove . . .' 'You might as well *live*', etc.
2. To embody some abstraction in one's working life or manner of existence. Thus, to *live* / embody 'clear direction allows organisational *alignments* and a *focus* on the *achievement* of goals'. To thus become insensible; to make of oneself a 'principle of business excellence'; to be a cliché; as good as dead.
3. To make like a *brand*.

> 'Our belief is that *values-based* behaviour and a positive *culture* build a strong *brand* and a successful organisation, so our priority will be on *growing* a high-performing *team* of people that is committed to *living our brand* in everyday *client* interaction'
>
> Ernst and Young

> 'Senior leadership's constant role-modelling of these principles, and creating a *supportive* environment in which to *live* these principles will help the organisation and its people to reach their full potential.'
>
> Gracedale Private Nursing Home

liveability

A word popular in Melbourne. *Environment* or context in which *lifestyles* get on *growth trajectories*.

> 'Melbourne 2030: Protecting our *liveability* now and for the future.'

look

1. To employ one's eyes in seeing.
2. Over there, see!
3. Agh. Blut. Mphh. Fusp.

> 'Alexander Downer: Well, some people claim he said that.
> Matt Brown: Oh no, it's quoted in the report.
> Alexander Downer: I think, I think, *look*, the, *look* the overall point, well maybe.'
>
> Alexander Downer, ABC, March 2004

> 'But, *look*, I mean we just think it's *calibrated* in the right way.'
>
> Alexander Downer, ABC, May 2004

> 'But, *look*, you know, our view is that we've made the protest, but in the end as time goes on, bearing in mind.'
>
> Alexander Downer, ABC, January 2001

look at

An expression of outrage (How dare you! By jingo!, etc.), as in:

> 'She (the Minister for Immigration) says she is outraged at the treatment of detainees and the Government is taking action.
> "That's been made very clear, when the Prime Minister and I responded to the Palmer Report that the contract will have to be *looked at*," she said.
> "Palmer recommended that it was, prior to that the Auditor-General put out his report, indicating his dissatisfaction of the contract [sic].
> "We said it will have to be *looked at* and it will be."'
>
> ABC, 30 July 2005

lower availability

Shortage.

> 'Mr Ballard said the *key issues* for the FY05 year were the strength of the Australian dollar and the *lower availability* of its super premium wines.'
>
> Southcorp media release, 2004

low key

Low pitch. Discussions and meetings which are informal, discursive, friendly and on which nothing much depends are described as *low key*. Meetings on which much depends are not so commonly called *high key*, and *mid key* meetings are unknown.

> 'A series of informal *low key* meetings for regional industry leaders, government officers and industry organisation managers to exchange information, develop *strategic* alliances and discuss regional *strategic issues* in a no recourse, non-threatening environment.'
>
> Sunraysia Mallee Economic Development Board

low-yield nuclear weapons

Nuclear weapons that cause less *collateral damage* than some others, bearing in mind the destruction is absolute if you're in the vicinity when one goes off. Aka 'Mini-nukes'.

> 'Moreover, as Congress understood in 1994, by seeking to produce usable *low-yield nuclear weapons*, we risk blurring the now sharp line separating nuclear and conventional warfare, and provide legitimacy for other nations to similarly consider using nuclear weapons in regional wars.'
>
> *Journal of the Federation of American Scientists*, 2001

Mm

main game

1. The most important game, match of the day.
2. The most important element in the mix. Where it's at.
What it's *about*. When you boil it down, *at the end of the
day*. What *the bottom line* is. That on which all else
depends, and to which all else is like unto a feather in a gale.

In the 1980s the *main game* was the economy. God,
getting a male heir, war, starvation and disease have also
been *main games*, and in some places remain so.

> 'Indeed, Rove's speech was no aberration. It was the *main game*.'
> Peter Hartcher, *Australian Financial Review*

make a difference

Internal clients key input. What every *team player*
wants to make. Corporate injunction to managers and
employees, possibly borrowed from football coaches. To
add value. To earn your keep. To do enough to survive
the next round of job cuts.

> 'I'm here to *make a difference*.'

See *large group awareness training*

make possession

Get (the ball), take, grab, grasp, gather, pluck, steal,
capture, spirit away, make off with, etc.

> 'Blokes were so often able to *make possession* . . .'
> ABC football commentator

'Moses *made possession* of Canaan; Agamemnon of Troy; Rupert Murdoch of the *Times*,' etc.

man of steel

John Winston Howard (according to President George W. Bush).

Iosif Djugashvili, i.e. Stalin.

management system

1. A system of management.
2. A system of blame. A system that allows management to absolve itself of responsibility and blame . . . the system; or some part of it, including abstract nouns.

'The development of Environment *Management Systems* for Australian agriculture is an important contributor to *sustainability* and to future trading and *marketing processes*. Our research, along with that of other corporations, *underpins* the development of *internationally acceptable accreditation systems* for *sustainable* agricultural production, environment management and new *agriindustry systems*.'

Australian Government Rural Industries Research and
Development Corporation

'*Capability gaps impacted* Captain Bligh's *management systems*.'

managing up, managing down

'I've *managed up and down* the generational ladder, gaining from my experiences a smattering of well-honed *skills* that go to the heart of this *issue*.'

Jennifer Lawton, www.score.org

mandate

The idea that recently elected governments have a right to do what pleases them. The tendency of recently defeated Oppositions to resist this concept may derive from an ancestral memory of governments that took their *mandate* to include the abolition of opponents. They could just as easily get it watching the SBS News.

'The people of Australia voted. John Howard won and he has a *mandate*.'

Shane Stone, *Age*, 2002

manhood

Thing.

'Well, on the *manhood* thing, I'll put mine up against his any time.'

George Bush Snr. after Walter Mondale said he didn't have the *manhood* to apologise

mapping

A job for a *consultant*.

'The *mapping* shows how the *outcomes* of the training program compare with the *outcomes* of the individual units

of competency from the Training *Package* qualifications . . .
It is these *outcomes* that have been *mapped* against the unit of
competency at the element and performance criteria
level.'

Industry Training Advisory Board

market (the)

1. Where goods are traded.
2. A force of nature; irresistible (and you're a fool to
try); more powerful than all of us; resistance is
hopeless, counter-productive (etc.). Like the weather.
An absolute wonder.
3. Value.

'The health system is a "*market*" and the Government's new
Medicare safety net has injected the system with "Coalition
values", Health Minister Tony Abbott has told a meeting of
Liberal Party supporters.'

Age, 22 April 2004

market failure

Where the pursuit of private interest is not in the public
interest; circumstance in which it used to be considered
appropriate for governments to intervene in the economy. Now obsolete.

'The most general statement about government intervention is that it should perform those functions for which
its powers of coercion give it an absolute advantage.'

Richard O. Zerbe Jr. and Howard McCurdy,
The End of Market Failure

See *transaction costs analysis*

market segmentation

Marketing's means of making certain that no one is left out; all human beings have a price, a *product*, a *need*, a *want*, a flow, a crack through which a *message* can be squeezed; 'No man is an Island, entire of itself', etc.

> '*Market segmentation* can be defined as the *process* of dividing a *market* into distinct subsets of *consumers* with common *needs* or characteristics and selecting one or more segments to *target* with a distinct *marketing* mix.'
>
> Marketing textbook

massage the figures

To loosen them up, make them *flexible*, improve tone and appearance, get them working as they should, make them look and feel like new.

mate, mateship

A cult.

> 'Socialism is just being *mates*.'
>
> William Lane, Australian utopian and mate

> 'We value excellence as well as fairness, independence as dearly as *mateship*.'
>
> John Howard, Draft Preamble to Australian Constitution

matrix

A situation or surrounding substance within which something else originates, develops, or is contained. E.g. *mateship* is the matrix of the *fair go* or the *true*

Australian. The company is the matrix of 'the suit'. The corporation has been described as 'The Matrix, the illusory world . . .' (Rose Michael, 'Inside the Matrix', *Cultural Studies Review*, 2003).

> 'It is not menstrual blood per se which disturbs the imagination — unstanchable as that red flood may be — but rather the albumen in the blood, the uterine shreds, placental jellyfish of the female sea. This is the chthonian *matrix* from which we rose.'
>
> Camille Paglia

> 'The Guerrilla *Matrix* for Business *Agility* presentation is distilled from the unique experiences of the speaker . . .'
>
> Global Profile

MBO (management by objectives)

A popular system of *management* that involves '*cascading* of organisational goals and objectives'; 'specific objectives for each member'; 'participative decision making'; 'explicit *time period*'; 'performance *evaluation* and *feedback*'; and a requirement that all employees regularly fill in report forms.

Coercion and control appropriate to *knowledge-based* industries.

> '*MBO* is a system in which specific performance objectives are jointly determined by subordinates and their superiors, progress toward objectives is periodically reviewed, and rewards are allocated on the basis of this progress.'
>
> University of Toronto, 1995

'The principle behind *MBO* is to make sure that everybody within the organisation has a clear understanding of the aims, or objectives, of that organisation, as well as awareness of their own roles and responsibilities in *achieving* those aims. The complete *MBO* system is to get managers and *empowered* employees acting to *implement* and *achieve* their plans, which automatically *achieve* those of the organisation.'

Cultural Intelligence and Modern Management
www.1000ventures.com/business

media

1. News *media*: (i) the newspapers, journals, radio, television that report the news (ii) the newspapers, journals, radio, television that decide what the news is.
2. Mass *media*: news *media* plus book publishing, film, recording, advertising, industries.
3. *Media* moguls: persons who control newspapers, radio stations, television stations and production houses, film studios and distribution companies, publishing conglomerates, recording companies, etc. People who decide what the news will be, what we will think about it, what we will eat, drink, wear, admire, think cool, think uncool, who gets elected, etc., to the extent that we can or cannot resist them. People of influence.
4. Alternative *media*: internet, al-Jazeera, *Guardian*, street posters, graffiti, text messaging, etc.

'"We think that there is so much *media* now, with the internet it's so easy and so cheap to start a newspaper or start a magazine that there's just millions of voices," Mr Murdoch told radio 2GB. "We don't really have to worry;

the old ideas of it being too concentrated, I think that's just fading away."'

Sydney Morning Herald, April 2004

'What really *drives* him, though, is not ideology but a cool concern for the *bottom line* — and the belief that the *media* should be treated like any other business, not as a semi-sacred public trust. The Bush Administration agrees. Rupert Murdoch has seen the future, and it is him.'

James Fallows, *Atlantic*, September 2003

'There are still places where people think that the function of the *media* is to provide information.'

Don Rottenberg

'Dogs need to sniff the ground; it's how they keep abreast of current events. The ground is a giant dog newspaper, containing all kinds of late-breaking dog news items, which, if they are especially urgent, are often continued in the next yard.'

Dave Barry

message

1. *Communication*, note, memorandum. Meaning, point, the sign within.
2. In politics, *marketing*, etc., the *story*, *takeout*, grab, line, *dog whistle*, underlying idea or theme, slogan, catchphrase, what they take away with them, that with which voters must be beaten senseless. *Messages* are verbal and non-verbal. They must be delivered in ways that *ensure* they *impact* and *engage* listeners. Politicians in particular must be always '*on message*', even if the effect is tedious, offensive and annoying.

'The successor to politics will be propaganda. Propaganda, not in the sense of a *message* or ideology, but as the *impact* of the whole technology of the times.'

Marshall McLuhan

'I just don't know, but I mean there's a very simple choice, Labor either supports the national interest on *border protection* or joins in sending a *message* to the people smugglers, a *message* to the people smugglers that we are starting to go soft. I don't think that is a *message the Australian people* want sent, it's not a *message* I want sent. And I say to the Labor Party, if you block this proposal you will be joining in sending a *message* to the people smugglers that this country is starting to go soft.'

John Howard, June 2002

See *PowerPoint*

metrics

1. Used to measure or assess a process.
2. Used to track trading trends, efficiency, productivity, etc.
3. Now used to measure business performance, as in: 'the *metrics* indicate that performance improved by . . .'

'The *Integrated Baseline Review* (IBR) . . . *focuses* on the assignment, definition, scheduling and *resourcing* of work, thus establishing early visibility into the acceptability of the Contractor's contract planning. The IBR also reviews the methods and *metrics* used to measure contract performance or progress.'

Australian Department of Defence

'The SCOR (Supply Chain Operations Reference) model provides a set of *performance metrics* and supply chain practices where the supply chain performance is contingent on the maturity of supply chain practices.'

Professor Umit S. Bititci, University of Strathclyde

migrate

To move issues.

'To this end, the Project *team* have undertaken a detailed testing *strategy* that unfortunately resulted in some un-expected results on *key* components of the *HR* module, as such we determined that it was more *appropriate* to defer the project by two weeks and resolve some of the open *issues* in a development environment rather than *migrate* them into a production system and try to resolve them through a support period.'

SAP Upgrade and Improvements Project

milk price level

The price of milk. Like 'carrot *price level*' or 'bicycle *price level*'. As in: 'What's that got to do with the fish *price level*?'

'We believe that the current industry *milk price level* is in advance of historical payment levels for the same external price factors in earlier years . . .'

Burra Foods letter to suppliers

'What's the *dog price level* of that doggy in the window?'

242

mindset

A set of assumptions from which escape is difficult. Mental inertia. Mental gridlock. The square outside of which one cannot, or is not allowed, to think.

> '. . . changing *mindsets* and *empowering people* to lead and *impact* in every sphere of life.'
>
> Hillsong Church Mission Statement

mind share

The proportion of a *consumer's* mind occupied by a brand. (Kleenex, Walkman, Google have a lot of *mind share*, for example.)

> 'A survey to assess satisfaction and *mind share* of the network was given higher priority, even whilst this was recognised as a lag indicator of *relationship building* activity.'
>
> Westpac

> 'Girl I'm sorry I was blind
> You always had a significant part of my *mind share*.'

See *front of mind*

mislead

1. To deceive (e.g. citizens, viewers, *customers*, *clients* etc.).
2. To lie, bear false witness, etc.
3. To deceive *non-core* citizens, viewers, *customers*, etc.

mission

'*Misleading* the ABC isn't quite the same as *misleading* the Parliament as a political crime.'

> Tony Abbott, ABC, August 2003

'It's not acceptable to *mislead* the public.'

> Tony Abbott, press release, August 2003

mission

Something to be *achieved*. Not yet *implemented*. Pre-*outcome* purpose. Like vision but different spelling.

See *mission statement*

mission accomplished

1. Mission successfully completed; victory is ours! Voilà! All over bar the shouting. Done deal. Game, set and match; we have a winner! Etc.
2. Not quite. Almost, nearly, soon, in the not-too-distant future, perhaps. It's not over till the fat lady sings. Don't count your chickens . . . etc. We never said it would be easy. There are *no quick fixes*, etc. Did I say *mission accomplished*? Who put that banner up there? One of my advisers has been a little too enthusiastic. Political *mission accomplished*.

Words on banner as President Bush, on board *USS Lincoln*, announced the end of 'combat operations' in Iraq, 1 May 2003.

'The battle of Iraq is one victory in a *war on terror* that began on September 11, 2001.'

George W. Bush

See *re-branding*

mission critical

Critical to the *mission*.

'Therefore, change in resource allocations will be more gradual than speedy, as ACIAR needs to keep faith with its *mission critical partnership* philosophy and hence with the priorities agreed in the rolling program of consultations with overseas partners.'

Alexander Downer, letter to Peter McGauran, undated
www.dest.gov.au

'Worked in partnership with the National Academy of Public Administration to begin developing *core competencies* for *mission critical* occupations.'

US Department of Labor

'. . . a provider of choice for *mission critical communications* and intelligence *solutions* for the Department of Defense . . .'

Titan Corporation

mission statement

Vision statement. Statement of principles, *core values* and *key goals*. Company creed. Usually seen in the reception area, but becoming less common.

'Every business needs a purpose that says what it is and a *vision* that describes what it wants to be. This purpose and vision come together in the *mission statement*.'

> e-Business Plan tutorial

'Our *Core* Beliefs and *Values*:
· Objectivity is the substance of intelligence, a deep *commitment* to the *customer* in its forms and timing . . .'

> CIA mission statement

'Therefore, policies, *strategic initiatives* and operational plans will be put in place to ensure that a *quality* service, relevant to this *vision* and *mission statement*, are maintained.'

> James Cook University, chaplaincy

'Where there is no *mission statement*, the people perish.'

See *bullet points*, *grandmother test*

misspeak / misspoke

1 To express oneself imperfectly.
2. To present the unknown as *known*; possibility as fact; speculative as certain; the desired as attained.
3. To lie; tell a whopper, a porkie; pull the wool, etc.
4. To not lie.

'He *misspoke*. That's all.'

> A spokesman for Paul Wolfowitz who, answering questions from a US House Appropriation Committee, understated the number of US soldiers killed in Iraq by one-third, April 2004

'Linda Chavez: I *misspoke*. I *absolutely*, I *misspoke*.

Al Franken: Okay, what does *misspoke* . . .?

Linda Chavez: I'm not going to do that. I'm just going to tell you I *misspoke*.

Al Franken: What does that mean though? . . .

Chavez: It's not a *lie*.'

> Linda Chavez, after calling John Kerry a 'communist apologist' three times in her syndicated column, Fox News, May 2004

mitigate

1. Lessen, alleviate, moderate, etc.
2. *Militate*, to have force or influence.

'Sector specialisation, regional diversification and an intense *focus* on *clients* differentiate Bovis Lend Lease from competitors, and helps *mitigate* against the *impact* of environmental and *market challenges*.'

> Annual report

MOAB

Massive Ordnance Air Blast. A 21,000-pound bomb.

mobilise

Walk.

Physiotherapist to elderly, immobile patient: 'Do you *mobilise*?'

'Yea, though I *mobilise* through the valley of death . . .'

'Rise, take up thy bed, and *mobilise*.'

moral clarity

Doctrinal equivalent to radical Islam: the US is the embodiment of good, its enemies the embodiment of *evil*. Enemy of all forms of *moral relativism*. Made popular by William J. Bennett, adopted in various degrees by President George W. Bush and the *neocons* advising him.

Moral clarity has nothing to do with (i) historical accuracy or, (ii) modesty, but it is useful – Churchill among others might say 'essential' – in war or imperial adventure.

> 'We defeated the twin menaces of fascism and Soviet communism. We advanced the wellbeing of people around the world, ameliorating suffering, improving human rights and promoting democracy. Such achievements wouldn't be possible without *moral clarity*.'
>
> William J. Bennett

moral relativists

Where believers in *moral clarity* insist that nothing is beyond the reach of moral reason and judgement, the *moral relativists* hold that 'man is the measure of all things' and moral judgements are contextual rather than absolute. For practical purposes this means that the US cannot embody pure good, a tenet that encourages those who believe in *moral clarity* to think that *moral relativists* are (i) unpatriotic; (ii) un-American and (iii) likely to think that Saddam Hussein and Osama bin Laden are no more the embodiment of *evil* than George Bush is.

See *cultural relativists*

most

1. A majority.
2. The ones one believes for the purposes of one's argument; not including those (from e.g. the State Department, Department of Energy, International Atomic Energy Commission, etc.) who doubt or dispute one's view.

> '*Most* US experts think they are intended to serve as rotors in centrifuges used to enrich uranium.'
>
> Colin Powell to UN, 6 February 2003

See *know, consensus, absolute certainty*

mouseholing

Urban combat technique of moving from house to house by blasting through interior walls.

move on

Also move *forward, going forwards* – whatever suggests progress or an absence of regression.

Popular form of escape from responsibility, *accountability* or discomfort – much favoured by cads, con-men, carpetbaggers, etc. Let's not dwell on the past; let's not wallow in the fens of history; let's not waste public money setting up inquiries; let's not waste time arguing the toss about who said what and whether they meant it. You and I might want to have this debate, Alan, but I don't think the Australian people want to have it, Alan. I think they want to *move on*. In fact I know they do.

'I think the public wants to *move on*.'

> John Howard, PM, moving on from the 'children
> overboard affair' in the 2004 election, ABC

'May the Lord be with us all as we *move* forwards.'

> Cardinal Pell Advent Letter 2004

'I'm through with you
too bad you're blue
I said *move on*
I said *move on*.'

See *forward-looking, going forwards*

multiculturalist

1. Advocate of cultural diversity and pluralism.
2. Reverse racist, member of minority group, cultural
or *moral relativist*, persecutor of the mainstream.

'. . . Aborigines, *multiculturalists* and a host of other minority
groups.'

> Pauline Hanson, 1996

'Then, compromising her own views on gender, she said,
"But I guess that's their *culture*." So she is a *multiculturalist*!'

> Web diary, July 2003

'The Republican Party of Bush, Hastert, Frist, Rove, et al.,
is a *multiculturalist*, diversity-mongering, pro-immigration
enemy of the interests of *ordinary Americans*.'

> View from the Right Web Forum, September 2003

See *reverse racism*

must-have

Something you don't have.

'This season's *must-have* accessory? Your music. Listen in style with iPod mini, from just $299.'

Apple.com.au

'So you can connect any number of compatible printers, scanners, DV camcorders and digital cameras, as well as such *must-have* peripherals as iPod, iPod mini, iPod shuffle and iSight.'

Apple.com.au

Nn

national offender managers

Name suggested by the Carter Report (UK) for Her Majesty's Prison Officers.

near earth objects

Asteroids, especially those that may collide with Earth and require *robust* detection.

> 'At present, only patchwork and under-funded research efforts are underway to *robustly* detect, track, catalogue and plot out *strategies* to thwart menacing asteroids and comets that place Earth at risk.'
>
> space.com

> '"The Moon could well be a base of operations that we could use as a means to defend this planet in a timely way, and a more effective way, against *near earth objects*," Rohrabacher explained.'
>
> Leonard David, space.com

needs

1. Whatever is required.
2. Whatever is desired.

> '*Marketing* is a human activity directed at satisfying *needs* and wants through the exchange *process*.'
>
> Philip Kotler, 1972

> 'What are the expressed information *needs* / wants of farmers as perceived by Intermediaries?'
>
> The Regional Institute Ltd, Key Evaluation Question

'Leave in for 1–5 minutes, according to your hair *needs*.'

Hair conditioner instructions

'He made it his mission in life to serve the poor and wanty.'

'From each according to his abilities, to each according to what he wants.'

negative health consequences

An illness *outcome* (US military); an illness *event*.

negative patient outcome

Bed sores, amputation, golden staph, etc. while a *client* of a hospital or nursing home. *The Times* (UK) once reported that the term was used to describe death. Also *negative care outcome*.

'. . . enabling the facility to demonstrate that based on available clinical evidence, a *negative care outcome* was unavoidable.'

US Department of Health and Human Services Appeal Board – Sanctuary at Whispering Meadows, June 2003

'In the midst of life we are in *negative patient outcomes*.'

'Till *negative patient outcomes* us do part.'

neglective

Neglectful. Not *supportive*.

networking

'The government has been *neglective* of the area.'

ABC radio caller, April 2004

'You have been *neglective* of my primary *needs*, Brian.'
'The only *need* I've been *neglective* of is my need to leave you, Noelene.' Etc.

networking

To exchange business cards, glances etc. Have a drink, take tea, dine with. Do what's necessary. (More if it's agreeable.)

'2.50pm. Coffee and *Networking*'.

Governance seminar brochure

'I *networked* my arse off.'

Participant in governance seminar

Neuro Linguistic Programming (NLP)

1. Variety of *knowledge management* derived from *Large Group Awareness Training* (*est*, *Landmark Forum*, etc.).
2. A 'methodology' taught by *consultants* (in 21 days) to other *consultants* who teach it to business.
3. Brainwashing, mind games, thought control, etc. Hogwash, etc.

'NLPers ask the question, "If another person can have fun playing with their pet spider, what can we learn about them that we could teach the phobic person so they can play with spiders, too?"'

www.nlpinfo.com

Alternatively: If one person is frightened of spiders, what can we learn about them that would teach others to be frightened of spiders too?

> '*Neuro Linguistic Programming (NLP)* studies the structure of how humans think and experience the world. Obviously, the structure of something so subjective does not lend itself to precise, statistical formulae but instead leads to models of how these things work. From these models, techniques for quickly and effectively changing thoughts, *behaviours* and beliefs that limit you have been deployed.'
>
> www.nlpinfo.com

> 'A methodology which allows you to track how people are thinking, what they *value*, and how they make their decisions, and how this helps or hinders their *processes*.'
>
> *The Consultant's Consultant*

> 'We can provide people with the ability to create the futures they want to *live*.'
>
> Chris Collingwood, *NLP* trainer assessor

See *human resources* (HR), *re-engineers*, *knowledge management*, etc.

neutral probabilities (very)

It may rain and it may not, very.

> 'When we are seeing these *very neutral probabilities*, we can't say one way or another whether it's going to be a wet season or a dry season.'
>
> Bureau of Meteorology, April 2004

nexus

1. Means of connection; link, tie.
2. A connection that would be sinister if it existed; a tenuous, possible or non-existent connection.

> '. . . the potentially much more sinister *nexus* between Iraq and al-Qaeda.'
>
> Colin Powell to UN, 5 October 2003

See *evil (axis of)*

nirvana

Ultimate solution.

> 'Well that's the *nirvana* of the ultimate solution, and if we could ever achieve that, or get along the way of achieving it, I think we would have done a great thing and a great legacy for those that are involved in it.'
>
> Bob Mansfield, ABC radio, May 2004

no blame culture

Culture of forgiveness, understanding and *moving on*. Anyone can make a mistake *culture*. Work out a *game plan* to avoid a similar *scenario going forward* culture. *Culture* in which blame has no place and people can be sacked without it.

> 'Our "*no blame*" *culture* underscored by a policy of "open disclosure" is a crucial facet of the Service ethos and staff

are encouraged to report errors and miscalculations immediately to *ensure* remedial and timely action is taken to
minimise future risks.'

CEO, West Wimmera Health Service

no child

1. Not one child, every single one, without exception.
2. Metaphorically speaking, as far as one can tell from
here, and who can say what's going to happen in the
future, you never know what's round the corner, etc.
A figure of speech.

'It is conservative to let local *communities* chart their own path
to *excellence*. It is compassionate to insist that every child
learns, so that *no child* is left behind.'

President George W. Bush, April 2002

'By 1990, *no child* will live in poverty.'

Bob Hawke, PM, 1987

'*No child* without a story book.'

Mark Latham, 2004

no doubt

1. Certain, positive, sure, *know* for a fact.
2. A *known known*.
3. They're going to invade anyway, so why have any
doubt about it. 'May as well be hung for a sheep,' etc.

'There is *no doubt* in our minds now that these vans were
designed for only one purpose, and that was to make
biological weapons.'

Colin Powell, 22 May 2003

'There is *no doubt* in our minds now that the monster we see here in Loch Ness is the Loch Ness Monster.'

See *absolute certainty*, *overwhelming*

node, nodes

Lump, bump. Join, intersection. *Strategic* point, especially where information is received and disseminated. Computer network, hotel, IT *community* or department, Singapore. (As in: 'Singapore is a major *node* for Russian businessmen to plug into Asia.')

'This 157-room hotel has a prime location in Eastgate, a fast developing business *node* just 10 minutes drive from Johannesburg International Airport.'

South African hotel guide

non-continuing

Dejobbed senior executives. Senior executives handsomely compensated for not continuing.

'*Non-continuing* senior executives.'

Annual report

'Bob's partner is Ailsa, Jeff's *non-continuing* wife.'

non-core

1. The truth, heart, essence, innermost part – not. A non-binding vow.
2. Non-*key*.

'The fleet business was *non-core* to our plant hire division and reflects *management's* intention to *exit* our *non-core* operations.'

CEO of Austrim Nylex

'*Core* promises and *non-core* promises'

John Howard

'You made a vow that you would always be true,
But somehow that vow was *non-core* to you.'

Non-ongoing position

Temporary.

'The current ongoing and *non-ongoing* positions at the Department of the Environment and Heritage are listed here.'

Brisbane job advertisement

'This is a *non-ongoing* position working three days per week until May 2006.'

Federal Court of Australia

non-powered tractor movement (unexpected)

To roll, forward or back and possibly over you or the dog; take off; bolt, run away.

'The Park Lock cable on your tractor may not be adjusted properly resulting in park not *engaging* after the transmission shift lever is moved to the "park" position. As a result, *unexpected non-powered tractor movement* may occur.'

John Deere Safety Notice

non-trivial

'A *non-powered* stone *movement* gathers no moss.'

See *product improvement program*

non-trivial

1. Very large.
2. Outrageously large, too much in the present circs. Piss off, and come back when you've got it down to trivial.

'In the circumstances 4 million is a *non-trivial* amount.'

Treasury official

'All creatures, *non-trivial* and small.'

notional functional hooks

Not real functional hooks; incomplete functional hooks; hooks in progress.

'Refine structural concept, develop *notional functional hooks* for *key processes* and *outputs*.'

Oo

ob products

1. *Products* for the use of obstetricians and gynaecologists. Also tampons.
2. New-born babies. Helen Edelman quit her job as communications consultant with a New York health care company when in a meeting she heard newborn babies referred to as *ob products* (*Houston Chronicle*, 6 June 2005).

> 'Don't throw the *ob product* out with the bathwater.'

Office of Special Plans

A neocon cell in the US Department of Defense that comes up with special *plans*, often despite the opposition, or without the knowledge of, other people in the Department. The invasion of Iraq was one such *special plan*.

> 'The OSP's task was, ostensibly, to help the Pentagon develop policy around the Iraq crisis . . . [but it] . . . was more akin to a nerve centre for what she now calls "a neoconservative coup, a hijacking of the Pentagon".'
>
> Interview Lt. Col. Karen Kwiatkowski,
> *LA Weekly*, February 2004

See *stovepiping*

off-line

To discuss an *issue* outside the meeting. As in: 'I think we should take that *issue off-line*, Jenny.'

offshored / offshorable

Sent *offshore*. Able to be sent *offshore*. Jobs done for lower wages and in much worse conditions abroad. Cheap labour; child labour; slave labour – whatever labour *grows* the company, is good for the *bottom line*, leads to *continuous improvement*, etc.

> 'A similar analysis of any company's corporate centre would show that about a quarter of those positions are *offshorable* as well. So the savings can be enormous even if some operations are kept onshore for redundancy.'
>
> American banker, 3 July 2003

See *decruitment*, *downsize*, etc.

on-balance judgement

A special kind of judgement using *balance*.

> 'This is an *on-balance judgement* . . . But it is an *on-balance judgement* . . . But it is an *on-balance decision*.'
>
> Alexander Downer, interview 2003

on-boarding

Training and orientation for new employees – in order to 'accelerate the time to performance from "hand-off"' (Human Capital Institute).

> '*On-boarding* accelerates a *hire's* progress by reducing the transition time between his or her starting date and full *productivity*.'
>
> Development Dimensions International

one-off basis

Once. Only once. Just once.

'Year of the Built Environment Grants are provided on a *one-off basis*. Projects must be time limited.'

Lotterywest, Western Australia's state lottery

'A lifetime opportunity on a *one-off basis*.'

'Bitten on a *one-off basis*, shy on a two-off basis.'

one version of the truth (across the organisation)

Getting the whole farmyard thinking the same way, dancing to the same tune, saluting the same *mission statement*. Everyone on the same page. Thought control; regimentation; fascism. 1984 has come late.

'Portraying *one version of the truth* by adopting a unified approach to your finance function.'

Conference brochure

See *Neuro Linguistic Programming*

ongoing

1. Going on. That which we're in the midst of. Time present. Time. Time continuing. Continuing *in terms of* the present moment. As in, 'You are asking me a question in the context of an *ongoing* investigation' (George W. Bush, 11 July 2005) – as opposed to a question in the context of something that has ended or

not yet begun. Continuing, and therefore beyond investigation, analysis, opinion or comment. Unresolved. *Sub judice*. It's not for me to say. These things are not for us to know.
2. A *time period* of indeterminate length. A lengthy *point in time*. Not an *appropriate* time. Proceeding through the immeasurable vastness of time. As long as a piece of string. A spin-doctor's special. As in, 'We're consulting with Congress now, *ongoing* consultations and that we are determined to do that [sic]' (Scott McLellan) . . . 'There are *ongoing* security *challenges* that we face and Prime Minister Allawi is determined to address those *ongoing* security threats' (Scott McLellan).

Q: Do you want to retract your statement that Rove, Karl Rove, was not *involved* in the Valerie Plame exposé?

A: I appreciate the question. This is an *ongoing* investigation at this point. The president directed the White House to cooperate fully with the investigation, and as part of co-operating fully with the investigation, that means we're not going to be commenting on it while it is *ongoing*.

Q: But Rove has apparently commented, through his lawyer, that he was definitely *involved*.

A: You're asking me to comment on an *ongoing* investigation.

Q: I'm saying, why did you stand there and say he was not *involved*?

A: Again, while there is an *ongoing* investigation, I'm not going to be commenting on it . . .

Scott McLellan, 11 July 2005

'. . . The difficulty for me in relation to these matters is I can't talk about *ongoing* activities in which our security agencies are *involved*. It compromises them. Traditionally we don't speak about them. But it would be naive to believe that matters that are reported on are not matters that the organ-isations that work in this area would not be aware of and wouldn't act on.'

Philip Ruddock, ABC, 8 June 2005

'All will be revealed in the fullness of the *ongoing*.'

'The *ongoing* is on my side.'

'. . . Creeps in this petty pace from day to day to the last syllable of the *ongoing*.'

on message

In election campaigns you must stay *on message*, or people will not know what you stand for. You stand for what the people stand for, or at least what your *focus* groups stand for, so don't start talking about Plato's *Dialogues* or reciting Emily Dickinson. Don't mention anything that you can't tie to the 'ladder of opportunity', or '*leadership*' or 'security', whatever is judged to be the *key message*. And jobs. Jobs, fairness, and opportunity. Mention these until they're sick, until you can see their knees buckling or your own are giving way. And when that happens mention them again. Recite them one by one. And don't forget to say 'Australian'. And 'we won't *cut and run*'. And 'all Aus-tralians'. And 'access and equity'. And mention '*mateship*', mate. And jobs. And *growth*. But keep it simple. And don't get personal. Of course he's a 'lying rodent'. We know that, but the mob don't like us saying it. And it only confuses them. It's noise. It's off *message*.

See *message*

on-selling

Selling – real estate, intellectual property, pork bellies, potatoes, underpants, hostages, etc.

> 'So criminal gangs according to security sources are taking people and then *on-selling* them to insurgents and terrorists.'
>
> ABC, July 2004

> *Death of an On-salesman* by Arthur Miller.

on strategy

On message in terms of strategy.

operational plans

Plans to deliver *plans*.

> 'A format for QSA business units to develop their *operational plans* to deliver the *strategic plan*.'
>
> QSA Strategic Plan Consultancy

operational release

A kind of release that *achieves* operational *outcomes*.

'The Royal Australian Navy has today accepted "*Operational Release*" of our six Collins class submarines, Defence Minister Robert Hill has announced. This important milestone acknowledged the submarine's ability to *achieve* defined *operational outcomes* laid down in the Defence Preparedness documentation.'

Department of Defence media release

Operation Decapitation (US military)

Chopping off heads from the air.

Operation Iraqi Freedom

A *coaling station* initiative.

opinion leader

Politician, cleric, columnist, talkback host, *lifestyle* program host, gym instructor, etc., Alan Jones, Jesus Christ, Jamie Oliver, Kylie Kwong, etc.

'A person who informally gives *product* information and advice to others.'

Marketing textbook

opinionnaire

An exciting new form of *stakeholder communication*.

'An *opinionnaire* was developed to gather data on students' attitudes toward the use of computer-based learning and their confidence in applying the cognitive objectives of Bloom's Taxonomy to their projects.'

Defying Gravity: A *paradigm* for developing teacher skills and attitudes in CBL courseware development, Australian Association for Research in Education

optimal position

Desired position requiring a plan to get there.

'So, if you don't have a *plan*, you can't end up in the *optimal position*, and we believe that with a *plan*, Australia can do a lot better in managing the water that it's got.'

Bob Mansfield, ABC Radio, May 2004

optimising

1. Maximising. Making the most of.
2. Augmenting and *enhancing outcomes* for companies and individuals.

'"Lifewise International Pty. Ltd. Optimising Personal Performance." Including "Practical tools for changing faulty self-perceptions, *achieving* life goals and improving general presence and image, *communication* and presentations."'

Lifewise International Pty. Ltd.

ordinary Australians (concerns of)

1. Australians whose opinions are a measure of relevance and worth, including moral worth. If ordinary people are not concerned by injustice, or famine, or fire-blight in New Zealand apples, the media should not be concerned, and people who are concerned are not

people who are *ordinary Australians* but likely members of an *elite*.
2. A rather patronising expression to describe not many Australians.

'I don't usually use the expression *"ordinary"* very often myself. I try and avoid using it, it sounds rather a patronising expression.'

John Howard, March 1999

'Prime Minister: And I think Australians, I don't like using the expression *ordinary* . . . I mean we are Australians.
Int: How many *ordinary Australians* do we know — not many.
Prime Minister: No, that's right. We're Australians.'

John Howard, radio interview, October 2000

'I mean, that is the sort of arrogant dismissal of the views of *ordinary Australians*, that many of them find disconcerting.'

John Howard, November 1999

'. . . to try and generate a momentum of hostility and concern about the *impact* of it on the lives of *ordinary Australians*.'

John Howard, June 2000

'. . . you suggest we are indifferent to the position of the *ordinary* worker.'

John Howard, debate 2001

'Coalition Government that has put more money, more disposal [sic] income, into the pockets of *ordinary Australian* workers.'

John Howard, June 2001

'No *ordinary Australian* family wants a situation of enormous medical bills for a major illness for one of its members.'

John Howard, December 2003

'I've always believed that good economic management is about giving *ordinary Australians* the freedom and opportunity to live their lives as they wish.'

John Howard, July 2004

'And, I mean, I said to him, in all honesty – I forget what his name was – I said: I don't have an immediate answer to that, but I said: I feel for you and I understand it. And he said: look, I am just an *ordinary Australian . . .*'

John Howard, Press Club Address, October 1998

See *real people*

organisational change

Just like *lifestyle* change.

'No one would make changes to their *lifestyle* or agree to surgery without running a series of tests [sic]. *Organisational change* is no different.'

www.growconnect.com.au/total

outcome

1. 'Natural result; consequence' (*American Heritage Dictionary*).
2. Result achieved after *targeting* and agreement. A consequence of *inputs* and *outputs*. Elements of a *scenario*. Companies, government departments, education curricula and schoolrooms are *outcomes-based*.

'Resource allocation decisions about which *outputs* to fund will be based on each *output's* contribution to government *outcomes*.'

Victorian Department of Treasury and Finance

'A *focus* on *outcome targets* without an emphasis on improved employment practices will not *deliver* support from men and will not result in *sustainable* changes in organisations to improve gender equity *outcomes*.'

www.eowa.gov.au

'A balanced agenda of *targeted outcomes*.'

Business speech

'. . . our little life is rounded with an *outcome*.'

out of the loop

To be a non-participant; a fringe-dweller or outsider; to be lacking essential information. (As in: 'I'm *out of the loop* on this one, will someone fill me in.') Countries are sometimes left *out of the loop*, on e.g. intelligence. It is possible to fall *out of the loop*, be kept *out of the loop* and to lack the means to get into the loop.

'It also says Colin Powell, the President's Secretary of State, was left *out of the loop* at one stage because he wasn't in Texas . . .'

ABC, 19 April 2004

out of touch

1. To not understand the desires or concerns of *ordinary Australians*; or some powerful constituency such as farmers or first home buyers. To understand but not care. To neither understand nor care.

2. To imagine that a principle or your own judgement should prevail over popular prejudice. Unpopular. Arrogant.

See *elite*, *chattering classes*, *café latte*, *ordinary Australians*, etc.

output

What comes out. All *inputs* have been *outputs* at some stage. A system of accounting.

> 'Government's desired or intended *impacts*/effects on the *community* resulting from a set of *outputs* and other factors including *community* action.'
>
> Victorian Department of Treasury and Finance

> 'This advice was provided to take account of the PNG section's uncertainty on how to *achieve* (i) the preparation of activity designs more *focused* on *outputs* and *outcomes*; (ii) more *flexible* approaches to project design and facility *management*; and (iii) the successful devolution of activity *management* to better *align* project *management* with contract *management*.'
>
> Company document

> 'In sorrow thou shalt bring forth *outputs*.'

See *input*

output management

Something for *output* managers to do.

> 'Process of linking funding *reporting and monitoring* of clearly defined *outputs* to government *strategic priorities* or *outcomes*.'
>
> Victorian Department of Treasury and Finance

outsource

(v) To sub-contract. To out-task. To *offshore*. To *downsize*.

To contract with other companies to provide goods and services and perform business *processes* formerly done in-house. To lower costs by doing this, especially by *outsourcing* to India and China where labour and skills are much cheaper. To keep your workforce *flexible* by this means. To *downsize* or *release capacity*. To multiply the number of *consultants* in the world. To strip jobs from the in-source and create them in the *outsource*. To *globalise*. To put us in touch with the people of Bangalore. An unstoppable trend, whatever you think of it.

'With the Government's emphases on improved efficiency, reduced staffing *levels* and *core* business activities in public sector agencies, training services are among those *non-core* activities which should be considered for *outsourcing*, either as an entire function or specific courses.'

Department of Transport, Victoria

See *offshore*, *Zippie*

oversight

1. (n) Unintentional omission.
2. (n) Supervision or care.
3. (v) To oversee, watch over, look over, supervise, run, keep an eye on, superintend, handle, guide, *monitor*.

'This includes *oversight* of activity *management* and close consultation with *key* officers within the MAFF.'

overwatch

'There's a somebody I'm longing to see,
I hope that he turns out to be,
Someone who'll *oversight* me.'

overwatch

To *oversight* in a military way.

'We have soldiers in *overwatch* on Iraqi citizens.'

US military

'I hope that she turns out to be,
Someone who'll *overwatch* me.'

overwhelming

1. Irresistible, overpowering, undeniable, tremendous.
2. Fragmentary, tenuous, just possible, unlikely, in the realm of *unknown unknowns*.

'There's *overwhelming* evidence that there was a connection between al-Qaeda and the Iraqi government.'

Vice President Cheney, 21 January 2004

See *absolute certainty, no doubt*

ownership (taking)

1. The state of owning – a house, a copyright, an idea, etc.
2. Military: 'You break it, you own it', where 'it' is a country.
3. Business: Making an idea one's own – or an *issue*, *problem*, solution, *process*, *plan*, *strategy*, *scenario*, principle, *values*, *mission*, *vision*, *input*, *outcome*, etc.

'You know you're gonna be *owning* this place.'

        Colin Powell to President George W. Bush, 2002

'Because of their involvement and *ownership* of the *issue* many *stakeholders* will have *knowledge*, *networks* and resources which can add significant *value* to your project.'

        NSW Environment Protection Authority

'Local *ownership* is more than "pressing of hands into concrete". It is about treating people with respect by openly sharing information and decision-making to allow under-standing whilst not apologising for the "constraints".'

        Vital Places, specialist consulting service

Pp

package

Suite of elements comprising an *initiative*, *plan*, *strategy*, policy, pork barrel, bribe, campaign, offer, etc. (E.g. 'Great Barrier Reef Marine Park Structural Adjustment *Package*'; 'Forest Industry Structural Adjustment *Package*', etc.) *Packages* are delivered. They contain *deliverables*. Broader than a code.

> 'This Code of Ethics is an integral part of the broader Ethics *Package*. The Ethics *Package* has now been revised to more closely reflect our changing work and our *values*. The complete Ethics *Package* is available on the EPA website. The Ethics *Package* will be a dynamic document and will be constantly amended as new *needs* and *issues* arise. All staff are encouraged to provide *input* into this process to *ensure* the Ethics *Package* remains a *relevant* and significant guide to assist our work.'
>
> EPA, New South Wales

> '. . . What we're doing today is expanding the reach of the *package* . . . to anyone who is *impacted* negatively by the *historic* rezoning of the reef.'
>
> Minister for the Environment, 27 August 2004

package (the complete)

1. A kind of footballer – as in: 'Michael Voss is the *complete package*'.
2. The real deal, the whole caboodle, the full kit. Also sometimes racehorses, greyhounds, entertainers.

3. Employment or disemployment deals. What comes with the job. What comes with the sack.

> 'This is the most complete swimming *package* I have ever seen.'
>
> Murray Rose on Ian Thorpe

packaging envelope

Off road envelope for a naturally aspirated unit.

> '. . . gives the engine impressive power output but keeps it within the *packaging envelope* of the naturally aspirated unit . . .'
>
> *Land Rover Owner International* magazine

painted into a corner

1. To trap oneself; leave oneself without any options, nowhere to run, hide; to have no means of escape, no *exit strategy*.
2. To be trapped by someone else in this way.

Painting others into corners without being so painted oneself is one of the arts of politics. The painting becomes intense before elections when politicians are asked to explain themselves and offer policies. At such times, politicians are also at greater risk of *painting themselves into corners*. The only remedy is to assert a principle and make a promise and worry about it after the election.

> 'The zero tax strategy has *painted* the Treasury *into a corner* before it has even been *implemented*.'
>
> Submission to Treasury, Isle of Man, 2004

paradigm (shift)

1. Model, exemplar or archetype. Movement from one model to another is a *paradigm shift.*
2. Change in the way you organise the office. What *consultants* claim to bring, and management after paying them, feels constrained to agree. The idea that a *paradigm shift* has occurred might serve as justification for new and constantly repeated terms – as a revolution is heralded by a new language.

Companies are attracted to the idea by the famous negative examples of IBM, which was so locked into an old *paradigm* of the computer business that it could not make the shift to the PC; and the Swiss, who invented quartz watches but, being caught in an older watch *paradigm*, left the Japanese to manufacture them.

> 'You've also got to measure in order to begin to affect *change* that's just more – when there's more than talk, there's just actual – a *paradigm shift.*'
>
> George W. Bush, July 2003

> 'Showing women wielding power – sexual and otherwise – over men has become a new advertising *paradigm*. It's a great way to get chicks to buy stuff.'
>
> Advertising agency creative director, *Sunday Age*, August 2004

partner / partnerships / partnering

Teams. Synergistic combinations. Teaming up. Joining forces. What you do <u>with</u> someone: As in, 'There are *ongoing* security *challenges* that we face and Prime Minister Allawi is determined to *address* those *ongoing* security threats. And we're there to *partner* with him in those efforts.' (Scott McLellan, 20 September 2004)

'Blackwater looks forward to *partnering* with you by offering its progressive design and execution approach to your specific requirements.'

Blackwater USA (military security contractors)

passion / passionate

1. (n) Infatuation, ardour; (adj) to be fevered, insatiable, crazy about, etc.
2. Common in management parlance, especially in *mission statements*, but with business you never know how long it will last.

'*Passionate* about food.'

Prêt à Manger

'. . . a *passion* to create a better society.'

Toyota mission statement

'The only thing that mattered . . . [the former Burger King CEO said], was very satisfied *customers* and that everyone involved in your company had to share that *passion*.'

'Bovis Lend Lease has a *passion* for facilitating educational excellence.'

Annual report

'Whatever I put my name to, I'm *passionate* about.'

Ian Thorpe

past (the)

1. Do not dwell on it, or in it. Don't live in it. *Achieve closure. Move on. Go forwards.* Be *forward looking. Embrace* the *challenge. Embrace* the future. *Embrace innovation. Embrace the vision. Implement the vision. Cascade the vision.* Etc.
2. Lest we forget.

> 'No, we are looking to the future, not *the past*. I have explained the context of those remarks and we've had a discussion, if you like, to clear the air, to clear the air about *the past* and *move forward* to the future. The important thing is that you can only win the *War Against Terror* for the future. Dwelling on *the past* is not going to add to the important responsibilities and *commitments* that we have to winning that *War Against Terror* and we need to *go forward*.'
>
> Mark Latham, December 2003

> 'I think it's fair to say Kim's made a contribution to the Labor Party but it's a contribution by-and-large that's in *the past*.'
>
> Mark Latham, *Courier-Mail*, October 2003

> 'Leverage *the past* for the present and the future. Separating what has happened from what is anticipated or planned helps people *translate* insights into concerted, well-informed *action going forwards* . . . This is of particular importance when *capturing best practices*. We ground our *action ideas going forward* in the *context* of specific *events* that are on participant's [sic] calendars already, rather than holding lessons vaguely in mind as "should dos."'
>
> Signet Consulting Group

Leverage the *past* for the present and future

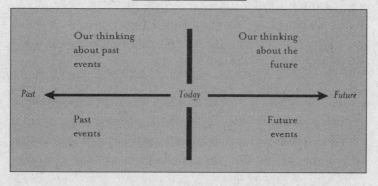

Signet Consulting Group

'*The past* is not dead. It is not even past.'

William Faulkner

pathways

1. Tracks, paths, usually leading somewhere.
2. Tracks you can strengthen. Tracks *going forwards* –
and sideways and underground. Tracks that make you
sleepy just following them on the page.

'The Youth *Pathways* Action Plan Taskforce will provide advice
to government on improving support for young people and
their families during young people's transition to independence and strengthening *pathways* for those young people
who do not, or are not likely to, go straight from school to
further education and training or full-time employment
and those who are not fully *engaged* with their *community*.'

Youth Pathways Action Plan Taskforce

penetration

1. To break into, pierce, force entry. To get through – a wall, a thick skull, etc. To gain insight.
2. To break into or pierce jobs; or break into or pierce with jobs . . .(?) Break into or pierce *clients*; pierce with telephone, etc.

'The trial looks at the *totality* of how we can bring together in the interests of reducing *frictional unemployment* the provision of the technology and the vacancy database and improve the *penetration* of a greater range of jobs from a much wider range of sources than in *the past*.'

Department of Employment and Workplace Relations

'You'll need proven ability to develop and cultivate new relationships, as well as increasing *penetration* within existing *clients*, combined with urgency, *passion* and a *commitment* to win.'

Hudson, job advertisement

'In areas with low telephone *penetration*, researchers have resorted to house-to-house in-person recruiting to overcome this problem. As telephone *penetration* increases, so does the randomness of telephone recruitment.'

Research company

'CareerOne: is Australia's leading online recruitment site, with unrivalled *penetration* of Australia through our association with News Limited.'

RMIT website

people (as a)

Popular construction of National Socialism. The national *zeitgeist*. People considered *holistically*.

> '*As a people* we have traditionally *engaged* the world optimistically. We are great travellers, whether for work, education or pleasure. Young Australians in particular go overseas in large numbers and we receive many visitors from other countries to our shores. Our open, friendly nature makes us welcome guests and warm hosts.'
>
> John Howard, *Let's Look Out for Australia*

> 'Nevertheless, the German *people*, who are by nature so ready to forgive and forget, felt no animosity toward that country.'
>
> Adolf Hitler, Berlin, May 1941

> 'We must recover for our people as one of its most elementary principles the recognition of the fact that a man is truly a man only if he defends and protects himself, that a *people* deserves that name only if in case of necessity it is prepared *as a people* to enter the lists.'
>
> Adolf Hitler, Munich, April 1923

> '. . . we, *as a people* and individually, always have reason to hope and trust in God, despite great adversity.'
>
> George W. Bush, November 2001

people-management

Not poultry management.

people (our)

'In the review *process* the team will aim to provide policies which fully utilise employees' *skills* and *knowledge*, and which present a range of mechanisms through which services can be delivered to increase the *people-management* effectiveness of UNE.'

University of New England

people (our)

Staff. A component of 'all our *stakeholders*'. *Human capital, human resources.* Internal *clients*.

'The priority we place on our *people* is what drives our *quality performance* and profitable growth, and in 2004 we made considerable investments in our *people initiatives*. Central to this was an *Accelerated Collaborative Event* (ACE) which enabled a broad cross-section of our *people* to have *input* into our *people* approach,. and has resulted in six project *teams* working to *embed* the *key initiatives* across our firm.'

Ernst & Young Message from the CEOs

performance arenas

The following: 'Our experiences working with senior managers on business *strategy*, *change management*, *leadership*, *culture change*, people interaction skills and *performance management* have led to the identification of *key competencies* that form an effective base for: assessing improvement areas, *targeting* action ideas and the preparation of development plans for the executive coaching *process*. These areas where *performance* improvement is built and maintained we call *Performance Arenas*.' (Executive Coaching Network)

performance-driven

Driven, and not by a concern for happiness, goodwill, loyalty, tradition, Christian or any other kind of fellowship, spontaneity, the pleasure principle, the principle of a fair day's work for a fair day's pay, an attachment to the ideas of Erasmus, J.S. Mill, George Orwell or John Curtin, etc., but by *performance*.

> 'From an *end-user* perspective, initially, there should be little change in the service. *Moving Forward* Facilities and Services will be developing a more user-*focussed* and *performance-driven* cleaning regime across the campus.'
>
> A message from the Deputy Vice-Chancellor,
> Monash University

performance management

An almost universal organisational method beyond the imagination of Soviet planners. *Performance* is measured by the difference between actual and desired results. Wherever the desired exceeds the actual there is a *performance problem* or *issue* which must be resolved by *performance* appraisal, *performance* improvement – by *performance management*. People, procedures, *teams*, programs, *communications* etc., are all measured. *Performance management* is justified by competitive *challenges*, especially global competition, which makes it imperative for every organisation to '*ensure strategies* are *implemented* effectively' to deliver *optimum outcomes*.

> '. . . the effective use of inter-related *strategies* and activities to improve the *performance* of individuals, *teams* and organisations . . . integrate and *align* organisational, business and

individual planning and *performance* . . . a means to recognise and reward good *performance* and to *manage* under*performance* of staff.'

Australian Public Service Commission

performance manage out

To sack. To fire. To cut. To dismiss. As in, 'Smith will be *performance managed out* of the enterprise.'

'HSBC's Chief Executive officer (CEO) Mr Michael Geoghegan has turned up the heat on *performance management* and is effectively exerting pressure on managers to "*manage out*" staff not *achieving* their sales *targets*. . . . It is clear that Mr Geoghegan subscribes to the philosophy that a successful organisation should "*manage out*" (sack) the bottom 10% of its staff each year in order to improve *performance*. This measure of *performance* is relative and therefore it does not matter how well your team is *performing*, managers should "*focus* on the bottom 10%".'

Amicus-Unifi HSBC

perhaps

1. Maybe. (As in: 'Thou shalt not kill, *perhaps*.')
2. Maybe not. (As in: '*Perhaps*, thou shalt not kill.')

'No one imagined that the task in Iraq would be easy. And *perhaps* the task is harder than we at first thought.'

John Howard, May 2004

'They *perhaps* for too long turned their backs on the situation in Bosnia and there's a strong sense in NATO that they

have to strike a lot earlier this time to stop the situation
getting out of hand, as it did in Bosnia some years ago.'

Alexander Downer, October 1998

'I did not have sex with that woman, *perhaps.*' '*Perhaps* I did
not have sex with that woman.' 'I did not have sex, *perhaps*,
with that woman.' 'I did not have *perhaps* sex . . . etc.'

'I did it my way, *perhaps.*'

'Thou shalt have no other Gods before me, perhaps' (1st
Commitment).

personal advice

The impersonal elided.

'This SOA is an important document. You are entitled to
receive a SOA whenever we provide you with any *personal
advice. Personal advice* is advice that takes into account any one
or more of your *objectives*, financial situation or *needs.*'

Car insurance renewal

personal business commitment (PBC)

Employee's undertaking to perform nominated tasks, on
time, within budget and with *focus* on *customer* satisfaction. E.g. 'To actively support the formulation and
achievement of the Database Management Service Line
objectives as part of the Global SSO initiative (if applicable). *Achievement* of all agreed objectives.' 'Support
the new SO *delivery* model by supporting new and
existing services within SSO to support new *product*
offerings across SSO Development of new offerings [sic].'

personality

Note: The nature of the *commitment* is determined by management.

personality

1. A cult. Katharine and Isabel Briggs say there are 16 types of personality. David Keirsey says there are four 'basic people patterns': Artisan (Ronald Reagan); Guardian (Nancy Reagan); Rationalist (Hillary Rodham Clinton); Idealist (Elizabeth Barrett Browning).

> 'By learning more about my own *Personality*, and about other *Personality* Types, I can come to a better understanding of my strengths and weaknesses. I can improve my interpersonal relationships, *realign* my expectations towards others, and gain a better self-knowledge that will help me define and *achieve goals.*'
>
> Web.page

> 'Which of the ten primary *personality* disorders do you suffer from?'
>
> quizzilla.com

> 'The #online *personality* assessment; Ph.D designed for career and personal development.'
>
> Internet advertisement

2. A marketing *challenge*.

> 'Each *consumer* has a unique *personality*.'
>
> Marketing textbook

personal life

The side of life which is not business but for *optimal outcomes* should be *aligned* with it.

> 'Inspiritive (Teaching lasting life skills) will help you to discover how *NLP* can *enhance* your personal and your professional *life*, and the relationships with the people you have in both.'

> '. . . this is our way of supporting a deeper *integration* of *NLP* into participants' lives.'
>> Neuro Linguistic Programming advertisement

personnel

People, staff, employees, soldiers, etc.

See *human resources* (*HR*), *friendly fire*, *collateral damage*. (Anti-personnel – usually refers to a bomb.)

phase

1. Stage of development.
2. Grade (Phase A = lowest grade. Phase E = highest grade).

> 'Children who do not show evidence of the sub-set of *key indicators* through the tasks are identified for consideration of further support in that *focus* area, along with children operating in *Phase* A of the *focus* area.'
>> Queensland Studies Authority, Diagnostic Net

'Heather will be all right. She's just going through a difficult *Phase A* of the *focus* area.'

plan

No person or organisation should be without one. Personal *goals*, objectives, etc. Without a *plan* there can be no *implementation*. Without *implementation* there can be no *outcomes*. Without *outcomes* there would be no *going forwards*. What would we do then?

'*Key indicators*: 1. Discharge Process Improvement. The development and *implementation* by health services of Discharge Improvement *Plans* is designed to improve current discharge *processes* and practices.'

Victorian Department of Human Services

The *Plan* to improve discharge is designed to improve discharge.

See *strategy*

planned learning

1. A conscious *process* to do with learning.
2. A *process* that renders one unconscious.

'*Planned learning* is a conscious *process*. It contrasts to the other two styles, occurring at any time an individual enters a situation with the clear *outcome* to learn and be *proactive* in that *learning*. A rather obvious observation, yet all too often, reality is that people miss out on significant *learning* opportunities when they enter experiences with no *plan* to learn, since they often leave the experience without reflecting on what has been gained.'

Melbourne University Leadership & Professional
Development Program

See *accidental learning* and *spontaneous learning*

plausible deniability

1. The ability to lie or disclaim responsibility convincingly.
2. The inability to lie or disclaim responsibility convincingly.
3. 'I did not have sexual relations with that woman.' 'I am not a crook.' 'I'm not aware / have no knowledge / know nothing of that.' 'We are determined to find the person or persons responsible for this enormity and you may be assured that the full force of the law will be applied.' Etc.

A political doctrine developed in the 1950s and applied to CIA operations. Deliberately loose chains of command enable the President and others in high office to deny giving any instructions that have gone wrong.

The doctrine failed in the case of Watergate because the President was not plausible. It also fails when those given the instructions take the combination of the President's blessing and his apparent unwillingness to know anything about the consequences as a licence to do what they like.

'The testimony that we did obtain from former CIA officials was often less than candid. A central axiom of

291

clandestine activities, such as the MKULTRA Program, is that CIA must maintain *"plausible deniablity."'*

www.turnerhome.com

'I am not denying anything I didn't say.'

Brian Mulroney, Canadian PM

plenty tough

Heaps tough. Masses, stacks, buckets tough. Capable of anything. Possessing very superior weaponry, technology. Overwhelming.

'I just know this — that we're *plenty tough.*'

President George W. Bush, April 2004

'Oh no, oh no not me,
I'm *plenty tough.*'

See *catastrophic success*

pockets of resistance

Groups, often small, of insurgents, fanatics or *dead enders*. In 1942, Hitler acknowledged that the German army was encountering 'small *pockets of resistance*' in Stalingrad. The US army ran into small *pockets* in Vietnam and again in Iraq. It is believed that they can be removed by 'mopping up activities'.

'Small *pockets of resistance* remain, said the spokesman, who acknowledged reports of looting in Basra.'

CNN, April 2003

'Some 7,000 enemy, well-equipped, crack NVA regulars blasted their way into the imperial city of Hue, overpowering all but a few *pockets of resistance* held by ARVN troops and the US Marines.'

History Ist Battalion, 5 Cavalry Regiment

point of contact

Someone to talk to; with whom to *touch base*, *dialogue*, *network*, exchange notes, etc. As in: 'Cleo, you're the *point of contact*, right?'

political correctness, politically correct (PC)

1. Of, relating to, or supporting broad social, political, and educational *change*, especially to redress injustices in matters such as race, class, gender, and sexual orientation.
2. 'Being or perceived as being overconcerned with such *change*, often to the exclusion of other matters' (*American Heritage Dictionary*).
3. Not believing in *moral clarity*, faith-based *initiatives*, the active presence of a partisan God, absolute good and *evil*, and the doctrine of *common sense*.
4. Thought police, intellectual *elites*, *chattering classes*, *café latte* set, femi-nazis, academic snobs, ideologues, 'fat cats, bureaucrats and . . . do-gooders' (Pauline Hanson), etc. Holding to some or all of their beliefs.

'. . . people can talk about certain things without living in fear of being branded as a bigot or a racist.'

John Howard, 1996

political internal exiles

'The 2UE radio announcer Alan Jones declared the 1996 Federal election outcome as "a defeat for *political correctness*", lamenting that Australia had been a place "where the voice of the people [was] never heard".'

Lisa Hill, *Policy*, CIS, 1998

See *common sense*

political internal exiles

'We have no political prisoners. We have *political internal exiles*.'

Pinochet, 1976

portal

Window, door, gate, etc. Means of entrance; '*portal of knowledge*', hence common in *knowledge management* and computer science.

'Human-oriented workflow is the next frontier for *portal* frameworks. The year 2004 will be "the *year of* the *process portal*" for *portal* frameworks, whereas 2001 was the year of the content *portal*, 2002 application access, and 2003 collaboration — with each year adding to the *capabilities* of those before it. This pattern of feature creep will end with composite applications in 2007, after which *portal* and composite application frameworks will merge and become indistinguishable.'

International Association for Human Resource Information Management

cf. 'Twas brillig, and the slithy toves,
Did gyre and gimble in the wabe,
All mimsy were the borogoves,
And the mome raths outgrabe'.

PowerPoint

Microsoft's presentation software; hundreds of millions sold and mainly used to present slide nights with intellectual pretensions, sales pitches dressed up as analysis and argument. Also used in schools as a substitute for writing essays.

Colin Powell used *PowerPoint* to present the case for invading Iraq at the United Nations.

> '*PowerPoint* allows speakers to pretend that they are giving a real talk and audiences to pretend that they are listening. This prankish conspiracy against substance and thought should always provoke the question, Why are we having this meeting?'
>
> Edward R. Tufte, *The Cognitive Style of PowerPoint*, 2003

> 'As we see in the organisational overview slide, four score and seven years ago brought forth on this continent a new nation . . . Next slide please . . . and that government of the people, by the people, for the people, next slide please, shall not perish from the earth.'
>
> Peter Norvig (after Abraham Lincoln)
> www.norvig.com

See *bullet points*

prejudice

A cliché.

prioritise

1. To make something a priority – e.g. goals, *challenges*, agreed *outcomes*, *implementation* of *strategies*, *alignment* of *strategy* and *outcomes*, buying paper clips, having a haircut.
2. To concentrate on, *focus*, make *front of mind*, give one's all to, do first, do in the morning or by the end of the month, do.

> 'So, how does one *prioritise*? First, write down all the *goals* you can think of, everything you want to have and *achieve*. Next, put them into categories based on how important they are to you. Decide what is the most important, and what is the most urgent. Try to realistically evaluate which and how many *goals* you can actively pursue at once.'
>
> Single-step.com

> 'If it were done when 'tis done, then 'twere well
> It were *prioritised*.'

privatise

To sell, unload, flog, cash in, hock, realise; award, apportion, transfer, vouchsafe, hand over, give up, surrender; abandon, cede, forsake, relinquish, pass up. Rationalise, modernise, capitalise. People's capitalism, popular capitalism, capitalism.

A window of profit opportunity.

proactive

Like 'active', but in a way that enables you to create your own 'perspective expanding experiences', etc. A relation of *pushing the envelope*.

> 'But if you're *proactive*, you don't have to wait for circumstances or other people to create perspective expanding experiences. You can consciously create your own.'
>> Steven R. Covey, *The 7 Habits of Highly Effective People*

> 'Their onballers have to get *proactive*.'
>> Football commentator

> 'It would enhance our *lifestyle going forwards*, Muriel, if you would more *proactively oversight* my porridge.'

problem

What one is if one is not part of the solution. 'I don't have a *problem* with that' means I agree, or I don't understand but it looks harmless, or I disagree but I'm not going to make an *issue* of it.

> 'Denis has had some major *issues* with neck *problems*.'
>> Fox Footy Channel, April 2004

> 'To be, or not to be: that is the *problem*.'

problem solve

(v) To solve *problem*(s).

'To this end, the AMU-TAF will assist the 3-AMCs to plan and *problem solve* taking full account of MAFF requirements and not simply the imperatives provided by milestones locked into contracts and annual plans.'

Company document

'To be, or not to be: if only I could *problem solve* . . .'

probletunity

A *problem* and an opportunity in one?

'Use "*Quality Tools*" to establish the procedures following the "*Probletunity* Story Board".' 'A *Problem* Statement is a *tool* used to document a *Probletunity.*'

New South Wales Education Department
document, after Langford International
Tool Time Education Handbook (See also
Tool Time Business Handbook)

'There is a *probletunity* in the affairs of men which taken at the flood . . .' etc.

See *portal*

process

Processes are subject to *continuous improvement*. As in: 'An outline of *quality* systems and *plans* which are *utilised*, including *continuous improvement processes*' (Victorian Department of Health Services). But this does not mean you will get a bed in the hospital.

product

'The *indicators* incorporate the *key processes* of care for an effective discharge and aim to complement existing *quality* activities whilst maintaining relevancy for the majority of patients and healthcare organisations.'

Victorian Department of Human Services

'In the beginning God created a *process*.'

processing centre

A camp in Papua New Guinea or Nauru in which refugees (see *queue jumper*, *illegal immigrant*, etc.) have their fates *processed*.

product

Arising from production, manufacturing, *innovation*, etc. *Output. Input. Outcome*. Goods, chattels, ideas, inventions, intelligence, concoctions, information, misinformation, art, novels, poetry, plays, football, pornography, apples, mental health services, correctional services, all services. Anything.

'"Jeffrey" has been working very well recently on the small group collaborative project which required students to develop their own *key* questions, research information and develop a variety of *products* to present their information.'

Year 7 History report

'. . . our processing infrastructure and development of innovative transactional banking *product*.'

Australian bank

'. . . and there was light. And God saw the light, that it was good *product*.'

product improvement program

'Raindrops on roses and whiskers on kittens,
Bright copper kettles and warm woollen mittens,
Brown paper packages tied up with string,
These are a few of my favourite *products*.'

product improvement program

Program to fix design fault.

'This repair to your tractor will be performed at no cost
to you for parts or labour expense . . . we hope this
Product Improvement Program will not cause any undue incon-
venience.'

John Deere, Safety Notice

'There are no quick *product improvement programs*.'

See *non-powered tractor movement* (*unexpected*)

product offering

Diverse is best.

Baked Beans in ham sauce. Baked Beans in cheese sauce.
Baked Beans in tomato sauce. Baked Beans in a three
pack. In a three pack with a lucky – 'Win a Weekend on
a Tropical Island' – coupon. Etc.

'There are more *product offerings* in heaven and earth,
Horatio, than are dreamt of in your philosophy.'

professionalisation

1. To make more business-like, including ordinary
existence.

2. To make your language more business-like, or like this.

> '7. Identify common "unhealthy" and "normal" group
> dynamics and the *impact* they have. 8. Transfer learning
> from the program to your lives.'
>> Melbourne University, Professional Development
>> & Leadership Program

> 'The *professionalisation* of ordinary existence: this is the enemy
> within.'
>> Martin Amis, *The War Against Cliché*, 2002

progress, progressed, progressing

(n) Growth, improvement, movement towards an objective, etc.
(v) To go *forward*, proceed, improve, kick it along, make
it work, get it off the ground, up and running, etc.,
implement. (As in: Who is going to *progress* the *implementation* of the change platform *going forwards*?) To
do – anything.

> 'The year has also been an important milestone as the
> Board vigorously *progressed* a wide-ranging review of CEDA's
> Charter . . .'
>> CEDA Annual report, 2001-02

> 'This process is *progressing*, and I look forward to reporting a
> favourable *outcome* in due course.'
>> Annual report

> 'QSA should *progress* the *assessment regime*.'
>> Queensland Studies Authority

'If it were *progressed* when 'tis *progressed*, then 'twere well It were *progressed* quickly . . .'

'I will rise and *progress* now, and *progress* to Innisfree . . .'

See *move on*, *going forwards* etc.

project facilitation

Key tool.

'*Project Facilitation* is the *key tool* to *leverage excellence* from the mediocre.'

Vital Places Consultancy

promise

1. Vow: to do something or not to do something, in all circumstances – in sickness and in health, etc. Unequivocal, binding and unbreakable. Absolute. To give one's word.
2. Vow: to do something, not to do something, depending on the circumstances, including the circumstance of what one was thinking when one made the vow. Equivocal, non-binding, breakable. As chaff before the wind, etc.
3. Lie.

'John Howard: I say to *the people of Australia*, there will be no GST, that it's not on our *agenda* and I mean it . . .
Reporter: Cross your heart type of stuff?
John Howard: Look, it's *absolute* . . . you can ask me again in two years time and you will find I've kept my word on that.'

Radio 2NC, 11 December 1995

prospect

(v) To go looking for *customers* – within their assigned vertical *markets*.

> 'We are seeking an experienced BDM to identify and *prospect* for new *customers* within their assigned vertical *markets*.'
>
> Advertisement for Business Development Manager

proud, independent people

Not cringing, yeller-belly milksops like as live in some countries.

> 'As *proud, independent people*, Iraqis do not support an indefinite occupation.'
>
> President George W. Bush

push the envelope

1. An aeronautical expression.
2. Go to the limits of *performance* or ability; take a risk (*risk-take*); stretch the boundaries; not habitual or until now assumed to be *core*.

> '*Pushing the Envelope*: Achieving High *Performance* in a Competitive Postal Environment'
>
> Accenture

> 'And God saw the light, that it was good: and God *pushed the envelope* . . .'

put in place

To *implement*, position, do, *bed down*.

> 'Many organisations experience backlash from men when *initiatives* are *put in place* for women. Commonly, this backlash results from a lack of understanding and a lack of *inclusion* of men, especially younger men. What is *critical* here is to position *initiatives* so that it is clear that they result in improved policies and practices that address the *issues* of all employees.'
>
> Equal Opportunity for Women in
> the *Workplace* Agency (EOWA)

> 'And God *put in place* great whales, and every living creature that moveth . . .'

Qq

quality

1. Feature or characteristic. (The *quality* of mercy, etc. Now rare.)
2. Value, excellence, high grade, superior, top, top-shelf, tops. (A *quality* real estate opportunity in the heart of Launceston.) See for example *quality tool belt*, *quality learning* experience, *quality* time, *quality* accommodation, *quality marketing*, *quality* health care, *quality* intelligence, *quality* information, *quality* team, *quality* player, *quality* management, *Total Quality Management*.

> 'To improve management infrastructure, *products* and services at all levels of sport to *ensure quality* participation opportunities and *sustainability*.'
>
> Active Australia

> 'And God saw the light, that it was *quality*.'

quality learning

Valuable, superior, worthwhile, excellent, good, substantial learning. Not worthless, inferior, bad, insubstantial, daggy, useless learning, or a waste of time *in terms of* learning.

> 'Langford *Quality Learning* 4-Day Seminars *focus* on the Deming philosophy of Profound Knowledge as it is applied to learning organisations. All organisations are learning organisations.'
>
> www.langfordlearning.com

> 'Much *quality learning* doth make thee mad.'

quality tool belt

1. A good tool belt?
2. A tool belt for qualities?

A *quality belt for tools* used in the '*continuous improvement* of *learning environments*' (i.e. classrooms?). It is conceivable that the belt might also serve for *notional functional hooks*.

> A *PowerPoint* Presentation.
> A *Quality Tool Belt: using Storyboards and Other Quality Tools*, Copyright Brenda Barnes and Jim Van Wormer.

queue jumper, queue jumpers

1. A refugee who jumps an orderly line of 14 million other refugees and arrives in Australia in an unauthorised fashion. An impatient, wilful, desperate foreigner; 'not the sort of person we want here', etc.
2. Persons fleeing persecution and catastrophe in Iraq, Iran, Afghanistan and other happy lands, and unwilling to wait their turn, etc.
3. Persons so foreign to *the Australian lifestyle* that they would risk their own lives and those of their children for freedom, democracy, etc.
4. Persons who would pay money to 'people smugglers' to save their families.
5. Persons who, in 'the familiar terms of doing good and fighting *evil*' (Philip Ruddock, July 2001), need to be fought.

> 'Thou shalt not covet thy neighbour's wife, nor his manservant, nor his maidservant, nor his ox, nor his ass, nor his place in the *queue*.'

'Ask, and it shall be given you; seek, and ye shall find; knock, and it shall be opened to you — not, dickhead.'

quick fix, quick fixes (no)

1. Type of speedy solution of which it is alleged that there are no successful examples. 'There are no *quick fixes*.' c.f. 'If it were done when 'tis done, 'twere well it were done *quickly*.'
2. Foolish remedy proposed by one's opponents or inherent in their question.
3. These things take time; we are bringing the best minds to bear upon it; let's *dialogue* on this; let's *strategise, stick to the game plan*, etc., there is no solution, at least not one we can sell. The *problem* is beyond us.
4. Our collective mind has gone completely blank.

'Those in our society who are uneasy about *change* — and, in particular, the economic *impact* of increasing *globalisation* — have turned to "*quick-fix*" solutions that involve raising barriers to trade, investment and migration. These are apparently simple solutions to the complexities of modern life. But, like most such solutions, they are unworkable.'

Alexander Downer, August 1998

See *product improvement programs*

quite frankly

1. To be honest with you; to spare you nothing in the way of truth, however unpleasant; what follows is my opinion unadorned and unambiguous.

2. I need you to believe this. Put this bit at the top of
the news. Here comes the grab.
3. 'Basically' substitute.

'She has got no respect from the veteran community and,
quite frankly, flip-flop floozies should go.'

> Graham Edwards, Labor backbencher, ABC,
>
> February 2004

'. . . what I'm saying to you, *quite frankly*, is I think the part
that has been played by the militias, for example, is a little
greater than what I recall anyway being anticipated.'

> Robert Hill, Defence Minister, March 2003

'It was then that it was arranged that, if it was operationally
possible, the photographs would be released. So I mean, I
didn't ignore that. Then, *quite frankly*, I got on to other *issues*
because we were in the middle of an election campaign.'

> John Howard, ABC, February 2002

'And unto Adam he said, *Quite frankly*, because thou hast
hearkened unto the voice of thy wife, and hast eaten of the
tree, of which I commanded thee, saying, Thou shalt not eat
of it: cursed is the ground for thy sake; in sorrow shalt thou
eat of it, *quite frankly*, all the days of thy life.'

Rr

ramp-up

(n,v) To elevate, give *priority*, increase, augment, expand, accelerate, make *key*, *very key*, etc.

'According to the GOP aide, the President said the White House will "seriously *ramp-up* the public relations effort" to counter Democratic criticism of the administration's Iraq policy.'

CNN, September 2003

'Revenue *growth* for the quarter was largely the result of continued *ramp-up* of existing large contracts with the military and intelligence *communities*, including the linguists' contract with the Army Intelligence and Security Command, the Enterprise Architecture and Decision Support contract with the National Security Agency, the Enterprise Information Technology contract with the US Special Operations Command, and the Affordable Weapon and X-Craft development contracts with the Office of Naval Research.'

Titan Corporation

'Police *ramp-up* search for missing teen.'

The Arizona Republic, July 2004

'The group resolved to *ramp-up* their efforts toward this channel as initially intended.'

Westpac

rapid response

Driven *implementation*.

rationalise

'I have asked the Secretary to position the department to be able to *rapidly respond* to whatever *changes* are required as a consequence of the Palmer report. I have also asked him to identify people suitable to be directly *involved* in driving and playing a lead role in the *implementation* of identified or necessary *changes*.'

Amanda Vanstone, 25 May 2005

rationalise

To simplify. To streamline, modernise, make more efficient, productive or 'competitive', economical, profitable, cheaper, easier to run. Cut costs, cut operations, cut branches, cut people: sack, *downsize*, *rightsize*, etc. Obey the *bottom line*. Achieve *best practice*, etc.

'To further *enhance* the efficiency gains, the Company will also consolidate more winemaking at these two wineries and *rationalise* the Australian distribution system.'

Southcorp media release, 2004

See *redundancy*, *rightsizing*, *involuntary career event*

rationalised footprint

A simplified *footprint*.

'Further productivity gains will be delivered from this *rationalised footprint*.'

Southcorp media release, 2004

It is possible that a *footprint* is a *key feature* of a '*blueprint*' because the *footprint* referred to in this document appears as a *bullet point* in 'The *key* features of the new *blueprint* for Southcorp's operations . . .'

real people

1. Inhabitants of the *real world*. *Battlers*, *aspirationals*, etc. Not *chattering classes* or *elites*, *café latte set*. Not liberals, intellectuals, artists, *bleeding hearts*, etc.
2. People of the above type known intimately to conservative newspaper *columnists*, and talkshow radio hosts who are on the same wavelength as them, on *the same page*, *at peace*, *at one*, etc.

See *ordinary Australians*

real time

Time without delays.

> 'A global economy is one whose *strategic core activities*, including *innovation*, finance and corporate management, function on a planetary scale on *real time*.'
>
> Martin Carnoy

real-time interactive scenario

A staged *event* involving people happening as it happens (with or without distributed simulations). As in: 'Mr and Mrs Rumsfeld request the pleasure of your company at a *real-time interactive scenario* this Saturday at 12.00 sharp.'

> 'Our *state-of-the-art* wargaming and modeling facilities give senior defence and business executives the ability to test advanced concepts, conduct integrated training, and *engage* in *real-time interactive scenarios*, including distributed simulations.'
>
> Booze Allan Hamilton consultants

See *learning tool*

real world

World lived in by *real people*. Where *the ducks are*. Not the world of the *chattering classes*. World lived in by people who know there are *no quick fixes*. *Common sense* world.

reality check

See if it works. What we call it if it doesn't.

> '*Reality check* on our service objectives.'
>
> International CEO Forum

re-brand

To deceive, dissemble, bullshit, bear false witness. To give something a new name when the existing one is passé, uncool and not selling to *consumers*. What you do when you don't have *buy-in*. What *marketing* and advertising agents do with product – e.g. motor vehicles, pre-mixed drinks and politicians – to lend them an attractive, if superficial or illusory character. The same is sometimes done with military campaigns e.g., 'Vietnamisation'.

Measures taken to defeat terrorists after September 11, 2001 were branded by the US administration as the '*War on Terror*'. President Bush was still using the term in June 2005 when with great passion he addressed US troops at Fort Bragg. But in July 2005 the administration said the operations would be *re-branded* as the 'struggle against violent extremism' (SAVE), and other 'more nuanced' language would be used.

A US official said, 'as the struggle evolves some of the language evolves'; but *re-branding* indicates *consumer* resistance rather than a change in the thing branded. It is therefore likely that the *War on Terror* was *re-branded* because of a deepening public perception that such a war could not be won.

recognise

1. To acknowledge.
2. To ask *you* to acknowledge.

> 'We believe that the current industry *milk price level* is in advance of historical payment levels for the same external price factors in earlier years but *recognise* that the industry is at present constraining investment in processing capacity and *growth* in order to maximise supplier returns.'
>
> Burra Foods letter to suppliers

recollect / recollection

1. To remember.
2. (I remember), but I don't have any *recollection* of it – not personally, not in the context of which the honourable member appears to be speaking. No. I move that all further questions be placed on the notice paper.

> 'Speaking for myself, I didn't personally have any discussions, from *recollection*, with any of them.'
>
> John Howard

recompetes

Renewal of a contract.

> 'Advantage Consulting, Inc. is prepared to provide you with *pro-active* Capture and Proposal services for your upcoming "must win" *recompetes*.'
>
> Advantage Consulting

recontextualise

'The record revenues and continued operation margin
improvements this quarter demonstrate our ability to
execute our *strategy* of generating new business, winning
recompetes, and *implementing* operational *efficiencies*.'

Titan Corporation

recontextualise

1. To think, write or speak of something or someone in
a different *context*.
2. To change the *context* or imagine a different one.
3. To use one's imagination, esp. for some analytic or
creative purpose.
4. To re-envision, reinvent, invent, make up, fantasise,
spin, deceive, delude, etc. As in, 'Stop the Destructive
Cycle: *Recontextualise* Your *Disempowering*
Roadblocks' (Robertson Lowstuter Career Development
Consultants).

'This involved the creation of usable learning objects out of
Toolboxes that assist teachers and trainers to *recontextualise* and
customise *Toolbox* content for their students and trainees
needs and learning styles.'

Australian Flexible Learning Framework

'Thus far philosophers have only contextualised the world;
the point is to *recontextualise* it.'

redeployment

To be *managed* into retrenchment. Rendered *vanilla*. To
become ripe for re-invention as an ideas *consultant*.

'*Redeployment* is the primary workforce *management strategy* to resolve situations where *ongoing* staff are unplaced due to *changes* to the organisational structure . . . The *processes* describe the arrangements for the management and resolution of excess staff situations in schools.'

Education Department Victoria

redundancy

The condition of being sacked, *downsized*, *decruited*, etc. Unemployed, lacking paid employment, unwanted, etc. *Efficiency-gain output*. An *involuntary career event*. *Implementation cost*. An *unlocked cost saving*. An excess *resource*.

'Write downs of the carrying values of fixed and other assets of $73 million and provisions for *redundancy* and other *implementation costs* . . .'

Southcorp media release, 2004

See *downsize*, *rightsize*, *redeployment*, *involuntary career event*

re-engineering

1. Restructuring, redeploying, renovating, rebuilding, changing.
2. *Decruiting*, *dejobbing*, destroying, obliterating. Achieving a solid *uptick*.

'*Business Process Reengineering* (BPR) was developed by former MIT professor Michael Hammer, whose original *Harvard Business Review* article gave examples of the application of his technique. The article, "*Re-engineering* work: don't automate:

obliterate" gave the example of Ford, which reduced its accounts payable staff by 75% as a result of *re-engineering*.'

Phil Cohen

'Ballard says the Australian operations are now poised for a solid *uptick*, with a strong management *team* now in place . . . As part of the fix-it plan, Ballard is overseeing heavy cost-cutting and process *re-engineering* in a push called Project Veraison, named after the ripening *process* of grapes.'

Australian Financial Review, October 2003

referent

See below.

'The deliberations of the symposium will be one *referent* to the development for the QSF.'

Queensland Studies Authority

reform

1. To form again.
2. To improve by altering. (As in: 1832 Reform Bill.)
3. (v) To alter. (n) Alteration. Any *change*, especially to legislation or an organisation. *Update*.

Reform is a *process* – *reform process*. *Reform*s often come in *packages* and are *wide-ranging* or *across the board*. They are *long overdue*.

'The program of *reform* known as the Corporate Law Economic *Reform* Program was initiated in 1997 to review and *reform* Australia's corporate and business legislation . . .'

Mrs Hull, Riverina, House of Representatives 2003

> '*Key initiatives* are that Australia will host a Ministerial meeting at the time of the UN General Assembly to "stimulate political momentum for *reform*" and Australia will also host a series of workshops to look at the practicalities of *reform*.'
>
> Philip Ruddock, media release, 2001

regime

1. System of management. Government. Regimen. Ruling group (hence *regime change*).
2. Watering (supervised).

> '"Pyongyang considers its nuclear weapons program critical to *regime* survival," Defense Intelligence Agency Director Lowell Jacoby said in congressional testimony in February.'
>
> David Ruppe, Global Security Newswire

> 'Maintain watering *regimes* under instruction.'
>
> Job description, groundsperson, *key* duties

relationship

1. Connection or association. Relations.
2. Commercial connection or association: between one organisation and another; an organisation and its *customers / clients*, including internal *clients*: an organisation and the *community*. Etc. *Relationships* are *valued*, even 'enjoyed'. *Customer-focused relationships* are common. *Relationships* are *grown* and *managed*. Some consultants are *relationship mana*gers. *High value* or *key relationships* are those which return the most commercial benefit to the *relationship-focused* organisation.

relationship builder

'At Western QBE, not only do we value the *relationship* we enjoy with each of our customers, but we also understand the importance of extending that *relationship* into our community, a *relationship* that we take very seriously!'

Western QBE letter

'Assist the Business Development Manager with the ongoing development and management of the Association *Relationship* Management Planning *regime.*'

Advertisement for Relationship Development Manager

relationship builder

How does one know?

'Are you a *relationship builder* and have a high desire to succeed in life?'

Job advertisement

release of resources

Decruitment, offshored, etc.

relocate

Never say 'move'.

'The bottling functions will be *relocated* to a venue in close proximity to the location of which the water is sourced.'

Bottled water company

'If Mohammed won't *relocate* to a venue in close proximity to the location of the mountain, the mountain must *relocate* to a venue in close proximity to the location of Mohammed.'

render

1. To hand over, give. As in: '*Render* therefore unto Caesar that which is Caesar's . . .'
2. To hand over detainees who have not responded to *torture lite* to foreign intelligence services who practise torture unrestrained.

> 'Those who cooperate are rewarded with creature comforts, interrogators whose methods include feigned friendship, respect, cultural sensitivity and, in some cases, money. Some who do not cooperate are turned over — "*rendered*", in official parlance — to foreign intelligence services whose practice of torture [is well known].'
>
> Press report, 2004

reposition / repositioning ·

1. (v) To move. (As in: deck chairs on *Titanic*). To hide, cover up, camouflage, etc.
2. (n) A make-over. *Rebranding*. Surface *change*. The *repositioning* is intended to take place in the *consumer*'s head. The trams and timetables are unchanged.

> 'A temporary, yet quirky, transit campaign to cover up former M Tram, Swanston Trams and The Met logos on trams has been launched alongside a major *repositioning* campaign for the entire Melbourne tram network, now run exclusively by Yarra Trams.'
>
> Yarra Trams

See *revenue protection officer*

resonate

To *drill down in terms of* understanding: 'We need to make this concept *resonate* with the staff' instead of just letting them understand it.

resource

1. Resource – employee, staff member or worker.
2. Under-resourced – under-staffed.

> 'The only reason for these words seems to be dehumanisation. "Shedding excess *resources*" sounds less upsetting than "sacking people".'
>
> Human Resources trainee

resource for everyday life

Health.

> 'To reach a state of complete physical, mental and social wellbeing, an individual or group must be able to identify and realise *aspirations*, satisfy *needs*, and change or cope with the environment. Health is, therefore, a *resource for everyday life*, not the objective of living.'
>
> NSW Health Department

> 'In sickness and when *resourced* for everyday life.'

resource re-balancing

Spilling resources – where the *resources* are employees.

> '5.51 Evidence received by the Committee indicated that in Darwin and Alice Springs, Telstra had commenced a *management*

program of "*resource rebalancing*" which was perceived as a euphemism for plans for large scale *redundancies*. All employees within Telstra are being rated on a scale of 1 to 5. The rating program has already commenced and, as early as July 1996, was said to already have had an *impact* on *customer service*.'

Parliament of Australia, 1996

See *redeployment*, *vanilla*, *downsizing*, *rightsizing*, *dejobbing*, etc.

responsible

A word with which to escape responsibility.

'These events occurred on my watch. As secretary of defense, I am *accountable* for them. I take full *responsibility* for them.'

Donald Rumsfeld

restatement of earnings

1. Restatement of earnings.
2. Fraud.

'Overall, our results indicated that the SEC's alarm over the shareholder wealth effects of *restatements* is valid, but primarily for a subset of *restatements* with large income effects that *involve* fraudulent activity and management that cannot or will not self-identify misstatements.'

Dr D. Jeanne Patterson, The Corporate Library

See *misspeak*, *lie*

results driven

An ability.

> 'Key Selection Criteria:
> Demonstrated ability to think laterally, question assumptions, *problem solve* and be *results driven*.'
>
> City of Port Phillip, job description

retail studies

An academic discipline; as in Professor of *Retail Studies*, University of Melbourne.

reticent

1. Reserved, taciturn, unforthcoming.
2. Reluctant (*in terms of back-ended* returns).

> 'With running yields below the cost of capital which were to be off-set by *back-ended* capital returns, the group was *reticent* to invest too heavily in this way.'
>
> Annual report

revenue enhancement

Tax increase.

revenue protection officer

Ticket inspector on Melbourne trams.

revenue side

The side the revenue's on. Best read aloud.

'On the *revenue side*, it's likely that the revenue benefits will come from taking *market* share from competitors, which is difficult to ascribe *value* to until we see it.'

Wilson HTM analyst Brett Le Mesurier,
Australian Financial Review, December 2003

reverse racism

Discrimination against the fortunate majority.

'We now have a situation where a type of *reverse racism* is applied to mainstream Australians by those who promote *political correctness* and those who control the various taxpayer funded "industries" that flourish in our society servicing Aboriginals, *multiculturalists* and a host of other minority groups.'

Pauline Hanson, Maiden Speech, 1996

revisit

1. To go back to, return.
2. To have another look, reconsider, check, refresh the memory.

'I think we should *revisit* the *implementation strategy*.'

'There's no point in *revisiting the past*.'

'Like dogs *revisiting* their vomit . . .'

See *look at*

revitalisation

Focused change process.

'It is common for existing Communities and Town Centres to use improvement projects as a *Revitalisation catalyst*. If your *challenge* is to *facilitate* the *delivery* of such a *critical* local *initiative* it may well be worthwhile to understand just what is *Revitalisation*? *Revitalisation* is a *change process focused* to improve *cultural*, economic and environmental vitality.'

Vital Places consultancy

rightsizing

Job eliminations; *downsizing*; *rationalising*; *business process re-engineering*; *decruitment*; *dejobbing*; efficiency gain; productivity improvement; offered the package; offshored; sacking; given the bird. *Involuntary career event*.

'Borders attributed the move to "*rightsizing*".'

Borders Group after sacking staff

See *unlock (the targeted cost savings)*, and above

ring-fence

Keeps out schizophrenia.

'Mark Rhoney, president of UPS's venture group, says this augurs [sic] for building a *ring-fence* around the venture group and taking people out of their line jobs to populate it. Says Rhoney, "You can't ask people to be functionally schizophrenic."'

Bain and Company, 2001

risk analysis assessment (form – 2D model)

1. Assessment of risk.
2. The following.

'The objectives of analysis are to separate the minor acceptable risks from the major risks, and to provide data to assist in the evaluation and treatment of risks. *Risk analysis* considers the magnitude of the consequences to personal safety of particular hazards and environmental *impacts* of particular environmental aspects, and the likelihood that those consequences may occur. Factors that affect consequences and likelihood may be identified.'

University of Melbourne

risk management

Managing risk. Minimising risk. Taking risks (*risk-taking*). Covering your arse. Having an *exit strategy*. Having insurance. Having *common sense*. Stating the obvious. Laying off.

'A risk is a potential *problem*. Managing the situation so that minimum loss or damage will result if the risk materialises.'

DM Review

'*Risk Management*: Titan Corporation provides a systems integration approach to risk mitigation and vulnerability reduction. In today's society, the *growth* and complexity of risk and its associated security *issues* has relegated single-source security *solutions* to *the past*.'

Titan Corporation

risk-take

Take risks.

> 'They *risk-taked* all night.'
>
> AFL football commentator

> 'Hardly surprising really that a *risk-taker* like Ms Russo was a wrong fit for the risk adverse [sic] environment of the legal profession.'
>
> CareerOne Job Network

> 'The best outcome is that the child will "*risk-take*" within the boundaries of personal safety.'
>
> RTA, NSW

road map

1. Road map.
2. Peace *plan*.
3. War *plan*.
4. *Plan*.

> 'Rebuilding America's Defenses' became the *road map* for foreign policy decisions made in the White House and the Pentagon; PNAC had the Vice President's office in one building, and the Defense Secretary's office in the other. Attacking Iraq was central to that *road map* from the beginning . . .'
>
> William Rivers Pitt, August 2004

robust

Full of health and strength; vigorous, strong; full-bodied (As in: 'a *robust* Hunter shiraz'), sturdy; stout.

'The community wants a *"robust"* curriculum framework that reflects expectations about meeting young people's *needs* and identifying and maximising individual talents and *capabilities*.'

Queensland Education Department

'Brooks also said that while the administration projected future budgets for possible development of a high-yield weapon called the *Robust* Nuclear Earth Penetrator weapon, no decision had been made to develop it and congressional approval would be required first to do so.'

David Ruppe, Global Security Newswire

'Dr Samuell contacted the Government expressing some concern over some material he'd seen and expressing concern over the *robustness* of that material . . . I mean, his concern is with the *robustness* of some work on which we're being asked . . . I think the *robustness* of this needs to be tested . . . but we do want the comments when they're held out as being informed and, you know, safe to rely on because of their academic nature. We do want to be sure that they are *robust* . . . As I've indicated to you, I think if someone raises a concern about the *robustness* of some research that's been done on which other people might rely, it's quite appropriate to have the *robustness* of that tested out . . . I mean I, I am turning my mind, as is the department in consultation with me, as to how we can be sure that we can get some *robust* and reliable information . . . The key thing that I'll be looking for, however, is, as I say, *robustness* and integrity of what's done . . . But it would only be on the basis of it having integrity and being *robust* and being free from bias either way in relation to this matter.'

Senator Amanda Vanstone, ABC radio, February 2004

rock star

1. Rock 'n' roll singer with charisma (Mick Jagger, Elvis, Little Richard, Johnny Rotten, etc.).
2. Member of a Muslim religious sect hired by CIA to spy on Saddam Hussein. 'Before the war, they recruit 87 of them all throughout the country and they give them satellite phones. And they report in regularly on secret things that are going on' (Bob Woodward, *Plan of Attack*).

> 'And Saddam went there at least once a year with his two sons. The security person at Dora Farm was a CIA spy, a *rock star*, and had a telephone, a satellite phone, in which he was reporting what he was seeing.'
>
> Bob Woodward

rocket science (not)

Easy, simple, straightforward, comprehensible, uncomplicated, not as hard as it looks, plain as the nose on your face, etc.

> 'It's not *rocket science*.'

> 'To be, or not to be: that is not *rocket science*.'

roll-out

(n) Commencement, beginning, *implementation* of the *plan* or *strategy* – e.g. military invasion, new computer program, etc. Go *live*.
(v) To put the plan into *action*, *implement*, *go live*, etc. (As in: When's *roll-out* on the monitoring *strategy*, the *empowering vision*, breakfast? etc.)

'Effective at knowledge transfer, training, and *roll-out* support, including development of training materials and user documentation.'

Resume

See *go live*, *implement*

rubber hits the road

Business as car, truck or bicycle tyre; what sort of tread, traction, grip. How fast it can go.

'Our mission and our values decide how *the rubber hits the road*.'

Business leader speech

'Where the *rubber hits the road in terms of strategies* and goals.'

Corporate document

'*Implementation*, that's when "*the rubber hits the road*".'

Expense Reduction Analysts, August 2003

'*At the end of the day* when the *rubber hits the road* and it comes to community *issues*, which House do the people turn to?'

Hansard NSW, March 2004

rumint

Rumour intelligence (US). Unreliable, 'tasty titbit' intelligence. Rumoured to be the sort of intelligence provided to President Bush, Secretary Powell, Prime Minister Blair, etc., before Iraq invasion. *Slam dunk* intelligence.

'*Rumint* is that George Tenet may stay on as DCI.'

www.intelforum.org

'*Rumint* is the varmints were wrong.'

rural values

The *main game* for country folk.

Ss

scenario

1. An imagined sequence of possible events.
2. Events.

Worst-case *scenario*; best-case *scenario*; nightmare *scenario*; last year's *scenario*; plausible *scenario*; possible *scenario*; future *scenario*; past *scenario*.

> 'Six floors above us flew up into the air, then came crashing down, taking all my staff members with me into a pancake *scenario* of all those floors.'
>
> Oklahoma bombing survivor

> 'In this *scenario* we'll use a dedicated root directory for each server, which is a personal *choice*.'
>
> Computer program

> 'Governing today means giving acceptable signs of credibility. It is like advertising and it is the same effect that is *achieved — commitment* to a *scenario*.'
>
> Jean Baudrillard

> 'We'll cross that bridge when the *scenario* presents itself.'
>
> The President of the USA, as a character on '24'

> 'To be, or not to be: they are the *scenarios*.'

scenario building

1. Imagining the future so you can plan for it.
2. Imagining the future and not planning for it.

'When you're *scenario building*, you know, you will only take action above that when you have information that leads you to a solid conclusion.'

Alexander Downer on intelligence before
Bali bombing, ABC, 2004

scenarios (common)

Those regularly experienced in activity centre planning.

'The purpose of the Activity Centre Design Guidelines project is to demonstrate how the Melbourne 2030 policies and objectives may be applied to *common scenarios* in activity centre planning (for example, existing street-based activity centres, mall-based centres and large stores, residential use in and around activity centres etc).'

Melbourne 2030

scientia ac labore

1. 'Knowledge through work' (university motto).
2. 'Participate actively and *innovatively* in their professional and social *communities of practice*' (university mission statement).

scope, scoping

To research, analyse, evaluate, document, study, look at, look over, peruse, read, check, scrutinise, skim.

'Traditionally, curriculum frameworks are descriptions of what is known to curriculum developers and which is then *scoped* and sequenced for the benefit of learners [sic].'

Queensland Studies Authority

sea change

1. Very slow *change*, gradual *change*; change without a *strategy* and no known *outcome*; not the sort of *change* a *consultant* could manage. A mysterious, haunting, melancholy kind of *change*.
2. As *proactive* is to active, *sea change* is to *change*. A lasting, thorough *change*. A *change* to the *culture*. A lifestyle *change*. *Change*.

> 'Nothing of him that doth fade,
> but doth suffer a *sea change*,
> into something rich and strange.'
>
> Shakespeare, *The Tempest*

> 'Now, the *sea change* has been *downgraded* and a growing number of city dwellers are doing a semi *sea change*.'
>
> *Sunday Life*, April 2004

> '*Sea change* needed in sick leave management.'
>
> Hallis People Skills

See also *about-face*

security contractors

Mercenaries. Companies (often new companies) that fight their country's wars, and provide their 'homeland security'. *Key stakeholders* in privatised warfare.

> 'A mercenary's dream at the outset of the war, Iraq is turning into a different *market* for security firms.'
>
> *Fortune*, July 2004

'Oh what a lovely war it's been for *security contractors* in Iraq. Taking on the many military tasks *outsourced* by the stretched-thin Pentagon, they have profited from a battle-zone gold rush: an instant billion dollar industry with a 20,000-person workforce.'

Fortune, July 2004

'But in a critical way the battle in Najaf represents the new face of modern warfare: most of the defenders were not soldiers but civilian contractors – employees of Blackwater USA, a private security firm based in North Carolina. The guns, ammo, and even the choppers all belonged to Blackwater.'

Fortune, 2004

seen

1. Perceived with the eyes; witnessed; apprehended; comprehended; to form a mental image; foreseen – perception.
2. Witnessed by the unseeing.
3. Caused.

'Meanwhile, an explosion at a factory in Calcutta has *seen* the deaths of hundreds of people.'

'A calf injury has *seen* the end of the big Swan's hopes of playing in a grand final.'

'My socks have *seen* the glory . . . etc.'

self-concept

How every *consumer* sees himself or herself '*in terms of
. . .* attitudes, perceptions, beliefs and evaluations'
(marketing textbook). The points of entry *in terms of
marketing*. Prejudice, insight, theology, calculus, etc.
Business's take on Thomas à Kempis: 'A true understanding and humble estimate of oneself is the highest
and most valuable of all lessons.'

> 'Hamlet had a *non-robust self-concept that he could not self-identify.*'
> Discuss.

self-harm

Hurting oneself (includes 'hanging gestures'). '*Self-harm*
is not a form of protest that the government condones'
(Immigration Department spokesman, June 2005).
(v) 'A group of people have *self-harmed*' (Immigration
Department spokesman June 2005).

The causes are partly cultural, according to former
Minister for Immigration, Philip Ruddock. 'Well, you say
it's desperation, I'd say that in many parts of the world
people believe that they get *outcomes* by behaving that
way. In part it's *cultural*' (ABC, August 2001).

> 'In 2003 there were 350 *self-harm* incidents, including 120
> hanging gestures.'
>> Lieutenant Colonel Leon Sumpter, army spokesman,
>> speaking about Guantanamo Bay, BBC News

> '. . . an organised *self-harm event.*'
>> ABC news, June 2005

senior living

Housing and other amenities for old or obsolete citizens. A category of real estate that *targets* those for whom the wheel is coming full circle, who hath borne most . . ., etc. A *lifestyle* category.

> 'Independent living units are designed for seniors who want to retain their full independence but also have *access* to the security, companionship, facilities and services of a *senior living* community.'
>
> www.primelife.com.au/lifestyles

> '. . . will you still feed me, when I'm in *senior living*?'

service profit chain

The link between good service and success recently redis-covered in some realms of business where it had been misplaced and nobody could remember where they had put it. The link is most profitable when the two elements are *aligned* – hence, one presumes, the 'chain', in which other links may be *focused on key drivers, key deliverables, key goals* and *core values*; staff training and incentives; staff *downsizing* or *rightsizing*; the global economic environment and *passion*.

> '. . . the central role of the *service profit chain*.'

service the target

To bomb. To attack and destroy.

set the agenda / agenda set

To decide what the game will be and how it will be played. Politicians try to *set the agenda* so that they can play the game on their terms. When they fail in this, they become defensive and reactive; they get 'on the back foot' and it may show up on television.

To set the agenda is to be *proactive*, positive, to get 'on the front foot', to show *leadership*, etc. This may involve *pushing the envelope* on policy. If there is no policy worth announcing, or you're losing on that front, you can always head for *the bush* and get in touch with *ordinary, common sense Australians* and *rural values*. This way you'll be *setting the media agenda*, and that's more important than the policy *agenda* anyway. Meanwhile the people will think <u>they</u> are setting the policy *agenda* which adds to the beauty of the whole initiative and proves the soundness of the *strategy*.

share of wallet

cf. pound of flesh.

> 'The percentage of a *customer's* requirements that are filled by a particular *brand* of *product* or service.'
>
> DM Review

shareholders

Easily forgotten category of human beings. Human beings to whom companies, who are also human beings, have obligations. *Stakeholder* subset.

'Interviewer: . . . do you think that executives of the company were somewhat blind to the moral responsibility and moral *issues* in all of this?

Meredith Hellicar: We are human beings. You cannot be blind to this awful, awful disease, and none of us has been blind to that . . . But — and we can't rewrite *history*. The fact of the matter is, we can't wish away our legal and fiduciary responsibilities and as much as we would like to in many respects, *at the end of the day*, we're custodians on behalf of the *shareholders*. We have obligations to our *shareholders* and you know, I think perhaps that's been forgotten in all of this.'

Chair, James Hardie Industries, August 2004

sharing (that)

'Thank you for *sharing that* with us, Henry,' where 'that' is an incoherent or tedious outpouring of personal angst, happiness or *closure*. 'Blessings, Henry. Shut up from now on.'

shifting the goalposts

Changing the rules while the game's being played. A low, unprincipled act, contrary to the spirit of business or politics.

shortfall

1. Not enough. Less than what is needed.
2. Less than what is generous or expected or just or proper, etc. An insufficient amount. Stingy, paltry, mean, etc.

'We were truly, truly sorry that there was a *shortfall* in our initial funding of the foundation. We do regret the anxiety and concern that that *outcome* may have caused sufferers and their families and the *community*.'

> Chair, James Hardie Industries, August 2004,
> speaking about an underfunded foundation for
> victims of asbestosis

shortly

(adv) Of, pertaining to or heralding a void of indeterminate dimensions, often set to music or advertising. The longest recorded *shortly* is five of Vivaldi's *Four Seasons*.

'A *customer service* representative/operator will be with you *shortly*.'

'*Shortly* the Rockies may crumble
Gibraltar may tumble . . . etc.'

'Better *shortly* than never.'

showcasing

What one does with talent and all *vibrant* things.

'Cr John Foss says he is looking forward to the festival, which *showcases* the *vibrant culture* and *lifestyle* of the Surf Coast Shire.'

> *Groundswell*, The Surf Coast Shire
> Community Newsletter

sidebar meeting

Extra meeting. Not the main one.
(As in: 'Not now. *Dialogue* it in a *sidebar meeting*.')

signage

More than one sign. One sign.

> 'For the purpose of the Comprehensive *Signage* Policy, this category of signs does not include regulatory, warning, guidance, destination and street *signage*.'
>
> Mornington Peninsula Shire

> 'Can't you read the *signage*?!'

> '. . . outward and visible *signage* of an inward and spiritual grace.'

> 'Oates was showing *signage* of exhaustion.'

significant

1. Important; substantial; *non-trivial*.
2. An undisclosed amount. You will have to take my word for it; but I am the President, after all. Enough to make several bombs to drop on us if that helps you get the point. (As in: '*significant* quantities of uranium . . .')

signs

1. Indication of something. A thing with a point on the end. Portent. 'Thrice the brinded cat hath mewed', etc.
2. Indication of something else, including something other than what you reckon it is or want it to be; a picture with an arrow on it; necromancy, reading tea leaves and giblets, etc.

> 'How do I know that? How can I say that? Let me give you a closer look. Look at the image on the left. On the left is a

close-up of one of the four chemical bunkers. The two arrows indicate the presence of sure *signs* that the bunkers are storing chemical weapons.'

Colin Powell to UN, 5 February 2003

A red sky in the morning is a shepherd's warning,
A red sky at night is a *sign* of Unarmed Aerial Vehicles.

silos

1. Storages for wheat, etc.
2. Storages for *knowledge*.

'Opening up the *silos* of expertise within individuals in some parts of the curriculum is a *challenge* for any curriculum coordinator.'

'Knowledge Management in Secondary Schools',
Australian Computer Society

'But if you look at their [teachers'] performance, from a *knowledge* perspective, they may in fact represent the ultimate in hermetically sealed knowledge *silos*.'

Wayne Hewett, Setting up Communities of Practice

sinister nexus

1. A sinister link, *linkage*, connection, series, associative relationship such as between Lady Macbeth and her husband. *Axis of evil* involving only two parties. *Nexus* of evil.
2. Absence of a relationship; never let the facts get in the way of a good story, etc.

'A *sinister nexus* between Iraq and al-Qaeda.'

Colin Powell

situational awareness

Awareness of a particular situation.

'As the Marines entered Nasiriya, their "*situational awareness* became clouded" because of deviations from the maneuver plan, the urban environment and *communications* problems, according to the report.'

CNN Report

six sigma

Leading cornerstones measured with a calculator.

'She uses tools like *Six Sigma* as cornerstones to lead *high impact culture change* . . . Ms Larson is a living example of how *multi-cultural* sensitivity is a must on our *global environment*. Her high *impact*, high action consulting style has enabled her to spread her *culture change* influence well beyond the borders of the US . . .'

www.isixsigma.com

'*Six Sigma* is a disciplined, data-driven approach and methodology for eliminating defects (driving towards six standard deviations between the mean and the nearest spec-ification limit) in any *process* — from manufacturing to transactional and from *product* to service . . . *Process* sigma can easily be calculated using a *Six Sigma* calculator.'

www.isixsigma.com

skill set

Personal collection, assembly, anthology, arrangement, etc., of skills. Employees of *quality* organisations, including football clubs, have *skill sets*. At this point in their development, farmers, mechanics, jockeys, people *engaged* in home duties and many other vocations may have extensive assortments or whole rafts of *skills*, but they do not have them in *sets*.

> 'Staff will have to work in new ways and develop wider *skill sets* than they have now.'
>
> Consultancy document

> 'Together the *"Circle of Strength"* team of experts provide the comprehensive and cohesive cross-functional *skill sets*, technology and knowledge *enhancements*, practical *strategic* service and support infrastructure, *communications* and fundamentally important business development *inputs* that are integral for successful long-term economic development and social benefit.'
>
> Sunraysia Mallee Development Board

> 'Achilles' *skill set* contained a *capability gap in terms of emotional intelligence*. Discuss.'

slam dunk

1. Certain goal in basketball provided you're 7 feet tall and know what you're doing. Sure thing; beyond a doubt; guaranteed; ironclad; no possibility it won't go through the hoop. Show of élan, hubris, etc.

2. Less than ironclad. ('Mr Tenet later told associates he should have said the evidence on weapons was less than ironclad', Bob Woodward, *Plan of Attack*.)

> '"It's a *slam dunk* case," Mr Tenet replied, throwing his arms in the air.'
> George Tenet (CIA) to President George W. Bush, 2002

smart bomb

1. Bomb, guided by laser or Global Positioning Satellite. 'Precision' bomb; one that limits *collateral damage*. Clever, bright, quick-witted, quick-on-its-feet bomb; elegant, stylish, smart but casual, etc.
2. Less than precise 'precision' bomb. Bomb that causes *collateral damage*.

> 'The GAO study concluded that, on average, it took four *smart bombs* to hit a target. In 20 percent of the cases, it took at least six bombs; in 15 percent, at least eight.'
> Fred Kaplan, *Boston Globe*, February 1998

See *daisy cutter*

smell

1. (v) To perceive a scent or odour.
2. Capacity to read people.

> 'They also state that a good independent director has the "ability to *smell* smoke coming from under the doors", i.e. the *capacity* to read people.'
> Colin Carter and J. Lorsch
> quoted by Arts & Recreation Victoria

> 'I can *smell* you like a book.'

social capital

Society. Society rediscovered, and found to be actually necessary and actually good for business. Recognition of an 'important *downside*': '*communities*, groups or *networks* which are isolated, parochial or working at cross-purposes to society's collective interests (e.g. drug cartels, corruption rackets) can actually hinder economic and social development' (World Bank). A surprise all round, actually. Education, health, welfare programs, charities, training, sport, networks, the arts, people are all social capital. Social resources; the resources of *communities*.

> 'Investment in *social capital* is investment in success.'
>
> Wayne Baker

> '*Social capital* refers to the institutions, relationships, and norms that shape the *quality* and quantity of a society's social interactions . . . Not just the sum of the institutions which *underpin* society − . . . the glue that holds them together.'
>
> World Bank

> 'Business has to *deliver*: by good *governance* on its own part, by building *social capital* on the part of *communities* and the nation.'
>
> Business speech

socialise

To circulate for *feedback*. As in, 'We need to *socialise* this idea with the management *team*.'

soft skills

Human skills. Soothing, tender, comforting skills. Massaging feelings, egos, etc. Making small talk. Humanist, romantic etc. Skills. Keats, Wordsworth, Sylvia Plath, etc. Wet skills. *Bleeding heart* skills. Bleeding edge skills. No *bullet points*.

> 'With a Big 4 background and experience in *BPR*, productivity improvement and training for influence, Cindy offers a unique mix of *soft skills* and hard-edged *process* change.'
>
> *The Consultant's Consultant*

> 'A *soft skill* turneth away wrath.'

soften up

1. To make soft.
2. To weaken resistance or strength by preliminary measures.
3. To kill, destroy and demoralise especially with heavy weapons such as *daisy cutters*.
4. To torture with *torture lite*.

> 'Rear Adm. John Stufflebeem, the Pentagon's designated spokesman on military operations in Afghanistan, said much of the US bombing is designed to *soften up* the Taliban for the northern alliance.'
>
> Associated Press, June 2001

> 'Sen. Robert Byrd, D-S.C., asked Taguba whether there was a policy in place for American guards to *soften up* prisoners before interrogation.'
>
> ABC News, May 2004

solution

Problem solved. (As in: Pacific *Solution*, long-term *solution*, short-term *solution*, medium-term *solution*, *solution* for the short to medium term, Final *Solution*, etc.)

'. . . our consultants are able to deliver the entire end–to–end *solution* for employers with the minimum of fuss.'

Hudson Human Capital Consultants

'We've outlined our policy in that regard and we are wanting a lasting *solution* in Iraq.'

John Howard, May 2004

'Well that's the nirvana of the ultimate *solution* . . .'

Bob Mansfield, ABC, 2004

'As a provider of national security *solutions*, the company has approximately 12,000 employees and annualised sales of approximately $2.0 billion.'

Titan Corporation

some concern (to us)

Unspecified amount or degree of concern. Hypothetical concern. Not a concern as yet. Not *non-trivial* concern. Unconcern.

'Well, if that is the case, that would be of *some concern to us* because, as I've said, we don't think there is a military solution to the problem of East Timor.'

Alexander Downer, December 1998

'We obviously have *some concern* about the security of the players, but yeah I would be very concerned about the political statement it would make.'

Alexander Downer, January 2004

'. . . if the spiritual leader of this organisation is to be released after a very short period of time, that would be of *some concern to us*.'

Alexander Downer, March 2004

source

(n) Where water, manganese, beans, grapes, oil, spare parts, labour, etc., come from.
(v) Getting the above by drilling, mining, picking, plucking, transporting, recruiting, purchasing, etc. Alternative to 'access'.

'Central to that *goal* is the ability to *source* fruit from diverse geographies . . .'

Southcorp media release, 2004

'But of the tree of the knowledge of good and *evil*, thou shall not *source* fruit from it.'

sovereign / sovereignty

1. Paramount, supreme, self-governing, independent, unmitigated power.
2. Not quite in charge of things, slightly not independent ('less than full-fledged', *New York Times*), unsovereign.

'They [the Iraqis] will be *sovereign*, but I think as a result of agreements, as a result of (*hopefully*) resolutions that are passed, there will be some constraints on the power of this *sovereignty*.'

Colin Powell, 8 April 2004

'That's what Mr Brahimi is doing. He's figuring out the nature of the entity we'll be handing *sovereignty* over.'

President George W. Bush, 14 April 2004

space

An imaginary . . . *space*. As in, 'We need to investigate what is happening in the curriculum *space*.'
cf. *bump space*.

spill and fill

1. To abolish jobs. Organisational *re-alignment*; restructuring; *re-engineering*, etc.
2. 'Professional assessment and *benchmarking* of internal candidates.'

'This is arguably the best chance to minimise resistance, confusion and cynicism. For example, *spill and fill* positions as rapidly and as fairly as can be done, *implement* changes in *key* areas such as pay and incentives from day 1, take the hard decisions up front.'

Consultant

spin / spin doctor

Story telling. Probably derives from '*spinning* a yarn'; but it might also refer to the *spin* bowlers put on a cricket ball or pitchers on a baseball with the intention of deceiving. In tennis and table tennis, *spin* is used to control the flight and bounce of the ball and to keep it in play, and it is the same in politics. *Spin* aims to control the interpretation of events where the events themselves cannot be controlled.

Any half-competent politician will instinctively put a *spin* on events, but in the interests of keeping the story consistent and leaving the pollie to practise being genuine and spontaneous, people calling themselves *Media* Advisers or *Media Strategists* are employed to persuade the *media* to buy or *buy in* to. Successful *spin* creates the political equivalent of *staff sign off* by the *media*. The government's *message*. These *spin doctors* or *spinmeisters* are often journalists on leave from the press gallery. Speechwriters are slightly glorified *spin doctors* but their jobs are less exciting. It is true that *spin* embellishes and manipulates the truth, and that sometimes outright lies are told. But just as often *spin* is the only way to *convey* the truth, to defeat lies and confusion, to properly counsel patience, to put words and events in context. As much as the media sneers at *spin*, they also depend on it. The relationship is interdependent if not downright incestuous. Companies, business leaders, NGOs and government departments all employ *spin doctors*.

See *buy in*, *staff sign off*

spiral dynamics

Who knows?

'You will be introduced to the *Spiral Dynamics* theory of *Values* Systems and *Leadership* and come away with distinct understanding into why "one size fits all" *leadership*, management and *marketing* approaches will never create the type of environment & ongoing business results demand that in an *increasingly competitive marketplace*.'

Senior Executive Leadership Seminar, Brisbane

'*Spiral Dynamics* can also be described as social *DNA*.'

leadervision.com

staff signoff

Stage in a *strategic plan*. Agreement. Get workers' names on it. On board, in the cart, etc. Give them ownership, *buy in*; pretend they have some say in things. Mug them in a *strategic context*.

'I *plan* to return to staff with an emergent QSA *Strategic Plan* for fine-tuning and *staff signoff*.'

Consultancy document

'Why was Mr Bligh unable to achieve *staff signoff* on the *Bounty*? Was it an *issue* of *emotional intelligence*? Discuss.'

See *buy in*

stakeholder challenges

Problems with the *triple bottom line*. Issues of *sustainability*. How to deal with the Greens and other *community* groups? Is 'good corporate citizen' an oxymoron? How to make *corporate social responsibility* look like it means something? Etc.

'. . . broader societal and *stakeholder challenges*.'

International CEO Forum

stakeholders

1. Person or organisation with a stake, i.e. a share or interest; people joined along the *triple bottom line*: *shareholders*, staff, *customers / clients*, etc.
2. People in a nursing home; people *engaged* in *senior living*. (As in: 'At Easter the *stakeholders* all wore bonnets and those who could joined in singing "It's a long way to Tipperary".')

> '*Sustainability* is determined by an organisation's ability to *create* and *deliver value* for all *stakeholders*.'
>
> Principles of Business Excellence,
> Gracedale Private Nursing Home

> 'Dear *Stakeholder*
> SAP Upgrade and Improvements Project — Deferred *Go-Live*
> I am writing this note to advise that the SAP Upgrade Project for Outcome One has been deferred by two weeks due to a number of unresolved *issues* identified during testing. The new *go-live* is now set to be Monday 29 March 2004 . . . The project *team* would like to thank the *key stakeholders* and business areas for their continued support and patience during this period.'

> 'And Moses called unto them; and Aaron and all the other *key stakeholders* returned unto him. And Moses *dialogued* with them.'

stakeholders (relevant)

People with a relevant stake. Not an irrelevant *stakeholder*.

'An *implementation strategy* for the NIQTSL (National Institute for Quality Teaching and School *Leadership*) will consider the roles, functions, *governance* arrangements, operational and funding requirements, *performance indicators* and relationships with *relevant stakeholders*.'

Federal Department of Education, Science & Training

'Co-ordinate and analyse *focus* groups as required to assess concerns, needs and ideas of *relevant stakeholders*.'

Position description,
Westgate Division of General Practice

'*Relevant stakeholders* (*key* and other) can be brought together through the Steering Committee to consider all relevant *issues* of the MPS proposal for the *community*, and to *drive* the *process* of development.'

WA Department of Health

state of the art

On the frontier of *innovation*; the *cutting edge / leading edge* of design, technology, management, ideas, fashion inc. facelifts, haircuts, etc. New in every respect except the term for it.

See *world's best practice*

step up to the plate

1. (US baseball) What a batter does when it's his turn.
2. To come forward; put oneself on the line; become engaged; take one's turn; do one's duty; be *accountable*; accept *responsibility*; do what's necessary, proper, right, appropriate, manly, brave, etc.

'The straight-talking was needed from the Prime Minister [and] if he won't deliver then it's not surprising Labor politicians will *step up to the plate* and give it a swing themselves.'

Mark Latham, June 2003

'When disasters strike our shores — whether they take the form of bushfires, earthquakes or mass murder — it is often local government leaders that *step up to the plate*.'

President of the Australian Local Government Association, 2002

story (the)

What every leader must have. The narrative that emerges from *spin*.

'Tonight my friends, I ask you to join me for the next 100 days in telling John Kerry's *story* and promoting his ideas.'

Bill Clinton, July 2004

stovepiping

To provide to powerful masters information that is likely to persuade them to the view or *plan* you favour; to protect them from contrary information or argument; in this way to delude your masters and make them zealous in some cause.

'This office [of Special Plans] which circumvented the usual procedures of vetting and *transparency*, *stovepiped* many of its findings to the highest ranking officials in the Administration.'

Seymour Hersh, *New Yorker*, 2003

'Did Iago *stovepipe* Othello? If so, how?'

See *Office of Special Plans*

strategic foresight analyst

A person who is paid to analyse *strategic foresights*?

strategic framework plan

Plan for a *strategic* framework. Framework for a *strategic* plan. *Strategic* plan for a framework. *Strategy* for a planned framework. Etc.

> 'SMEDB's approach to cohesive and more equitable whole-of-region positive *outcomes* is addressed in the following organisational structure, created to maximise the *capture* of valuable resources, transfer of *knowledge* and information, improve opportunity awareness, eliminate costly organisational and dissemination duplication and best manage the delivery of desirable *outcomes* via the *Strategic Framework Plan*.'
>
> Sunraysia Mallee Economic Development Board

strategic oversight

1. Something missed in the *strategy*. Something missed e.g. position of the enemy forces; resistance of the enemy forces; failings of one's own forces. Stuff-up, cock-up, etc.
2. Not the other way of doing it. *Oversight* at the *strategic* end of the *spectrum*.

strategic planning

'*Strategic oversight* of resources by government.'

Victorian Department of Treasury and Finance

strategic planning

Planning with a *plan* in mind.

See *future directions*

strategies, strategised, strategising, strategic

Strategic (adj) *Strategy* (n) *Strategise, strategising* (v) *Strategically* (adv). Clever, smart, far-sighted, very clever. (As in: a *strategic* plan, policy campaign, etc.) Anything better than stupid, misguided, wrong, etc. Well-planned, well-husbanded, well-marshalled. Tactical, considered, measured, etc. Antonyms: non-strategic, unstrategic, myopic, playing it by ear, ad hoc, flexible, adaptable, free, light on one's feet, exceedingly clever.

'I think the more you want to become more and more creative you have to not only elicit other peoples' *strategies* and replicate them yourself, but also modify others' *strategies* and have a *strategy* that creates new creativity *strategies* based on as many wonderful states as you can design for yourself.'

Richard Bandler, co-founder of NLP

'*Customer service*. Each *strategy* then has attached to it, *strategic issues* in *achieving* the overarching *strategies*. *Performance* measures are also included to determine if *goals* are met.'

Community Plan 2004-07, Strathbogie Shire
Community Bulletin, February 2004

'*Strategic* Process Improvement.'

> Toorak (Vic) business offering massage and
> chiropractic therapy

strategy elicitation model

Not a real one – a model.

> 'There are constraints inside this model since it was built by reducing things down. The *strategy elicitation model* is always looking for the most finite way of accomplishing a result. This model is based on sequential elicitation and simultaneous installation.'
>
> Richard Bandler, co-founder of NLP

structural adjustment

1. Adjusting structures – of economies, industries, regions, businesses, etc., in the name of efficiency, prosperity or survival. When governments make structural adjustments they are usually obliged to compensate people who lose jobs or business.
2. As above, but don't call it 'compensation'. It might start a stampede.

> Interviewer: '. . . you're opening the door here for massive compensation claims?'
>
> Senator Ian Campbell: 'I think it's a very, this isn't compensation, it is *structural adjustment* . . .'
>
> ABC, 27 August 2004

structural envisioning

As it sounds.

See *envisioning*

stuff

1. Bits and pieces, odds and ends, bric a brac, anything.
2. Rioting, looting, mayhem.

> '*Stuff* happens.'
>
> Donald Rumsfeld on Baghdad
> after the *mission* was *accomplished*

submodalities

Best if *advanced*.

> 'The program provides a *flexible* Master Practitioner approach to training based on five *core* component areas: *values* and *value* development, expert performance modeling, pattern elicitation *strategy* and *strategic* abundance, exploration of *advanced* language patterns, and facility with advanced *submodalities*.'
>
> Erickson College, Vancouver,
> A Systematic *NLP* Master Practitioner Course for Coaches

suite

A group. A tribe of goats, flock of sheep, school of fish, a *suite* of indicators, etc.

> 'During 2000, a *suite* of *indicators* reflecting the phases of an effective discharge was developed and four of the five *indicators* were *implemented* in all acute hospitals, sub acute services and MPS on 1st July 2001.'
>
> Victorian Department of Human Services

> 'For each *output*, a *suite* of *output performance* measures and *targets* (at least annual) have been identified covering

quantity, *quality*, timeliness and *cost* characteristics of the *output*.'

Victorian Department of Treasury and Finance

supply end of the spectrum

End farthest from the demand end.

See *spectrum*

supportive / supportiveness

Supporting, friendly, helpful, thoughtful, generous, charitable, kind, loyal, faithful, solid, a brick, etc. offering or providing support; i.e. comfort, reassurance, money, guns, explosives, bodyguards, psychological and other counselling, sympathy, empathetic understanding, a hug, a cup of tea. Not *neglective* or merely *acceptant*. Some environments are also *supportive* /provide *supportiveness*.

'The Council's emphasis on grants will continue to be of great importance in *ensuring* the *ongoing* viability of the arts in Australia. However, *support* at the *demand end of the spectrum* has the potential to provide multiplier benefits for artists which grants alone cannot provide.'

Australia Council

'I want to thank my mum and dad for being *supportive*.'

'And be *supportive*, in sickness and in health . . .'

'Wilt thou love her, comfort her, honour, and be *supportive* . . .'

surgical strike

To blow up, eliminate, wipe out, obliterate, *attrite*, *degrade* or take out a target with bombs, as one would an appendix or pancreas with a scalpel, i.e. without harm to the surrounding environment.

'The idea of American planes suddenly and swiftly eliminating a missile complex with conventional bombs in a matter of minutes — so-called *"surgical" strike* — had appeal to almost everyone first considering the matter.'

Theodore Sorensen, *Kennedy*, 1964

sustainable, sustainability

1. What can be kept in existence, maintained.
2. *Sustainable* business practices are those that allow businesses to say they have met the *triple bottom line*, *stakeholder challenges*, *corporate social responsibility*.
3. Art of *achieving growth* without *downsizing* to zero.

'Meeting the *needs* of the present generation without compromising the ability of future generations to meet their *needs*.'

Brundtland Commission, 1987

'As AusAid *strategic* planning emphasises (i) program *outcomes* orientations (ii) better measurement of program *impact*, and (iii) more *innovative* ways of *achieving sustainability*, IDSS feel comfortable with the AMU-TAF as these *values* form the *core* of IDSS project *implementation* and management.'

synergy

Said to occur when the sum of two parts is greater than two – hence 'synergistic combination'. Organisational equivalent to certain forces in nature. Salvation is believed to be produced by the combination of divine grace and human will.

'We are *leveraging* scale to *harvest* global and regional *synergies* and maintaining *flexibility* to adapt to individual *markets*.'

Annual report, 2003

'*Achieve synergies* intended by the amalgamation.'

QSA Strategic Plan Consultancy

'. . . targeted cross *synergies* between each business unit.'

Annual report

'Love and marriage,
synergise like a horse and carriage.'

systems enhancement

A change.

'. . . a *systems enhancement* in late March will allow day-one commencements in *Community* Work'.

'Referrals to *Community* Work Coordinators before MO Gate', Department of Employment and Workplace Relations

'Thus far philosophers have only interpreted the world: the point is to *systems enhance* it.'

'*Systems enhancement* is in the wind.'

tactical pant

1. Faking it.
2. *Plenty tough* trousers for mercenary soldiers.
Strategic pants.

> 'The 5.11 *Tactical Pant* is the ultimate blend of convenience,
> efficiency and durability. It has been designed as a piece of
> equipment – not just a garment. Our *commitment* to *quality*
> can be seen by the components used to make these remark-
> able pants, from the high density tactical canvas to the
> Prym® snap and YKK® zipper . . . as *tough* as the men and
> women who own them . . .'
>
> > Blackwater USA (security contractor)

takeout / takeaway

1. Food one takes away.
2. Life one takes away.
3. The 'take'. (n) The story, the gist, the main bit.
A journalist's term.
Also (v) To eliminate a person or target.

> 'What's the *takeout*?'

> 'My *takeaway* from it was, "Hey, we didn't play things
> properly on the front page . . ."'
>
> > Erik Wemple, *New York Times*, August 2004

> '"All day, you build up for the moment when you fire the
> shot," Field, 23, says as he and his partner take positions in
> a hostile zone. "Then there's a feeling of exhilaration, and
> you feel like you've really done something for your country.
> You've *taken someone out.*"'
>
> > *Chicago Tribune*, 25 April 2003

See *light up*

talent management

Formerly what an agent for a pop star did. Now a form of *consultancy*.

> 'By working over the period of a full day with a select group of the *target* audience . . . we are able to cut through to the essence of required organisational imperatives to take their *talent management endeavours* to new heights of effectiveness.'
>> The Stephenson Partnership Pty Ltd, which helps executives 'free up more air-space in their diaries' and poses the question: 'What if *restructuring* did not leave any executives in new roles or reporting relationships demotivated . . .'

talk us through

Tell us about. Describe. As in, '*Talk us through* your feelings.' '*Talk us through* what went through your mind when you found out you were going to die?'

> 'Hamlet *talks us through* his *liveability issues*.'

target / targeting

(n) Something to aim at – such as a tree, a terrorist or a monthly sales figure. An objective, *focus*, goal, esp. *key goal*. (v) To aim, *focus*, pursue, concentrate upon, make your main mission, the *achieved outcome* of choice etc.

> 'Victoria Police: Now *targeting* drunk drivers'

target of opportunity

A *window of opportunity* onto someone you want dead (US military). A chance to *light up* or *takeout*.

team

Basic unit of corporatism. Everyone is a member of a *team* and no one who was not a *team* player ever got the job. It's a *team* game, with *team* values, *team* goals, *team* meetings and *team* language. Political leaders speak of their *teams*. Organisations work through *teams*. For individual self-expression workers must make do with karaoke.

> 'Must be adept at working in a multi-functional *team* environment.'
>
> Job advertisement

> 'But when you have a complex *customer* service *challenge* or *marketing* campaign that needs expertise from several *areas* of your company, a great *team* can *step up to the plate* and come up with a wildly successful *plan* that never could've been *implemented* — much less conjured — by one person alone.'
>
> Entrepreneur.com

team building

Fostering *team* work, *team* spirit, *team* consciousness, *team* loyalty, *team* solidarity, *team* creativity, *team* fun, *team* bonding, *team* excitement, *team* hysteria, a sense of *team*, *gestalt*, *team zeitgeist*, etc., through often senseless, juvenile, embarrassing, sadistic, quasi-military exercises.

'In the late 80s and 90s, *"Team Building"* has been recognised by many companies as an important factor in providing a *quality* service and remaining *competitive*.'

The Basics of Team Building

team player

Non-individualist, holist, cooperative type, all round good person or SMEDB.

'SMEDB is a *committed team player* providing an effective and convenient *catalyst* for the region's many players to come together in one cohesive *team*, the SMR's *"circle of strength"*, dedicated to achieving positive economic *outcomes*, environmental *sustainability* and social benefits for our region.'

Sunraysia Mallee Economic Development Board

'Macbeth was not a *team player*.' Discuss or *recontextualise*.

tear up

1. Rip apart.
2. Cry, weep, sob, howl, bawl, snivel, snuffle, blubber, grow tearful.

'Belic listened as Brando . . . sipped tea and Perrier and reminisced about his life, sometimes *tearing up*.'

Who Weekly, July 2004

temporary protection visa

A visa for *unauthorised arrivals* affording little protection.

Ten Commandments (The)

Ten bullet points. Judeo-Christian *mission statement*.
Ten Commitments. (Deuteronomy 5; Exodus 20)

That they represent the foundations of Judeo-Christian
civilisation is at once evident in their prohibiting the
worship of idols, killing, stealing, lying, coveting, etc.

Much quoted in the United States, where separation of
church and state is not well understood by everyone, and
recommended to Australians by the Federal Treasurer as
'the foundation of our law and our society' and the principles from which our morals and values derive. John
Howard PM also speaks of our 'historic Christian faith'.
The Governor-General is adamant that 'faith in God has
been an important establishing and unifying principle for
our nation'.

These statements bear a certain amount of false witness
to Australia's secular institutions, *history*, temper and
traditions, but these days who's going to notice?

> Thou shalt not *light up* thy neighbour's ass.'

terminological inexactitude

A *misspeak* of sorts.

> '25. SOCOG takes over the Club. As a result of a mediation
> on 30 July 1999, it was agreed by AOC, SOCOG, TOC and
> Synthesis that SOCOG should take over responsibility for
> running the Club . . . Although it contained some *terminolog-
> ical inexactitudes*, such as saying that the purpose of the transfer

was to achieve *"synergistic* benefits", it did truthfully say that SOCOG was to "assume sole control of the Olympic Club".'

Zhu v The Treasurer of the State of New South Wales [2004], 17 November 2004, High Court of Australia

terms

1. *immediate to short.* Between now and when the short *term* starts.
2. *short term.* Not as long as the medium *term* and much shorter than the long. (As in: '. . . and the life of man, solitary, poor, nasty, brutish and short *term*'.)
3. *short to medium term.* This is self-explanatory.
4. *medium term.* A *term* that is not as long as the long *term* or as short as the short.
5. *medium to long term.* See short to medium. (As in: 'If you can look into the medium to long *term* / and say which grain will grow and which will not . . .')
6. *long term.* Longer than the medium *term*. Out there. Well down the track. Barely foreseeable *in terms of* the future, even with twenty-twenty vision.
7. *longer term.* Not as long as long term; even as short as short to medium.

terrorists

People who hide in holes (especially *evil*doers, varmints, etc.).

'The best way to find these *terrorists* who hide in holes is to get people coming forth to describe the location of the hole, is to give clues and data.'

George W. Bush, December 2003

text

1. Original manuscript or book, essay, poem or other written work; written work specifically for study – *text* book.
2. Anything containing words that is studied or conceivably can be studied, including film, television and advertisements.
3. (v) To send a written message on a mobile phone.

> 'At High Achievement, the student has consistently shown knowledge and understanding of how *texts* are constructed across a range of *texts* in a range of social and cultural contexts.'
> Queensland Education Department

> 'Would that mine adversary had written a *text*.'

> 'I can read you like a *text*.'

See *author*

theatre mortuary evacuation point

Morgue (US military).

> 'The *Theatre Mortuary Evacuation Point* occupies a forlorn cluster of tents at the back corner of this sand-covered base in Kuwait.'
> Press report, AP, March 2004

> 'I went down to St James *Theatre Mortuary Evacuation Point*,
> Saw my baby there,
> She was stretched out, on a long white table . . .'

think outside the square / box

To think of something different. To think differently. Don't think like everyone else. Think creatively. Think any thought that the rest of the team aren't thinking. Think outside the rut, hole, morass, etc. Think. (But don't do it too often or you'll get a reputation for not being a *team player*.)

> 'A Keynote Speaker, Lateral Thinking Trainer, *Facilitator* and Entertainer helping organisations *think outside the square*.'
>
> Consultant

think tanks

Institution for solving problems, some of them of their own making. Political parties sponsor *think tanks* and vice versa. The Liberal Party is the political arm of the Institute of Public Affairs, a *think tank*. Labor has not been able to get a good *think tank* going. Recent American foreign policy, which is somewhat like American foreign policy at the turn of the 19th century, was dreamt up by a neo-conservative *think tank*, and several members of the *think tank* are members of the administration. President George W. Bush was not a member of the *think tank*. *Think tanks* are not elected by the people which should make their members *elite* intellectuals, but many of them deny this.

> '*Network* and *participate* in *think tanks* and *harvest* ideas to learn practically about the balancing of the [sic] *managerial risk taking*, entrepreneurial energy and *high capability*, with *monitoring*, so that management direction is *aligned* with the interest of those

who have entrusted their resources to the organisation and
to the interests of the other *stakeholders* — including . . .'
'Governance' Benchmarking Partnerships

'Our *mission statement* had also been *enhanced* to recognise our
role as a *think tank* and a *forum* of business and *community*
leaders. These *enhancements* are reflected in a simpler structure and a new contemporary constitution . . .'
CEDA Annual Report, 2001–02

third wardrobe (leader)

A *'people-focused'* leader; soft, loose, fallible, broad
church, *team-oriented* sort of leader.

'The *third wardrobe* — the increasing adoption of a new "neat
casual" executive dress code that bridges the gap between the
"suits" and the rest — is symbolic of the need to place people
and *team* factors at the centre of the *leadership agenda*.'
Jeff Floyd, CEO, *Australian Chief Executive*,
October 2002

See *agenda, hard and soft*

thought shower

'Other creative devices suggested by Michael include lateral
thinking and *brainstorming* (or *thought shower!*).'
Speak Easy, journal of Professional
Speakers Association

See *brainstorming*

time (at this point in)

Now, then, before, earlier, later, next Wednesday, *at the end of the day*, etc.

'But *at the end of the day* we have to say it is not *appropriate at this point in time*.' (after Alexander Downer); cf. 'The whole life of man is but a *point in time* . . .' (Plutarch)

'At this *point in time* I lay me down to sleep.'

'On a day like today,
We passed the *points of time* away.'

'Excuse me, can you tell me the *point in time*?'

time budget

The time one has available. Schedule. Diary. As in, 'Alison, check my *time budget* and see if I can squeeze in a couple of hours with Sharon.' 'We'd just love to catch up with you, but there's no time in our budget.'

'Frequently students try to do too much with their 168 hours and their study *commitments* suffer because that is the only place they can make cuts in their *time budget*.'

TAFE NSW

'The mating system and *time budgets* of colour-banded comb-crested Jacanas were studied at two sites near Townsville, Queensland, Australia.'

CSIRO

time crunch

> 'A time to weep; and a time to laugh; a time to mourn and a time to dance; a time to love and a time to hate . . . etc. and a time to put them all in one's *time budget*.'

> '*Time budgets* wait for no man.'

time crunch

Not crunch time (As in: 'Crunch Time Looms for PM', etc.). Time that is crunched (by, e.g., work and *family commitments*). Lack of time. No time. As in: *7 Ways to Win the Time Crunch* by Ken Leonard Jr. and 'The Time Crunch Workout'.

> 'Oh dear, oh dear,
> I shall be in a *time crunch*.'

See *zero latency*

timeframe

If someone asks, 'What's the *timeframe*?' don't look at your watch.

> 'For example, if a course requires a person to complete a task within a particular *timeframe* this does not necessarily mean that the course would therefore *map* against the project management "Manage Time" unit of *competency* as the *competency* is not being demonstrated within a project management environment.'

> Industry Training Board

time horizon

The end – *in terms of* time.

> 'The *time horizon* is three years.'
>
> Education consultancy

time period

At that time; then; just then; now. In those days.

> 'Go ahead, make my 24 hour *time period*.'
>
> George Bush Sr., 1988

> 'In this *time period* I'm not talking to him.'
>
> George Tenet, CIA Director – about President Bush before 9/11

> 'There were giants in the earth in that *time period*.'

time-poor

An affliction of our age. In the past people had heaps of time.

> 'People these days are *time poor* . . .'
>
> *Gardening Australia*, June 2005

> 'RMIT online masters targets *time-poor* medical scientists.'

time (through)

Over time. In the course of time. In time. As time goes by. *Going forwards.*

tools

'You must remember this,
a kiss is still a kiss,
a sigh is still a sigh,
the fundamental things apply,
as *time* goes through.'

tools

Any implement, utensil or machine used in the performance of work or any operation, including things like economic policy and words. 'Think of the *tools* in a *tool*-box: there is a hammer, pliers, a saw, a screwdriver, a rule, a glue-pot, nails and screws. The functions of words are as diverse as the functions of these objects' (Ludwig Wittgenstein). cf. 'Models such as meta-model, metaprogram, sensory acuity, Milton-model, representational systems and submodalities among others, provide a diverse set of *tools* for creating change in yourself and others' (www.nlpinfo.com).

Any concept, proven or not, alleged to serve a real or invented end is called a *tool*, and collections of these are called *tool-boxes* or *tool-belts*, depending on their arrangement. Such *tools* are often *quality tools* serving, and sometimes *implementing*, *quality learning outcomes in terms of skill sets*. Tools are also used for *Neuro Linguistic Programming* (NLP) of people.

'Our Assertiveness Course is a practical *workshop* designed to give you the *tools* you need to communicate with *clients*, colleagues or business partners in a view [sic] to maintaining a good working relationship.'

Odyssey training

'Strike, while the *tool* is *quality*.'

'For thou art with me,
thy *quality tools* comfort me.'

top line growth

Sales?

'Our ability to improve on our FY04 performance will ultimately depend on our success in profitably driving *top line growth* from this *strategy*.'

Southcorp media release, 2004

torture lite

1. To keep 'detainees' standing or kneeling for hours in black hoods or spray-painter goggles; deprive them of sleep and keep them in painful positions. To sodomise with flashlights; force men to wear women's underwear; force them to masturbate and commit gross acts; to renounce their religion and declare their love of Jesus; etc. To beat (in some cases to death), rape, smear with excrement; tell them their families will be killed, etc. and thus 'set physical and mental conditions for favourable interrogation of witnesses'.
2. To have a good time. To release emotions. The military equivalent of a 'college fraternity prank'.

totality

> 'The White House denied he was being tortured, although there is speculation that a variety of techniques known in the intelligence community as *"torture lite"* would be used to get information from him.'
>
> *Guardian*, March 2003

> 'No physical or mental torture, nor any other form of coercion, may be inflicted on prisoners of war to secure from them information of any kind whatever.'
>
> Article 17, Third Geneva Convention

See *emotional release*, *rendered*

totality

State of being total. Not partial, fragmentary, narrow or slipshod.

> 'The trial looks at the *totality* of how we can bring together in the interests of reducing *frictional unemployment* the provision of the technology and the vacancy database and improve the *penetration* of a greater range of jobs from a much wider range of sources than in *the past*.'
>
> Department of Employment and Workplace Relations employee at Senate Estimates Committee, 19 February 2004

> 'It's very clear, I think, from the *totality* of the Opposition's question and the *totality* of the Prime Minister's answer exactly what the context of the answer was.'
>
> Tony Abbott, MHR

See *holistic*

total solution proposals

Say yes. Or whatever.

> 'Are you able to formulate *total solution proposals* and tender responses?'
>
> Job advertisement

touch base

To make contact, speak to, phone, meet. (US baseball)

> 'I'll just *touch base* with the wife.'

> 'Let's *touch base* at the full moon.'

See *networking*

tough

Tough (tough, tough). Tough. *Plenty tough*. Hard.

> 'Mr Bush admitted this himself, saying recently there was "no question it's been a *tough, tough, tough* series of weeks for the American people".'
>
> *Independent*, 24 April 2004

See *plenty tough*

tough decisions

'I'm sorry but you no longer have a job here. It hurts me as much as it hurts you,' etc.

tough weeks

Texan. See *plenty tough*. *Tough* Daffy Duck, etc.

> 'This has been *tough weeks* in that country.'
>
> President George W. Bush

track record

Not as in: 'She broke the *track record* for 1000 metres.' But as in: The record, curriculum vitae, experience, history, resume. What the record shows. *Track records* are usually 'demonstrated'.

> 'The firm also has a demonstrated *track record* in the successful management of ADB, World Bank and UNDP technical assistance projects for *capacity building* of supreme *governance* institutions overseas.'
>
> Company document

tradition / traditional (clash)

Any sporting event more than five years old; as in: '*Traditional* Anzac Day Clash', 'Clash of *traditional* rivals', 'Tooheys New Cup *clash* between *traditional* rivals Randwick and Warringah will be a fully fledged contest . . .', '*Traditional clash* between Carlton and Collingwood AFL Clubs', 'We are underway at Aussie Stadium for the *traditional clash* between the Roosters and the Rabbitohs'. Etc.

traditional values

Fading but important, rhetorically speaking.

See *community values*

transaction costs analysis

Economic / accounting theory that has largely supplanted *market failure* and, with this, most justifications for government participation in the economy. (As in: 'The only general statement that can be made about government intervention on efficiency grounds is that governments should intervene where the costs of intervention are less than the benefits.')

> '*Transaction costs* are the resources necessary to transfer, establish and maintain property rights.'
>
> Richard O. Zerbe Jr and Howard McCurdy,
> *The End of Market Failure*

transfer cases / tubes

(US military) Metal coffin packed with ice in which corpses are removed from *theatre mortuary evacuation points* in Iraq. Formerly bodybag or human remains pouch.

> 'Outside the main tent, a hundred or more metal caskets — or "*transfer cases*" — sit at the ready . . .'
>
> Press report, AP, March 2004

> 'She was stretched out in a *transfer tube*,
> So cold, so sweet . . .'

See *theatre mortuary evacuation point*

transformation

'A discipline of being in the domain of being.'

Werner Erhard, *est*

transformative moment

1. Big moment, transforming moment, sort of epiphany.
2. Finding that each group's *strategic* goals are very much the same.
3. You could have knocked me down with a feather. Stone the crows. Blow me down a hatch. Well, suck a dog's nose. Etc.

> 'When the negotiators returned from their caucuses, we listed out each group's *strategic goals*, side-by-side, and found, amazingly, that they were very much the same. The graphic representation of these goals, repeated almost word-for-word beside one another, was a *transformative moment* in the *process*.'
>
> Strategic Solutions, Consultants

transition

Hard work.

> 'But it is hard work *transitioning* from a brutal dictatorship to a democratic Iraq.'
>
> Scott McLellan, 20 September 2004

transition out (transition in)

A gentle kind of *dejobbing*. What follows a *management spill and fill*.

'I was very conscious that I had to *transition out* of Manpower, as well as *transition in* to my new position at Coates.'
> The Managed CEO Transition, Ceoforum.com.au

'Further *ongoing* savings will be achieved in 2004-05, especially as Defence Integrated Distribution System staff *transition out* of the organisation.'
> Defence (Aust) Annual Report, 2003-2004

transition (undergo a)

To change, alter, develop, mutate, become something else, grow whiskers, etc.

'It is generally expected that, at some point between the ages of 12 and 25, young people *undergo a transition* from economic and social dependence to independence.'
> Report to the National Youth Affairs Research Scheme

'The more things *undergo a transition*, the more they remain the same.'

'We will have a picnic if the weather doesn't *undergo a transition*.'

See *change*, *sea change*

transit lounge

The waiting room in some hospitals.

translate

To change, alter, perform miracles. As Jesus *translated* water into wine, five loaves into enough for five thousand. As Dr Jekyll *translated* into Mr Hyde. Etc.

> 'Mutually agreed plans *translate* organisational direction into actions.'
>
> Principles of Business Excellence,
Gracedale Private Nursing Home

> 'And found in the temple, those that sold oxen and sheep and doves, and the *translators* of money sitting.'

transparency

Able to be seen through, clear, open to view, not opaque, dark, hidden or inscrutable. Companies and other organisations that believe in good *governance* and *accountability* also believe in *transparency*.

> 'But any fair-minded student of the mechanism that I am releasing today would say that this is *about transparency* and *accountability*.'
>
> Tony Abbott, July 2004

transparent

> 'Our member firms are taking steps to better retain top talent, help employees create a stronger *work-life balance*, and make the link between *performance management* and recognition more *concrete* and *transparent*'.
>
> Deloitte.com

trickle-down

Theory that wealth accumulated by the upper strata of society makes the lower reaches richer too.

> 'Our results provide an argument against a *"trickle-down"*, or *growth*-oriented, view of intra-household distribution as it relates to inter-generation disparity . . .'
>
> Centre for Economic Policy Research, ANU,
> October 2003

See *fair go*

trigger events

Triggers. *Events* that pull them. Causes. *Catalysts*.

> '. . . if the nature of the revisions arising from a *trigger event* were such that the derogation would be maintained, or if the adjustment mechanism did not operate to revise tariffs during the period of the derogations, there would appear to be little benefit in undertaking a review process.'
>
> *Issues* paper, ACCC, January 2001

triple bottom line

The *bottom line* extended to include social and environmental concerns. Hence the refrain – 'all our *stakeholders*'.

> 'Our *vision* is the creation of a region with a life-long *passion* for discovery and *innovation*, excellence in business, commerce, industry, education and government and the enthusiastic practice of environmentally *sustainable* enterprise and social

activities that benefit all in the *community* with *ongoing triple bottom line* economic development.'

Sunraysia Mallee Economic Development Board vision

See *sustainability*, *greenwashing*, *corporate social responsibility*

true Australian, true Australians, truly Australian

An Australian (or New Zealand) film star who lives in LA, but comes home regularly.

trust

1. Belief in the honour, integrity, truthfulness, etc., of another. Reliance on his, her or its word. (As in: '*Trust* in God.')
2. A word used in politics and *marketing*. (As in: '*Trust* British Paints? Sure can.')
3. A relative term. (As in: '*The Australian people . . .* will make a decision about who they better *trust*.')
4. A scarce *commodity*. Not a word to be *trusted*.

'I can agree with the prime minister in saying the election is about *trust* — people don't *trust* this government anymore, with good reason.'

Mark Latham, 28 August 2004

'Eight people in ten disagree that "Directors of large companies can be *trusted* to tell the truth", according to the MORI poll conducted for the *Financial Times* last week . . . nearly two-thirds of those in full-time employment, 65 per cent, say they do not believe that "companies can be *trusted* to honour their pension *commitments* to employees".'

MORI

'Don't even think about going down that road. Politics pits people against each other while *leadership* inspires people to come together, *enhancing trust.*'

John C. Maxwell, *Enterprise*, 13 August 2004

'There is little that Blair can do about this. As he is said to have recognised earlier this year, he has simply lost public *trust* — essential in forging a *consensus.*'

Jonathan Freedland, *Guardian*, 13 September 2004

'Well, the Australian people will make a decision about who they better *trust* to keep their interest rates down, who they better *trust* to protect their living standards, who they better *trust* to deliver a strong budget so we can spend more on health and education and who they better *trust* to lead Australia in the fight against international terrorism.'

John Howard, ABC radio, 30 August 2004

See *truth*

truth in water entitlements

A factor in water entitlements? *Truth* in all things, therefore *truth in water entitlements*?

'The second document we're putting out is one called *truth in water entitlements* and simply speaking, when some state governments have allocated more than 100 per cent of the water they've got, we have a *problem*, and we have to go back to the drawing board on getting that fixed as well, so that the water entitlement factor has security in it.'

Bob Mansfield, ABC radio, May 2004

'Thou shalt not bear false witness about your *water entitlements.*'

truth, truthful

What is not false.

'We want to assert the very simple principle that *truth* is absolute, *truth* is supreme, *truth* is never disposable in national political life.'

John Howard, August 1995

'The question is not *truthfulness*, the question is *credibility* in a *moment in time.*'

Colin Powell, ABC Radio, July 2003

'"What is truth?" said jesting Pilate and would not stay for an answer.'

Francis Bacon

See *absolute fact, known known, mislead, honest, misspeak, core promise, believe, clear evidence, spin, come concern to us, stovepiping, your call is important to us,* etc.

turn key business paradigm

A sort of paradigm.

'The GRAVITY SYSTEM is a revolutionary *turn key business paradigm* you use to consistently draw new interest and attract greater profits . . . Encircling the GRAVITY SYSTEM are the four disciplines that drive profits your way — group strength classes, Pilates, personal training, and post rehab — all on the GTS machine, your premium *space* utilizer.'

24/7

24 hours a day, seven days a week. Flat out. Burning the candle at both ends, etc. Show of *commitment, focus, actioning the agenda, back-ending, adding alpha, passion, a competitive environment, living the core values, enhanced implementation procedures, going forwards,* avoidance of an *involuntary career event,* etc.

'I've been working on it 24/7.'

Uu

ultimate

1. Final, definitive, critical.
2. Essential, supreme, greatest.

> 'We at Balmoral are in business to provide the *ultimate* coffee service whilst working with courtesy, enthusiasm and *professionalism*.'
>
> Balmoral Dispense, Kettering UK

unacceptable behaviour(s)

Not acceptable, e.g. telling porkies, farting at dinner, using bad words, torturing people, harassing people, being rude to people, killing people, not killing people.

> 'For every fatal shooting, there were roughly three non-fatal shootings, and, folks, this is *unacceptable* in America. It's just *unacceptable* and we're going to do something about it.'
>
> George W. Bush, May 2001

un-Australian

Person, attitude or remark held to be inconsistent with or hostile to Australia's interests, essence, identity, traditions, customs or *zeitgeist*. Whatever is at odds with her *icons* or sport. To foul one's own nest or piss in one's own backyard. To be a smart-arse or wanker. *Latte* drinker. *Elite*. *Out of touch*. Aka 'Not the Australian way'. *Black armband historian. Anti-American.*

> 'Echoing the political philosophy of the two Josephs — Goebbels and McCarthy — [Shane] Stone claimed that the

recent "negative outpouring against the Howard Government" was "*un-Australian*".'

Mark McKenna, *Age*, April 2002

'It's not the Australian way *to cut and run*. It's the Australian way to stay and do the job and see it through.'

John Howard, ABC, March 2004

'That is entirely *un-Australian* and I think that the pressure he has been put under is quite outrageous, *quite frankly*.'

Robert McClelland, March 2004

uncertainty

Apparent in the speech patterns of some Texans.

'There's a lot of *uncertainty* that's not clear in my mind.'

Texas House Speaker, Gib Lewis

underdog, underdogs

Not to love them is *un-Australian* – unless. (See *refugees*, *illegals*, etc.)

underpin

Underneath somewhere.

'Teachers plan learning and assessing based on those things that are valued – the explicit *learning outcomes* described in syllabuses and guidelines, and the explicit and implicit *values* and principles that *underpin* the orientations and emphases of the different *phases* of learning.'

Queensland Studies Framework

unexpressed needs

A *marketing* concept. Repressed wants.

unlock

1. To unlock. Open.
2. To axe. Cut. Blood let.

> 'CBA says it will need to axe 3,700 jobs over the next three years to *unlock* the *targeted* cost savings.'
>
> *Australian Financial Review*

unmanned aerial vehicles

Vehicles which, if they existed, could kill Americans in their homes.

> 'Iraq has a growing fleet of manned and *unmanned aerial vehicles* that could be used to disperse chemical and biological weapons across broad areas.'
>
> President George W. Bush

unpack the text

To understand the writer.

> 'Helpful hint: print out your passage(s) double — or triple — spaced on blank sheets of paper. Then *unpack the text* by underlining, circling and connecting anything that seems important.'
>
> English syllabus

See *issues*: they are also *unpacked*.

unsettled

The arse fell out of it.

> 'Meanwhile, a series of *leadership changes unsettled* the *core* pension equity advisory business.'
>
> Annual report

update

(n) News, information, what's happening, breaking, etc. Statement, description, announcement, account, accounting, etc.
(v) To provide any of the above. To bring up to date. To create an illusion of progress, that life and business is in constant change; *innovation*, moving on, *going forwards*, heading for *time crunch*, etc.

> 'Mr Ballard also provided an *update* on the anticipated earnings position.'
>
> Southcorp media release, 2004

upside

Not the downside.

> 'The ducks appear to be lining up in favour of our "buy 1" rating on CBA as we enter the 2004 year, given *restructuring upside*, valuation, *leverage* to wealth management and bias to rising rates.'
>
> USB analyst, Jeff Emmanuel, *Australian Financial Review*,
> December 2004

See *downside*

uptake

Take up (e.g. drugs). Buy, consume.

> 'The Action *Plan* identifies seven *key strategy areas* for preventing the *uptake* of illicit drug use . . .'
>
> > Department of Health and Aged Care

uptick

Not a down tick. Positive tick *going upwards*. Tick up.

See *re-engineering*

upward bullying

Oppression of the strong by the many. Manager-bashing.

> 'Workplace mobbing is a term used to describe *upward bullying* of managers and supervisors which is ignored by senior executives and employers. This signals that bullying, abuse and vicious-ness will be tolerated, increasing the vulnerability of employees in the workplace.'
>
> > West Australian Government Notice advertising an address on the subject by Dr Jocelynne Scutt, the 'imminent barrister and writer'

user-friendly

Warm, kind, hospitable, approachable, loyal, faithful – as a dog is to man – to a user. That which is easy to use is called *user-friendly*; e.g. some mobile phones and audio visual equipment can be operated by people of ordinary intelligence and sensibilities. Government departments are also caller *user-friendly*, meaning that people of average intelligence work in them and people of ordinary intelligence and sensibility will not be grievously mistreated by them. Others are called *can-do*, meaning they can do pretty well anything that pleases them at the time. Nevertheless, a *can-do* department can *transition* into a *user-friendly* one because it is a *can-do* department with a *can-do culture*. Can a *user-friendly* department *transition* into a *can-do* one? This question should be directed to Senator Amanda Vanstone, Minister for Immigration, Parliament House, Canberra, ACT 2600.

See *can-do*, *robust*

utilise

To use, make use of.

> 'I *utilise* a range of modalities including Shiatsu, Bowen Therapy, Traditional Chinese Medicine and Relaxation / Remedial techniques etc.'
>
> Masseur's advertisement

value-adding, value-added, value-addeds

Washing the potatoes before selling them; turning grapes into wine; loaves into fishes, etc. Advertising, design – anything that adds *value* to a *product* is *value-adding*. (And adds to the price of the *product*.) Cutting in the middle man.

> 'That the organisation identifies which performance management activities provide the most *value-add in terms of* individual and organisation *performance.*'
>
> Centrelink

value (your call, we)

We are so not indifferent to or contemptuous of your call. We have ascribed a *value* to it which bears no relation to the time we are taking to pick up the phone. If we wanted you to piss off, do you think we'd be playing you such beautiful music? For your enjoyment we will now advertise our services.

values

1. Ethics, morals, beliefs, creeds, customs, principles, propriety, conscious of right and wrong, etc.
2. What a thing is worth.
3. *Key*.
4. Lubricant.

> 'A leader needs to determine the *values*, behaviour and mores of the company and personally live these *values*. The "leaching" of these *values* into the *culture* of the company will not come by pronouncements from on high, but by the way leaders act on

a day-to-day basis, continually reinforcing that these *values* are the essential *lubricant* and *key* to the company's success.'

Jeff Floyd, *Australian Chief Executive*, October 2002

vanilla

Obsolete skills or skills to be *outsourced*. A person with such skills. One who has been overtaken by technology or progress of any kind. A redundant or expendable person, one ripe for *dejobbing*. A person in the *churn*. *Vanillas* often re-invent, transform or *recontextualise* themselves as ideas *consultants*.

variability (exhibit)

1. Of a variable or varying nature; the quality of not being fixed; lacking a pattern; not predictable.
2. Must be kept to a minimum, especially when your *clients* are so *senior*.

'All systems and *processes* exhibit *variability*, which *impacts* on predictability and *performance*.'

Principles of Business *Excellence*,
Gracedale Private Nursing Home

vertical and horizontal associations

Up and down associations. Allows a higher as well as a broader understanding of *social capital*.

'A broader understanding of *social capital* accounts for the positive and negative aspects by including *vertical as well as horizontal* associations between people, and includes behaviour within and among organisations, such as firms.'

World Bank

very draft

1. ???
2. Even earlier than the early stages. Fairly unformed.
Too early to speak with confidence. Not as yet.
Unbegun, as it were. Ask me again next month.

> 'What stage is the program at?' 'It's still *very draft*, but it's got
> an *aggressive timeline* on it.'
>> Report of an exchange in the
>> Victorian Education Department

very key

1. *Enhanced in terms of key*ness.
2. More important than very important. Crucial.
Very *strategic*. The whole *implementation* architecture
hangs on it. The *underpinning* of the *game plan*
depends on it.

> 'Is it important?' 'Yes, it's *very key*.'
>> Victorian Education Department, same meeting as above

vibrant

Absolutely buzzing. Arts, *communities*, *cultures*, *multicultures*, business *cultures*, business addresses are *vibrant*.

> 'Delfin Lend Lease is committed to the development of
> employment and investment opportunities by encouraging
> *vibrant business addresses* where business can *grow* and
> prosper.'
>> How We Create Special Places, Delfin Lend Lease

'*Vibrant* Health For All'
>> Hampstead Seventh Day Adventists' banner

'A time to be *vibrant*, and a time to be *robust*.'

vintage operations

Fruit crushing.

'From 2005, *vintage operations* (i.e. fruit crushing) for all for-
tified wines will be relocated . . .'
>> Southcorp media release, 2004

virtual skin wear

Condoms (British).

vision

Something one can see – anything. Hence 'visionary' –
the one who sees it. *Mission statement.*

'Have an ability to be able to *solution* sell and have the *vision* to
see opportunities of *value adding* to the businesses of *customers*
and potential *clients*.'
>> Microsoft job advertisement

vision (executing)

It's not much use having a *vision* if you can't *execute* it.
But don't blame the *vision*. The *vision* was good. And the
executives were fine. It was external factors *impacting* on
the thing.

visioning / vision setting

'The difficulty in *executing this vision* was compounded by the deteriorating global economic environment.'

Annual report

visioning / vision setting

Not, as one might think, looking, seeing or foreseeing. Not as in: 'Can I help you, ma'am?' 'No thank you, I'm just *visioning*.'

'[*visioning*] . . . creates a *Mission*, *Values* and qualitative, time-based *Vision* using a SWOT (Strengths, Weaknesses, Opportunities and Threats) Analysis to define the *strategic* context.'

The Growth Connection, www.growconnect.com.au

vision statement

Envisioned *mission statement*.

visitation

Visit: particularly of an official, ordained, calamitous or supernatural kind.

'Council Arts Development Officer says *visitation* to the toilet block has risen significantly since the installation of the murals.'

Surf Coast Shire Bulletin, 2003

'Excuse me, I must pay a *visitation* to the lavatory.'

'On the way home I decided to *visitate* my aunt Hilda.'

visual integrity

Town planning, architecture, landscaping, design, environment, etc. The view. The *visual integrity* of a tree is retained by not chopping it or decorating it in any way, except perhaps if Christo does it, in which case the *v.i.* might be *enhanced*. Also cooktops, awnings, websites, restaurants, etc.

'The Trinity combines quality, safety and *visual integrity* . . .'
Highland Trinity Gas Cooktop, Australian Design Awards

'. . . maintenance of the *visual integrity* of the University's marks and logo'

University of Newcastle, NSW

'The resulting logo was *iconic* yet polished enough to uphold the *visual integrity* of the interior space.'

Cracker New Media

'3.0 Policies. 3.5 *Visual integrity*. Explanation: . . . Maungakiekie (along with Rangitoto) is the landscape "*icon*" of Auckland, with immense *values in terms of* heritage, geology, *culture* and landscape.'

Auckland City

'Maintaining *visual integrity* is believing.'

voluntary departure package (VDP)

What you get when you go. Incentive to depart, perhaps to take up a career in *consulting*, perhaps to the organisation that just gave you the *incentive*.

Ww

War on Terror

A *misspeak*. They meant to say 'Global Struggle against violent extremism' (Global SAVE) but it wouldn't fit on the Fox News banner.

watchdog

1. Dog that barks at or bites intruders. Guard dog. Fierce dog. Good dog, etc.
2. A person or persons *tasked* to *oversight* corporate *behaviour*.

> 'A federal *watchdog* tasked with tackling "spam" emails has had to investigate its own staff for distributing pornographic and racist emails, it was reported.'
>
> *Age*, January 2004

watershed

1. A place where water is stored, or a line dividing two drainage areas.
2. Metaphorically a moment that divides one epoch from the next and irrigates the new one. A '*watershed in terms of* staff' might fit this definition for the company. A watershed <u>for</u> the staff will depend on their *packages*.

> 'The year has also been a *watershed in terms of* staff.'
>
> Annual report

See also *sea change* and *paradigm shift*

we

1. You and me. 'You and me, can *we* be partners . . . etc?'
2. Me.
3. Me and the wife.
4. Queen Victoria and her successors. '*We* are not amused.'
5. The state.

> '*We* decide who comes to this country and the circumstances in which they come.'
>
> John Howard, 2001

> 'People should listen to us when *we* say, again and again, *we* determine the order at our border! And *we* ensure that it is maintained . . .'
>
> Karl Eduard von Schnitzler, East German propaganda chief 1965, after two people had been shot trying to get over the Berlin Wall. From *Stasiland*, by Anna Funder

weapons of mass destruction

Thingamebobs, jiggers, hoozits, doodads, watchamecallits, wigwams for a goose's bridle, etc. Weaponish sorts of things. Destructive sorts of things. Destructive items possibly related to weapons. Weapons developed by countries that are not free.

> 'See, free nations are peaceful nations. Free nations don't attack each other. Free nations don't develop *weapons of mass destruction*.'
>
> George W. Bush, October 2003

---

weapons of mass destruction related program activities

1. Activities related to programs related to *weapons of mass destruction.*
2. Activities (e.g. Game Boy, snooker, gymkhanas, belly dancing, etc.)

> Search *teams* in Iraq 'identified dozens of *weapons of mass destruction-related program activities*'.
>
> > President George W. Bush, January 2004

> '. . . dozens of *weapons of mass destruction-related program activities* and significant amounts of equipment that Iraq concealed from the United Nations.'
>
> > Congressman Peter Hoekstra, Rep. Michigan,
> > October 2003

> 'Oh, you don't believe,
> We're on the eve of *destruction-related program activities*.'

web organisation

A unique *culture.*

> 'The City of Port Phillip serves a diverse municipality, and has developed a unique *culture* to deliver the organisation's *commitment* to Same Day Service and Economic, Environmental, Social and *Cultural Sustainability*. The CEO, David Spokes, has described this *culture* as a *Web Organisation* . . .'
>
> > City of Port Phillip

wellbeing (enhanced)

Lifestyle, health, complexion, joie de vivre; whatever can be *enhanced* with lip balm and a spray of Evian water.

> 'This functional bag contains specially selected *products* chosen for their ability to *enhance* your *wellbeing.*'
>
> Qantas toiletry bag

wet work

Assassination. Terminate with extreme prejudice. *Take out*, neutralise in the sense of killing, etc. Work done by military organisations with multiple 'S's in their ranks – SS, SAS etc.

whole of (organisation, industry, region)

Economic development in the whole region.

> 'The structure is based on the *"Circle of Strength"* model, deemed to be the most appropriate for the broad participation of multi-sectoral and *diverse stakeholders* such as is required to drive *whole of region* economic development.'
>
> Sunraysia Mallee Economic Development Board

window of opportunity

If it were a door you might not be able to see the opportunity. An opportunity that might not be there tomorrow, or one you can reach only if you move quickly. A fleeting opportunity. A glimpse. Go for it. Chance for a *quick fix*.

'Gather ye rosebuds while ye have ye window of opportunity.'

See *target of opportunity*, *portal*

winnebagoes of death

Weather balloon launching platforms sold to Iraq by Britain.

with the effluxion of time

In time; in good time; over time; in due course; whenever. Have a little patience, these things take time; Rome wasn't built in a day; there are *no quick fixes*; it can't be done overnight. This year, next year, sometime, never. Not on an *aggressive timeframe*.

Bureaucratic (esp. Department of Immigration) for 'the sands of time', 'time's winged chariot', 'All time is irredeemable' (T.S. Eliot), 'Time is on my side' (M. Jagger).

See *through time*

working smarter

1. Working more efficiently. Using technology. Also; '*Work smarter*, not harder', as in, 'Wouldn't it be easier if you used a brush and pan? . . . faster if you rode a bicycle? . . . speedier and more *empowering* if we had a teleconference?'
2. Cant. A mantra. An old chestnut; a good one. Spare us, please!

Many people who have *worked smarter* say it often means the opposite: that it may mean nothing more than new and more complex bureaucratic procedures replacing simple ones, and that the service provided is 'dumbed down' in the process. Some say that, if not always harder, people now work much longer. Others believe that it is common for the injunction to follow job losses, and just as often it precedes them.

'For several years now, economists from Alan Greenspan on down have been praising the tech-driven improvement in the *productivity* of the US workforce. The theory is that, as computers allow us all to produce more with less work, our incomes will continue to grow and our standard of living will rise. But there's a darker side to *productivity* that some economists are now beginning to look at more closely. Simply put: Are we all really *working smarter*? Or just a lot harder?'

John W. Schoen, MSNBC

See *help desk*, *management systems*

workplace

1. Place of work.
2. Not a place of work.

'A *workplace* should act as a *tool* from which you can *leverage* your business and a means to effecting the most efficient use of your resources. Our fitout feature illustrates how Colliers International has redesigned its own office from a place to work in, to a place that works for them.'

Colliers International advertisement, August 2004

workshop

1. (n) A place of work.
2. (v) To take to a committee; ring around; think about; *dialogue*; talk to a standstill. (As in: 'OK, I think we need to *workshop* that.')
3. A *facilitator's* natural environment.

> 'Facilitated *workshop* on practical solutions and *the way forward* regarding your *issues* in senior executive *leadership*.'
>
> *Benchmarking Partnerships*

> 'If there's one word that sums up everything that's gone wrong since the War, it's *Workshop*.'
>
> Kingsley Amis

world class

Excellent, good, competent, passable, pretentious, insecure, silly.

> 'Welcome to the definitive Internet starting point for learning about *World Class* Giant Pumpkins!'
>
> www.backyardgardener.com

world's best practice

State of the art. Leading edge. Cutting edge.

See *best practice*

Yy

your call is important to us

Please hold the line.

See *call centre*

zero latency

No time.

> 'There is no time lapse between receipt of critical informa-
> tion and the ability to analyse and act on that information.'
>
> DM Review

> 'Hold on, we'll have you out of here in *zero latency*.'

> 'Oh my ears and whiskers, how zero latent it's getting.'

See *time crunch*

Zippie

A person, commonly Indian, 15–25 years old, who works in a *call centre*. So called, according to Thomas Friedman, because having the job puts 'a zip in their stride'.

Acknowledgements

Many words and quotations owe their presence in this dictionary to people obliged to use them in their work, or affronted by their appearance in the media or their letter boxes. For passing them on to me, and for keeping a sense of humour, I thank them all. I acknowledge in particular John P. Hall, Rowen Wilken, Upjay Aksi, Mark Hetherington, Brian Lowe, Lois Fraser, Monty Stephens, Dennis O'Donnell, Deb Doyle, Deb Watson, Mike Corder, Peter Watson, John Sullivan, Mary Edwards, May Lam, Rupert Freeman, Michael Doogan, Ross Alford, Margaret Morgan, Marc Peake, Matthew Broad, Steve Forsyth, Kathy Moyo, Peter G Dellys, Branko Bulovic, Vince Baldwin, Dennis Perry, Andrew Cox, Barry Stuart, Stephen Merrall, Paul Brice, John Cohen, Graham Giblin, Jane Smart, Sarah Monaghan, Steve Booth, Roger Jones, Imogen Boas, Bob Galligan, Steven Smith, David Burch, Jeremy King, Barry Stuart, Judith Holmes, Sally Williams, Andrew Manning, Michael Hewitt, Chris Fowler, Murray Whitlocke-Jones, Gus Paull, David Boyd, Rod Metcalfe, Rob Nethery, Susannah Chambers, Peter Scott, Arne Lindquist, Jo & Garth Jenkinson, David Small, Gary Max, Jeremy Press, Bernie Wriede, Jenny Tetlow, Ben Lawson, Ian Lyall, David Burch, Jamie Wodetzki, Dennis T, Dave Annetts, Kim Mason, Cris Cordeiro, Vanessa Petterson, Stephanie Boldeman, Jeremy Gilling, Elli Housden, Bruce Donald,

Tom Wilson, David Burch, Steve Sutherland, Charlie Myres, David Whelan, Derek Lewis, Holly Shorland, Arne Lindquist, Alasdair Baird, Chris Mitchell; and for peerless and generous technical advice, Dennis Perry.

I must also acknowledge Helen Smith for all the varieties of her assistance, especially her unerring and imaginative research. Her *competencies* and *skill sets* were invaluable. Thanks also to Bruce Petty (again), Jane Palfreyman (again) and Hilary McPhee (again and again).